Sourcing *in the* Public Sector

SECOND EDITION

Carole Pettijohn, Ph.D.
and
Ken S. Babich, BCom., CPPO

Prepared for the National Institute of Governmental Purchasing under the LEAP Program. All rights are conveyed to the NIGP upon completion of this book.

Sourcing *in the* Public Sector

National Institute of Governmental Purchasing, Inc. (NIGP)
151 Spring Street
Herndon, VA 20170
Phone: 703-736-8900; 800-367-6447
Fax: 703-736-9639 Email: education@nigp.org

This book is available at a special discount when ordered in bulk quantities. For information, contact NIGP at 800-367-6447. A complete catalog of titles is available on the NIGP website at www.nigp.org.

ISBN 1-932315-17-9
ISBN 978-1-932315-17-2

This book was set in Berkeley Oldstyle
Design & production by Vizüal, Inc. - www.vizual.com.
Printed & bound by HBP.

With Appreciation

Procurement professionals have historically risen through the ranks of government employment with little or no formal education in their chosen profession. Out of this awareness, the idea behind the LEAP program was conceived. In the fall of 2000, the program was first presented to the Board of Directors of the National Institute of Governmental Purchasing (NIGP) and given a vote of confidence to continue. From that time on, work has not ceased to make this vision become reality. With a mission to build a new educational framework that provides the procurement professional with knowledge and the potential for more rigorous formalized educational opportunities supported by academia, this project is just the beginning of what we perceive to be the commencement of public procurement education reform.

We cannot do justice to the many people who have been a part of the formidable effort required in the writing and production of these books. We would be remiss however, if we did not acknowledge the staff of NIGP, who contributed countless hours of work to the project with commitment and dedication. Donna Beach, CPPO, CPPB, C.P.M., Rick Grimm, CPPO, CPPB, and Carol Hodes, CAE, have offered insights, editorial comments, revision expertise and emotional and physical support to all involved. A special thanks to Bill Hertwig, CPPO, CPPB, C.P.M., A.P.P., Mr. John J. Zeyer, CPPO, CPPB, Ms. Myra D. Smith, CPPB and Mr. David P. Gragan, CPPO who spent numerous hours reading the text to ensure quality, credibility and consistency throughout. Members, NIGP instructors and committed professionals, too numerous to mention here, volunteered their time to read countless drafts and offer suggestions to the authors as the work began to take form.

This project is dedicated to the men and women who serve the public by striving to make quality public procurement decisions. Such commitment to excellence will undoubtedly change the face of public procurement in academia and in the workplace.

Acknowledgements

When Rick Grimm, Chief Executive Officer of NIGP, called inviting me to participate in the development of the new LEAP Program by co-authoring one of the foundation course text books, I initially received the telephone call in disbelief, then followed feelings of honor, pride, and privilege. It was several days later, when the invitation arrived by letter, that I knew this was not a dream. Reality set in!

The 1st Edition was published in July 2004 and has been a foundation level core textbook in NIGP's LEAP Program. It was always one of my goals to author a text reflecting public sector procurement from a practitioner perspective that addresses relevant theory, process and perspective.

I want to thank Michele (the significant other within our household) for all her support and encouragement to complete this 2nd Edition. I want again to acknowledge my employer, The University of Victoria, for continuing to support and provide me with the opportunity to develop my expertise in an academic environment pioneering in public procurement, including engagement of electronic technology. This provided me the ability to apply and articulate these principles and practices within the core material of this text. John Braybrook, CPPB, my associate in Purchasing Services continues to reflect upon and provide considerable insight and editorial checks and balances on theory and practice, as well as being an ongoing contributor to specific content. Material in the form of examples and specific documents were drawn and referenced from a number of public sector agencies and associations, and their contributions are recognized within each chapter of the text.

When the National Institute of Governmental Purchasing Education Department asked me if I was interested in contribution and co-writing the 2nd Edition, my first reaction was "how am I going to do this with everything I already am committed too and involved with" ? When I committed to co-authoring this 2nd Edition, I did so on the basis that many changes have taken place in public procurement processes over the past three plus years. These are reflected within the content of this 2nd Edition. Fortunately, my engagement with the University of Victoria, who are leaders and pioneers in ocean science research, has enabled our procurement office to trail-blaze new and innovative concepts in public procurement. Some of these are in the areas of "Joint Solutions Procurement" (JSP), strategic sourcing through "Strategic Alliances" (SA's), Level 1 and Level 2 Mandatory provisions of RFP/RFI/REI/RFQu submission requirements, and Stewardship, Social Responsibility, and Sustainability. These are all incorporated into this 2nd Edition.

At the risk of missing any contributors, I sincerely appreciate the input and efforts of my team and all others. I will forever be indebted to my colleagues in public procurement and my mentors for their wisdom, insight, and guidance in the stewardship of taxpayer's dollars.

Ken S. Babich, BCom., CPPO

Dedication

This book is again dedicated with love to my late parents, Alan and Marjorie Pettijohn, my children, Erin and Lynne, and my grandson, Drew.

Acknowledgements

Writing a book is never completed without the assistance of so many. It would be impossible to name everyone who provided support, inspiration and encouragement. The NIGP staff, reviewers, and proofreaders have provided insightful comments and have been incredibly patient awaiting this second edition. Thank you for all of your help. Thank you again to Rick Grimm, Carol Hodes and Dr. Khi Thai for giving me the opportunity to participate in the LEAP project.

I want to thank my family for supporting and understanding me when I needed to spend time away writing and researching. I am grateful for all of my teachers and colleagues who gave me the tools and intellectual curiosity. I wish to thank my colleagues at the University of South Florida. Conversations with them have provided most of the insights that I have gained, especially Dr. Jamil Jreisat. It goes without saying that any inaccuracies are all my own. So many friends understood when I needed to disappear - too many to name them all individually, but especially Harriet. All of you have my gratitude and love.

Carole Pettijohn, Ph.D.

Contents

Preface 1

Part I — The Theory and Value of Public Sourcing 3

Chapter 1.   A Framework For Sourcing 3
Goals of the Procurement Process.. 3
Structural Models for Procurement Organizations.................................... 8
Multidimensional Model of Public Sourcing 9

Chapter 2.   Introduction to Sourcing...13
Stages in the Solicitation Process 14
Methods of Solicitation.. 17
       Small Dollar/Purchasing Card... 18
       Emergency Purchases 19
       Sole Source Purchase 19
       Request for Quotation (RFQ) 21
       Invitation for Bids (IFB)/Invitation to Tender (ITT)............... 21
       Request for Proposal (RFP)... 22
       Request for Information (RFI)/Request for Expression of Interest (REI)................... 24
       Reverse Auction 24
       Invitation to Negotiate (ITN) 27
       Request for Supplier Qualification (RFSQu) 28
       Notice of Intent (NOI) 28
       Joint Solutions Procurement (JSP) 29
       Public-Private Partnerships (P3) 30
       Strategic Alliance (SA) 30
Solicitation Categories 32
eProcurement as a Strategy 33
Green Procurement.. 35

Part II — Public Sourcing: Analysis Before Action 39

Chapter 3.   Requirements Analysis 39
Gathering Information.. 39
The Purchase Requisition (PR) 40
Strategic Sourcing 41
Identifying the Need and Requirements Definition 42
       Surveying the Market 42
       Initial Cost Analyses 43
       Make or Buy Cost Analysis... 43
       Leasing and Renting 45
       Requirements Definition.. 46
       Requirements Characteristics... 47
       Requirements Relationships... 49
       Requirements Descriptions 50
       Requirements Quality 50

Determinants of Cost - Manufacturer and Supplier Pricing Considerations 51

Chapter 4.   **Sourcing Suppliers..53**
Creating and Maintaining Supplier Lists... 54
Determining the Appropriate Sourcing Strategy 57
Electronic Sourcing (eSourcing) 59

Chapter 5.   **Specifications and Standards.................................61**
Specifications... 61
General Definition 63
Purpose of Specifications.. 64
Types of Specifications... 65
        Design Specifications.. 66
        Performance Specifications... 67
        Combination Specifications.. 67
        Brand Name or Approved Equal 68
        Qualified Products List (QPL) and Samples 68
        Regulatory and Testing Agency.. 70
        Restrictive Specifications—Proprietary Products 70
        Industry Standards—Generic Products 71
        Market Grades 71
        Material and Manufacturing Method 71
        Tolerances... 72
        Part Drawing and Part Specification 72
        Finishes 72
Standards... 72
Standardization Program 73
Standards Committee 74
Sources of Standards.. 75
Requirements Analysis.. 75
Establishing Mandatory and/or Optional Sourcing Criteria..................... 76

Chapter 6.   **Authorization and Approvals..................................79**
Introduction... 79
Identification of Need... 80
Establishing Specific Requirements 81
Budget Commitment Approval.. 81
Formalizing the Acquisition 81
Generating a Purchase Requisition—"Law of Agency" 82
Purchasing Organization Authority 82
Selection of Supplier or Contractor and Approval of Award 83
Assessing and Establishing Delegated Authority.................................... 84
        Other Forms of Authority.. 85
Determining Approval Levels 85
Solicitation Approvals.. 86
        Electronic Authorization.. 86
        Other Authorizations... 87
Payment Authorization... 89
Sole Source Authorization 89

Other than Low-Compliant Bid/Quote/Proposal 90
Local Preference/Regional Restrictions... 90
Technical Reviews and Approvals.. 91
Policy and Procedure Compliance 92

Part III — Assembling The Sourcing Document..95
Preface 95

Chapter 7.   The Sourcing Document: Instructions and General Terms/Conditions 97
Instructions to Bidders 97
Schedule and Calendar of Activities 97
Closing Date and Time 98
Public Entity's Contact Information for Inquiries 99
Terms and Definitions 99
Inquiries Prior to Pre-response Conference 100
Bidders Conferences 100
Bidders Conference Calls... 101
Communications Guidelines 101
Issuing Addenda Due to Changes and Extensions 101
Site Visit and Examination.. 102
Oral Presentations.. 102
Receipt and Confirmation Form... 103
Withdrawal Conditions 103
Copies of Response Documents.. 103
Notification of Award.. 103
General Terms and Conditions 104
Statutory and Legal Terms 104
Governing Law and Compliance 104
Workers' Compensation 105
Occupational Safety and Health—Infractions and Compliance................. 105
Workplace Hazards... 105
Ownership and Intellectual Property.. 105
Disclosure, Confidentiality, and Public Information 106
Indemnity 106
Personal Harassment 106
Infringement 106
Administrative Terms.. 107
Acceptance.. 107
Rejection of Responses 107
Force Majeure.. 107
Non-Waiver 107
Funding.. 107
Financial Conditions 108
Non-Collusion 108
Amendments and Withdrawals 108
Error in Response 108
Error in Pricing.. 109
Dispute Resolution 109

Disqualification...109

Termination for Convenience 109

Performance and Default 110

Purchase Order/Agreement Number on Invoice...110

Chapter 8.   **The Sourcing Document: Special Terms and Conditions 111**

Pricing 111

Fixed Price..112

Variations of Fixed Priced Contracts..112

Fixed Firm Price..112

Fixed Price with Escalation (Fixed Price with Economic Price Adjustment)............113

Fixed Price with Incentive 113

Fixed Price with Redetermination 114

Cost Reimbursement 114

Variations to Cost Reimbursement Contracts 114

Cost Plus Fixed Fee 115

Cost Plus Incentive Fee 115

Cost Sharing..115

Time and Materials 115

Method of Award..116

Life Cycle Cost based on Bids Submitted 116

Multi-step Bidding...117

Privilege Clause/Best Interest 117

Risk Management 119

Insurance 119

Bid Deposit, Bond and Security..119

Performance and Payment Bond 119

Financial 120

Liquidated Damages 120

Prompt Payment...120

Volume Discounts..121

Invoicing and Payment 121

Holdbacks..121

Taxes..121

Bid Deposit—Plans and/or Drawings 121

Purchase Order or Agreement Number on Shipment 122

Shipping and Delivery 122

Definite Delivery...122

Indefinite Delivery..122

F.O.B.—Delivery and Transportation...123

International Commercial Terms (Incoterms)...125

Customs and Brokerage 126

Delivery and Installation...126

Returns and Refunds 126

Over Shipment and Errors in Shipment..126

Recycling and Packing...127

Safety Stock Levels..127

Master Standing Offer (MSO) and Blanket Contract Releases 127

Packaging..127
Waste Removal 128
Restocking Charges...128
Time is of the Essence 128
Performance..128
Quality Assurance Program 128
Safety Procedures Review 129
Inspection, Testing and Acceptance...129
Defective Work 129
Claims for Damage, Shortage, or Loss in Transit 129
Supplier Obligations for Remedial Action 129
Reporting..130
Regulatory Reporting Requirements 130
Reports and Records...130
Records Management..130
Reporting Methods/Frequency 130
Audits and Inspections of Financial Reports 130
Warranty...131
Warranties and Guarantees..131
Warranty Briefings 131
Product-Related Information 131
Brochures, Catalogs, Operating and Reference Manuals...............................131
New Product Testing and Sampling...131
Risk of Loss—Demonstration or Trial of Products or Equipment 132
Brand Name or Equal 132
Royalties and Patents 132
Purchase Quantities 132
System and Equipment Demonstrations...132
After Warranty Parts and Repairs...133
Inspection and Takeover Procedures 133
Manufacturer's Instruction Manual 133
Administrative Issues 133
Agreement Extensions and Renewal Options 133
Professional Errors and Omissions 134
Alternatives, Equivalents, and Substitutions...134
Assignments and Conveyance 134
Title—Lien Protection 135
Business Registration Required by the Public Entity 135
Disclosure of Factory Locations...135
Debriefing...135
Limitation of Damages..135
Sub-suppliers..135
Travel and Other Related Expenses 136
International Labor Organizations...136

Chapter 9.   The Sourcing Document: Technical Specifications or Statement of Work 137
Writing Technical Specifications 138

Sources of Specifications..140
    Suppliers and Manufacturers..141
    Colleagues and Governmental Sources...141
    Professional Associations 141
    Online Resources..142
    Other Resources 142
    Specification Content..142
Writing a Scope/Statement of Work (SOW) 144
    Preparing the Scope/Statement of Work (SOW)...........................144
    Introduction and Scope of Work/Project 145
    Nature and Description of the Project 146
    Background 146
    Objectives and Purpose of the Solicitation 146
    Public Entity 146
    Executive Steering Committee...146
    Project Advisory Committee..147
    Project Coordinator 147
    Project Team...147
    Project Scope of Work and Requirements Definition 147
Use of Standard Terms to Define the Scope of Work......................................148
    Administrative Issues...148
    Legal Issues..150
Work and Materials 151

Chapter 10.   **The Sourcing Document: The Bid Proposal Form............................155**
Minimum Components of a Bid Proposal Form...155
    Proposal Instructions...156
    Cover Letter..156
    Technical Proposals...156
    Proposed Pricing..157
    Exceptions and Variances 157
    Required Attachments..157
    Conflict of Interest Form 157
Optional Components of a Bid Proposal Form..158
    Executive Summary..158
    Bidder's Profile and Information 158
    Project Approach and Work Plan 158
    Subcontracting and Alliances..158
    Schedule of Subcontractors...159
    References...159
    Financial Guarantees 159
    Ineligibility of Responses 159
    Agreement Documents 160
    Bidder/Proponent Checklist..160
    Stewardship, Social Responsibility and Sustainability 160
        Recycling and Removal of Packaging and Debris 161
        Waste Removal 161

Sustainability Provisions and Social Responsibility 161
Leadership in Maintaining Sustainability, Social and
Environmental Responsibility 162
eWaste Program 163
Local Preference 163
Employee, Student and Alumni Discount Programs 163
Disposal Certification 163
Environmental Management Act - British Columbia Recycling Regulation 164
Vehicle Idling 164
Bio-Fuel Delivery Vehicles 164

Chapter 11.   **Receiving, Opening, and Evaluating Bid/Proposal Responses 165**
Receiving Bids and Proposals 166
Closing Date and Time 166
Responsibility for Late or Lost Bids 166
Receipt of Bids prior to Opening 166
Acknowledgement of Receipt of Response Submittals 167
Validation of Bid Submittals 167
Security and Safeguards of Bid Submittals 168
Modification or Withdrawal of Bid Submittal prior to Opening 168
Rejection of Late Bid Submittals 168
Opening Bids and Proposals 169
Bid Opening and Proceedings 169
Compliant or Non-compliant Determination 171
Discovery of Bidder Errors or Mistakes After Bid Opening 173
Bid Surety and Bid Bond Deposits (Bonds, Insurance) 173
Bid Protests 174
Bid Debriefing 176
Responding to Protests 177
Evaluating Bids and Proposals 178
The Evaluation Process 179
Small Dollar/Purchasing Card Acquisitions 179
Emergency Purchases 179
Sole Source 179
Request for Quotation (RFQ) 183
Invitation for Bids/Invitation to Tender (IFB/ITT) 183
Request for Proposal (RFP) 184
Request for Expression of Interest/Request for Information (REI/RFI) 184
Reverse Auctions 185
The Evaluation Plan 185
The Evaluation or Selection Committee/Team 186
Safeguarding Original Submittals and Duplication 188
Response Evaluation Process 188
Evaluation Criteria 188
Mandatory Evaluation Criteria 189
Other Evaluation Criteria 190
Determining Responsiveness of Proposals to Agency Needs 191

Variances in Bid Responses 192

Minor Informalities and Irregularities 194

Handling Confidential and Proprietary Information 195

Evaluation of Payment Terms Offered 196

Documentation and Certification 196

Site Visits and Demonstrations 197

Samples, Tests, and Inspections 197

Determining the Best Value Bid 198

Negotiations 198

Best and Final Offer (BAFO) 199

Contract Award 199

Award Recommendation and Approval 200

User Sign-off 201

Finance Office/Funding 201

Executive Level and Governing Body Approval 201

Award Notification 202

CHAPTER 12. In Conclusion: Putting It All Together **203**

The Value of Competition 203

Barriers to Competition 204

The Future of Sourcing in the Public Sector 205

Electronic Sourcing (eSourcing) 206

Impact of the Internet on Procurement 206

Electronic Bid Boards and Bid Notification 206

Third-party Electronic Sourcing 207

Final Thoughts 207

Appendix A   Sole Source Procurement Request **209**

Appendix B   Directed Contract Procurement Request **211**

Appendix C   Notice of Intent (NOI) **215**

Appendix D   Levels of Mandatory Requirements (University of Victoria Model) **217**

Appendix E   Purchasing Services Strategic Objectives and Stewardship Considerations **220**

Appendix F   NIGP Code of Ethics **221**

Index **225**

Preface

To many, the idea of purchasing is not a complex matter. Individuals buy goods and services regularly, shopping for reputable suppliers and trying to get the best price for the highest quality, most affordable item. So why develop a book about purchasing for public organizations? Purchasing, or sourcing, by government organizations is a different and complex process, filled with rules, regulations, procedures, court decisions, conflict of interest prohibitions, and a plethora of issues that can complicate and confound the lives of government officials charged with procurement responsibilities.

The definition of public sourcing is the acquisition of goods or services by government organizations (Warrillow, 1995). Once considered an administrative support function, the role of the public procurement officer has evolved into an important strategic position as public organizations plan and conduct business. This role of public procurement has been expanded upon as public organizations are faced with the demands of outsourcing or privatizing services. The move toward increased privatization is virtually a demand for contracting for services (Auger, 1999). Contracting for services is the privatization tool of choice for most public organizations. As such, the demand for professional and knowledgeable procurement officials has resulted in the need for information and training with respect to procurement options and practices.

The National Institute of Governmental Purchasing (NIGP) entered into a partnership with Florida Atlantic University in 1999 to create a series of textbooks covering the important aspects of public procurement. The textbooks are to be used in professional training and will be the foundation for academic coursework and professional certification. Part of the collaboration process included the teaming of procurement practitioners and academic researchers in the field of procurement to encourage a balance and interaction between theory and practice. This collaboration has produced several symposia and has influenced a new journal (*Journal of Public Procurement*) in order to raise the visibility and increase the public perception of professionalism within the field.

This book is one of six in the first collection of foundation texts developed under this partnership. The book is divided into three parts. Part I, incorporates the theory and value of sourcing within public procurement. The book addresses several mechanisms for sourcing in the public sector. It frames the sourcing process and discusses the goals and objectives of the process.

Part II covers the preparatory work required before the solicitation document is released. It will describe the supplier and product development/information gathering and analysis phase of procurement and factors that help procurement officers in choosing an appropriate method of sourcing. The need for approved supplier lists, gathering information, and deciding on a procurement strategy will be discussed. This section will focus on needs assessment and requirements definition, where, in defining the procurement requirements, initial cost estimates are developed and suppliers are pre-qualified. The text deals with the topic of determining standards and developing functional and technical specifications for procurement items and discusses the concept of authorization and the importance of understanding who controls procurements and why control of the procurement process is necessary.

Part III represents all of the steps required in developing the bid solicitation document as well as the various processes to be considered in conjunction with the receipt, evaluation, and award of bids. It describes the steps in creating instructions to bidders and the general terms and conditions—often referred to as the boilerplate. This section provides a detailed assessment of special terms and conditions and addresses the development of the technical specifications or the Statement of Work. It addresses the mechanics of the bid proposal form utilized to submit bid responses and discusses several key issues related to the receipt, evaluation, and award of bids. The section focuses on the critical importance of receiving bids and proposals to ensure the perception of fairness and professionalism in the process. It also addresses how bids should be evaluated with particular emphasis on the selection of the evaluation team. Finally, there is a summary of the critical issues that frame the concept of public sector sourcing and discusses future sourcing challenges.

References

Auger, D. A. (1999). Privatization, contracting and the states: Lessons from state government experience. *Public Productivity and Management Review*, 22, 435-454.

Warrillow, C. (1995). Market-oriented public procurement systems. *International Trade Forum*, 3, 24-29.

Part I: The Theory and Value of Public Sourcing

Chapter 1

A Framework for Sourcing

Goals of the Procurement Process

Public procurement is governed by thousands of rules and regulations. According to McVay (1991), 4,000 federal laws were enacted that specifically affected the federal procurement process. According to the National Performance Review (1993), the Federal Government has 1,600 pages of the Federal Acquisition Regulations (FAR) plus another 2,900 pages of agency-specific supplements. Purchasing officials in state and local governments are faced with numerous rigid procurement regulations (Short, 1992). The purpose of these rules and regulations has always been to provide equity, integrity, and efficiency in the public procurement system.

Early in the history of the United States' Government, Congress passed laws prohibiting public officials from personally gaining as a result of their position of power or engaging in activities considered to be a "conflict of interest" to their position. The early framers of the administrative process were mindful of the public's expectation of fair and equitable treatment.

Highly publicized incidences of corruption and bribery of public officials, especially in the arena of public procurements, offend the public's sensibilities and undermine confidence in the public administration process. In order to maintain adequate control over the process, many procedures, rules, and regulations now govern public acquisitions.

Most of the administrative processes with respect to public procurements support various goals and objectives that are key to maintaining public confidence in the procurement process. Kelman (1990) and Warrillow (1995), among others, identified equity, integrity, and efficiency in defining this confidence.

- **Equity:** to provide fair access to bidders in competing for government business. At the heart of the need for equity is the process of fair and open competition. Competition lowers prices and supports the goal of economy.

- **Integrity:** to reduce the chance of corruption in the procurement process and maintain public confidence in the objectivity and fairness in awarding public contracts.

- **Efficiency:** to procure goods or services of the quality desired at the lowest possible price. Efficiency measures take a variety of forms, from decentralizing the process, to increasing approval thresholds at the department level, or increasing training opportunities that ensure the procurement staff is knowledgeable with respect to the myriad of procurement procedures and regulations. Efficiency is a measurement of the outputs in relation to pre-established goals and objectives and encompasses procedures and actions intended to lower the administrative transaction costs of procurements. Many eProcurement initiatives have been undertaken with this goal in mind.

These are by no means the only goals and objectives surrounding the public sourcing process. Others include:

- **Economy:** The essence of the economy goal is purchasing the exact amount of the right good or service at the best price from the best source at the right time. This goal is strongly supported by the notion of competitive acquisitions of which the competitive bid is one of the primary sourcing vehicles.

- **Transparency:** The public procurement process must be performed according to defined and well-publicized policies and procedures, especially with respect to the awarding of a contract. Both the public organization and the supplier community benefit when sourcing activities have clearly defined guidelines and procedures. The public organization benefits by maintaining the professionalism and integrity of the process, while the supplier community is well served by knowing in advance whether they are technically qualified to legitimately compete for the business. Given the cost of preparing competitive proposals in the current environment, this information allows the supplier community to determine in which competitive procurements they want to invest their resources.

- **Delegation of Authority:** The prevailing model of public procurement has been to use a centralized purchasing authority in order to maintain control and take advantage of organizational economies of scale. This model, however, has the disadvantage of creating levels of approval and causes a slow-down in the procurement process. Procurement reform efforts have acknowledged that delegating authority to field units and increasing the approval threshold has the potential to avoid some of the stumbling blocks in the process. Delegation of authority is just one of the measures intended to expand decentralization and has enabled the streamlining of the process. This downward delegation of authority entails some risk to the process and requires that adequate documentation of policies and procedures exist as well as ensures that effective audit mechanisms are in place. There are a number of different types of authority other than "delegated authority" that are often an integral part of the procurement process. These are described later in this text.

- **Law of Agency:** Agency theory is based on the idea that an organization consists of contracts between the owners (principals) of resources and their formally designated agents who are charged with managing and controlling the owner's resources. The principal is responsible for the acts of his or her agent when the agent is acting within the scope of his or her employment. Procurement officials act as agents of their respective employers (public organizations standing in for the interests of the public at large). Within agency theory is also the idea that agents have more information than the principal, which affects the principal's ability to effectively monitor the actions of the agent. An interesting dimension of agency theory becomes apparent when the provision of services is privatized, at which time private organizations become agents of government-employed principles. Procurement specialists must ensure that these private "agents" are held accountable through internal and external controls, even with the inherent information asymmetry within the principal-agent relationship.

  Procurement officials act as agents of their respective employers.

- **Non-discrimination:** Closely linked to developing neutral, functional, and technical specifications, this goal allows for all bidders to have an equal chance to supply the needed good or service. Avoiding specific manufacturer trademarks to remove bias from the procurement document is one way to achieve neutrality. This goal is closely aligned with the principle of open competition. Free and open competition is the "centerpiece around which the public contracting process turns" (Council of State Governments, 1988 p. 24). This principle requires that public acquisitions be conducted in an environment that fosters participation from many responsible suppliers covering a broad spectrum of goods and services.

- **Accountability:** Public procurement officials are being held accountable for acts preformed in the exercise of their duties. Increasing incidence of accountability legislation, both domestic and international, makes it necessary for procurement officials to be mindful of the damages awarded to aggrieved bidders who have been able to prove bias in the procurement process. Accountability is important throughout the stages of the procurement process but especially important during the monitoring and evaluation stages and post contract award. Accountability refers to the obligation of government organizations to provide efficient and effective services to assure compliance with contract provisions (Peat & Costly, 2001). The ability of public officials to hold contractors accountable depends on their ability to provide clearly specified and measurable goals and objectives within the contract.

- **Promotion of Domestic Industry:** Domestic preference policies are still prevalent in national legislation. This is changing with the creation and implementation of international agreements, such as the General Agreement on Tariffs and Trades (GATT), the North American Free Trade Agreement (NAFTA) created in 1994, and the more recent World Trade Organization (WTO) Agreement on Government Procurement. In Canada public sector agencies may be governed by the Agreement on Internal Trade (AIT). This is a Federal-Provincial-Territorial agreement restricting certain types of trade practices between jurisdictions, and applies to all levels of government, crowns, municipalities, educational institutions, etc. In July 2007, the Provinces of Alberta and British Columbia went further and signed a Trade, Investment, Labour Mobility Agreement (TILMA) that currently applies to all Ministries of both Provinces, and on July 1, 2009, applies to all levels of government as noted above. TILMA further eliminates restrictive trade barriers between the two Provinces, and reduces the dollar thresholds that require electronic competitive sourcing for goods, services and construction. For more information on AIT go to http://www.ait-aci.ca/index_en.htm and for more information on TILMA go to: http://www.gov.bc.ca/ecdev/down/BC-AB_TILMA_Agreement-signed.pdf.

- **Foster Socio-economic Objectives:** Some procurement policies currently in place give advantage to certain historically underutilized supplier groups, e.g., minorities, firms that employ individuals with disabilities, or green procurement/ sustainability issues. This constitutes what is known as "set-asides." A set-aside is a policy that allows an established percentage of the business conducted with the government organization to be excluded from the general competitive pool and purchased from a specialized class of businesses (MacManus, 1992). Proponents of set-asides argue that the policy is a means of leveling the playing field for small or historically underutilized businesses and demonstrates the impartiality within the public purchasing process. Opponents of the process argue that the favoritism inherent in the process violates the open competition, efficiency, and impartiality objectives of public sourcing.

These goals were developed in an environment in which government tasks were relatively simple and straightforward. Rules and regulations work well when procurement deals with simple commodities. However, as government jobs become more complex, many rules have become outdated and severely limit the central procurement office's ability to respond to these changes (Kelman, 1990; National Association of State Procurement Officials (NASPO) database, 1999). None of the goals and objectives can be implemented in isolation; and, while some of them are mutually supporting, others conflict with each other (Adams, 1994; Warrillow, 1995). Providing equity and non-discrimination in the sourcing process for all prospective suppliers conflicts with policies that favor promoting socio-economic objectives or favor domestic industry. Gaining efficiency by decentralizing sourcing decisions may conflict with accountability and transparency policies and the advantages of economies of scale. Different procurement environments need a different combination of balancing rules and discretion in order to achieve the best blend of the conflicting goals and objectives in the procurement process.

In order to provide guidance on how best to balance these conflicting goals, procurement organizations such as the National Institute of Governmental Purchasing (NIGP) and the Logistics Management Institute (LMI), have attempted to develop guidelines and performance standards for measuring quality, efficiency, and effectiveness of procurement operations. Performance outcome measures can be used to indicate how well the procurement process assists government organizations in meeting the goals of the procurement process (Kestenbaum & Straight, 1995). Based on the research done by the previously named organizations, various suggested performance criteria have been developed. Quality measures, which are among the most difficult to quantify, include measures of:

- Reliability: the ability to perform the service dependably and accurately;
- Responsiveness: the customer service aspect of the function; and
- Assurance: the ability of procurement officials to instill confidence in their knowledge and abilities.

Effectiveness criteria include measures relating to the:

- timeliness in meeting deadlines and other scheduled procurement activities, such as obligating funds, issuing procurement documents, and preparing contracts; and
- ability to solve problems related to procurement procedures.

Finally, suggested criteria for evaluating efficiency include measures of the:

- cost per output, i.e., the number and dollar amount of contracts awarded per procurement specialist;
- cost of the contracting organization as a percentage of the total award; or
- cost of the contracting operation as a percentage of the agency budget.

Evaluating the performance measures to be used is equally important, because "what gets measured is what gets done." Sometimes performance measures result in counter-productive behavior, as is the case if the number of contracts issued per specialist increases yet ultimately poorer quality procurements are produced. When determining the sourcing policies that guide procurement decisions, governmental organizations must consider the importance of each goal or objective in relation to their own organizational culture and values.

Structural Models for Procurement Organizations

The institutional infrastructures found in procurement organizations must also be considered. Cavinato (1992) explored the evolution of procurement organizational structures with respect to private sector procurement. Three organizational structures—centralized, decentralized, and a hybrid structure—seem to be prevalent in the public sector procurement organization. Centralized purchasing organizations have long been perceived as being necessary to ensure the integrity and accountability of the purchasing function. It is believed that centralizing the process will assure professionalism, standardize the purchase of commonly used goods, and achieve economies of scale. The centralized organization provides the ability to control procurement policies and allows for a minimum of procurement staff to perform the function.

...every procurement official is faced with challenges in determining the most appropriate mechanism for buying goods and services.

In recent years, though, centralized purchasing has been criticized for increasing red tape, prolonging the procurement period, and being less responsive to those in need of purchasing services. As a result, a movement to decentralize the procurement function exists. Re-engineering initiatives have identified procurement as a key opportunity for achieving greater efficiency by eliminating unnecessary procedural obstacles. Empowering service managers to procure necessary goods and services without having to seek approval from the central procurement office expedites the process and, ultimately, makes government function more effectively. In the totally decentralized model, the field staff can be empowered, and there is no centralized coordination of procurement activities other than those policies developed as a result of previously defined financial or operating policies. Such procedures may prevent a purchasing synergy or economy of scale for the organization as a whole and can lead to differentiated pricing by the supplier community and substantial cost increases to the organization.

A study by McCue (2001) evaluated the degree to which the procurement function is being decentralized and whether the change has, in fact, increased efficiency and effectiveness in organizations. His findings indicated that larger organizations are decentralizing at a faster rate than smaller ones, but decentralization represents different things to different organizations. Many local governments report a decentralized procurement function when, in fact, many controls still exist, and managers do not have complete control over managing their own procurement needs. Large organizations tend to decentralize the process in two ways: (1) increase the dollar limit approval levels or (2) assign purchasing responsibilities to staff in the organization's functional departments. Smaller organizations may appear to decentralize by issuing procurement cards and identifying staff in the functional areas that manage some purchasing responsibilities. McCue's study also indicated that both centralized and decentralized procurement staff perceived that they had, in fact, significantly improved efficiency in the purchasing function. The results of McCue's study suggest that the answer may not be either a centralized or decentralized procurement process but, possibly, a hybrid based on the characteristics of the procurement required. With this in mind, a model that matches procurement strategies to characteristics of procurements may be helpful in allocating sourcing responsibilities.

The third model, the hybrid procurement organization, is a combination of several models found in the Cavinato (1992) study. Aspects of both centralized and decentralized organizations exist in this model. Cavinato found a "centralized coordinator model" with a central procurement coordinator in charge of establishing procurement policies overall, with field unit procurement teams in charge of daily operational aspects reporting to an operations manager in the field. He also identified an "area planner model" which utilizes a central procurement group that establishes supplier relationships using various sourcing mechanisms, such as commodity term contracts that allow field units to purchase the commodities. These hybrid models incorporate elements of centralization in an attempt to reap the benefits that centralized control and mass purchasing provide, while streamlining the process to speed up the procurement function. Many of the efforts to reform the procurement process in the public sector have resulted in the expansion of the hybrid model throughout public organizations.

Multidimensional Model of Public Sourcing

Given the goals of procurement and the various organizational structures found in the public sector, how will the procurement officer choose among the different sourcing strategies available? Keeping in mind the goals of the public procurement process, every procurement official is faced with challenges in determining the most appropriate mechanism for buying goods and services. The model used to help choose an appropriate strategy is multidimensional. The formula must incorporate the availability of suppliers (one or more vendors competing for the business), the cost or complexity of the procurement, and the level of uncertainty or risk involved in the procurement.

When evaluating the appropriate strategy, the higher the dollar value of the projected procurement or the more complex, the greater the difficulty there is in choosing an appropriate procurement strategy. As uncertainty increases in the desired product or service, the higher the risk to the organization and the harder it is to create good requirement specifications. Uncertainty arises when multiple solutions/products could fill the need and if the requesting organization is open to a proposed product or service solution.

As uncertainty increases, a number of risk factors must be considered. Risk is a combination of threats to a project as well as opportunities that may arise during a project and may consist of many different types (Abi-Karam, 2001). Abi-Karam suggests that every project should be evaluated for six types of risk:

- **Proposal Risk:** How well does the supplier understand what the proposal requires?
- **Price Risk:** Does the price accurately reflect what the procurement will cost?
- **Schedule Risk:** Will the required item(s) be delivered on time?
- **Performance Risk:** Will the supplier deliver the item(s) with the expected quality?
- **Contractual Risk:** Will the contract documents cover unforeseen issues and protect the public organization in case of problems?
- **Surety/liability Risk:** What are the potential liabilities that may be encountered by the public organization or supplier?

Procurement officials must take all elements that may affect all procurements into consideration. Not evaluating each element and determining its importance may result in choosing an inappropriate strategy or a strategy that does not completely fulfill the procurement needs.

A multidimensional model has been created based on the elements of cost, complexity, uncertainty, risk, and supplier availability. These elements, carefully arranged in the model, can be used to provide guidance when determining which procurement strategies are the preferred options based on the projected cost, complexity, level of risk, and uncertainty. Figure 1 provides a model for addressing these elements and maps various procurement strategies based on the elements. Cost or complexity involved is mapped against the amount of uncertainty or risk, and the appropriate strategies for each situation are placed in each quadrant. The third leg of the multidimensional model addresses the availability of suppliers to compete for public business. If there is only one supplier, then the procurement method is a sole source or directed contract procurement, regardless of the other elements.

High	Emergency Purchases Invitation for Bid Reverse Auction	Request for Proposal Invitation to Negotiate Request for Information/ Expression of Intent
Cost/Complexity *Sole Source*	Small Dollar Purchases pCards Notice of Intent	Request for Statement of Qualifications Request for Quotation
Low	Risk/Uncertainty	**High**
Vendor Availability		

Figure 1. *Methods of Solicitation*

When the value of the procurement is relatively small or of little complexity and the product or service desired is very specific, procurement strategies in the lower left-hand corner (pCard, Notice of Intent or Small Dollar Purchases) are appropriate for consideration.

As cost or complexity increases, even though the desired product or service is specifically identified, a different group of strategies may be considered as shown in the upper left-hand quadrant (i.e., Emergency Purchases, Invitation for Bids, and Reverse Auction). Emergency purchases would be placed in this quadrant because the procurement official should be fairly certain that the object of the emergency purchase meets the need. The degree of uncertainty with respect to specifications is low. Emergency purchases almost always carry some measure of risk and should not be executed without careful examination of the issues.

When uncertainty or risk is high but the cost or complexity is low (possibly because the procurement is at the information gathering stage), the strategies in the lower right-hand quadrant should be considered (i.e., Request for Statement of Qualification and Request for Quotation). The upper right-hand quadrant illustrates the most difficult and most risky procurement strategies. If cost or complexity is high and a high level of uncertainty or risk exists, the organization should gather as much information as possible prior to acquisition (Request for Proposal and Invitation to Negotiate).

Evaluating procurement strategies in light of cost/complexity and uncertainty/risk enables procurement officials to categorize procurement strategies according to areas of greater flexibility. Autonomy could be allowed and decentralization of the purchasing function could achieve efficiency without risking problems with violations of procurement guidelines and rules. On the other hand, trained procurement officials who have experience with complex acquisitions should closely monitor procurements where cost/complexity and uncertainty/risk are high.

Every procurement organization should ensure that adequately trained individuals, capable of offering suggestions and advice on complex and risky procurements, are an integral part of their team. Sole source or directed contract acquisitions should always be justified so that the integrity of the process is never threatened. Procurement policies intended to reform the process should reflect organizational strengths in light of the elements described in the multidimensional model.

The stages in the sourcing process are the topics for the remaining chapters in this book. Each stage in the sourcing process is discussed in detail, and its applicability to the various sourcing mechanisms is identified. Unless identified as being applicable to only one region or nation, the information applies to procurement organizations globally. Templates for many of the documents referenced in the book are available for the reader's use. Any templates included in the text are for explanatory purposes and should be reviewed by an organization's legal office prior to use in an official procurement.

References

Abi-Karam, T. (2001). *Managing risk in design-build*. Morgantown, WV: American Association of Cost Engineers International Transactions.

Adams, M. B. (1994). Agency theory and the internal audit. *Managerial Auditing Journal, 6,* 8-12.

Cavinato, J. L. (1992). Evolving procurement organizations: Logistics implications. *Journal of Business Logistics, Oak Brook 13,* 27-37.

Council of State Governments (1988). *State and local government purchasing* (3rd ed.). Lexington, KY: National Association of State Procurement Officials.

Kelman, S. (1990). *Procurement and public management: The fear of discretion and the quality of government performance.* Washington, DC: AEI Press.

Kestenbaum, M. I., & Straight, R. L. (1995). Procurement performance: Measuring quality, effectiveness and efficiency. *Public Productivity and Management Review, 19,* 200-215.

MacManus, S. A. (1992). *Doing business with government.* New York: Paragon House.

McCue, C.P. (2001), *Organizing The Public Purchasing Function: A Survey Of Cities And Counties.* Government Finance Review, 1, p 9-13.

McVay, B.L., (1991). *The History of federal procurement: How we got to where we are.* Woodbridge, VA: Pan-optic Enterprises.

National Performance Review (1993, September). *Reinventing federal procurement.* Washington, DC: U.S. Government Printing Office.

Peat, B., & Costley, D. L. (2001). Effective contracting of social services. *Nonprofit Management and Leadership, 12,* 55.

Short, J. (1992). *Issues in public purchasing: A guidebook for policymakers.* Lexington, KY: The Council of State Governments.

Warrillow, C. (1995). Market-oriented public procurement systems. *International Trade Forum, 3,* 24-29.

Chapter 2

Introduction to Sourcing

Public organizations are spending enormous amounts of money annually on goods and services. The United States Federal Government alone is the largest buyer in the world with annual procurements in excess of $400 billion. When you add procurements by U.S. state and local governments, the annual procurement exceeds $700 billion annually. With this level of investment at stake, it is important that public procurement officers increase their knowledge and awareness of appropriate sourcing methods and develop an awareness of best practices in the field to ensure that the public's confidence in the public procurement function is increased.

Because of the purchasing power of public organizations, the temptation toward favoritism and abuse has resulted in a profusion of rules and regulations designed to restrain and control the process and the amount of discretion afforded by government officials. By the late 1980s, public procurement seemed bogged down in red tape and the administrative process. A call for procurement reform resulted in a number of sourcing strategies designed to improve and streamline public sourcing. Procurement officials needed to act strategically in support of jurisdiction/agency missions, goals, and objectives and had to develop processes, practices, and systems of checks and balances that were effective and efficient to safeguard the public interest and best serve the organizations' overall needs.

Public and private sector procurement procedures differ dramatically. While both sectors are interested in acquiring the best quality for the least price, the public sector is faced with obstacles that often tie the hands of procurement officers. MacManus (1992) provides seven characteristics that contrast public sourcing with its private sector counterpart.

- The funds expended are public and may be used only as prescribed by law under careful budgetary, oversight, and auditing procedures.

- The goods and services acquired are for the use of government organizations and are not usually intended for resale or manufacturing purposes.

- The procurement process is managed by public employees who are not motivated by profit-centered objectives, as are private sector employees.

- The procurement process is conducted in public view and under public scrutiny where everything related to the process is a matter of public record.

- Public procurement officials have little discretion, bound by the rules and regulations inherent in the administrative process that leave little room for innovation.

- Public managers are subject to censure and prosecution for mishandling any public procurement, while only the most grievous private sector procurement catastrophes are reported to the public.

- The size and scope of public procurement allows government to dominate the market unlike most private organizations which place public procurement officials in a position of considerable power and leverage.

These characteristics indicate why the public sourcing arena is filled with bureaucratic processes. The bureaucracy involved in public procurement has led many to criticize public procurement and search for ways to improve the process. In order to make improvements, there needs to be an understanding of the stages within the procurement process and how they relate to procurement strategies.

Stages in the Solicitation Process

There are nine stages in the procurement process. Depending on the method of procurement, not all stages are required. The following list provides only a basic overview of the process, which will be expanded later.

- **Information Gathering/Analysis/Supplier and Product Development:** collecting information with respect to procurement needs and identifying supplier and product lists.

- **Identifying the Needs and Requirements Definition:** identifying specific functional needs for defining accurate requirements.

- **Specifications and Standards:** writing detailed technical descriptions of the characteristics of the requested goods and/or services.

- **Review and Authorization:** assessing and endorsing prior to the actual procurement as a part of the oversight process.

- **Source Document Preparation and Competitive Sourcing:** compiling formal paperwork for release to the supplier community, which may be very simple or extraordinarily complex.

- **Review, Evaluation, and Recommendation:** deciding to procure goods and services and considering and assessing all submitted responses following predetermined guidelines.

- **Approval, Award, and Contract Formation:** assessment and endorsement by the official, presenting a formal contract to the supplier and negotiating, if necessary.

- **Acceptance, Certification, Payment, and Reporting:** arriving at an agreement with the supplier in areas such as accepting terms; ensuring fulfillment of contractual requirements; initiating payment schedules; determining documentation and reporting requirements.

- **Post Award—Ongoing Supply Management and Planning Activities:** evaluating the process; documenting any discrepancies; making inspections, processing payments; beginning to plan for future procurements. (See Figure 2.)

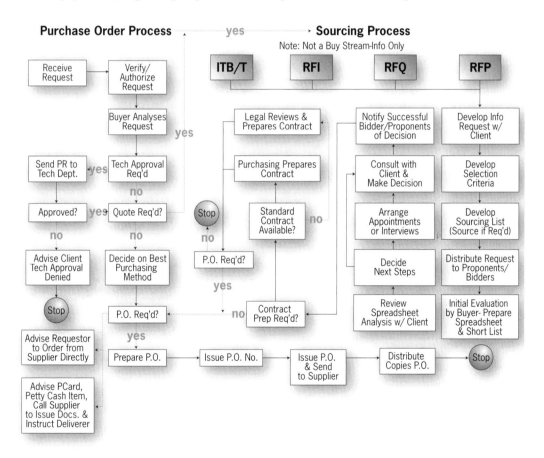

Figure 2. *Purchasing process flow chart*

The three Phases and nine Steps or Stages in the procurement life-cycle are further detailed in Table 1 below.

STAGE/DESCRIPTION	INPUTS - OUTPUTS - ACTIONS
Pre-sourcing Phase	
I. Supplier & Product Development	Supplier Registration
	Product Registration
	Product Testing
	Market Research
	Supplier Performance
	Regulatory Provisions
	Environmental Assessment
	Pre-Qualified Suppliers
	Pre-Approved Products
II. Needs Identification & Requirements Determination	Specifications
	Standards
	Suggested Products
	Suggested Suppliers
	Risk Assessment
III. Acquisition Review & Authorization	Program Needs
	Funding - Budget Provisions
	Approval Record
	Commitment Recorded
	Internal Control - Approval on Non-Budget Items
	Account Holder Signing Authority & Spending Levels
	Establish Acquisition Team
	Establish Terms of Reference
Sourcing Phase	
IV. Determining the Sourcing Options & Methods	Preparing the Sourcing Plan
	Preparing the Sourcing Documents

V. Conducting the Sourcing Exercise	Issue Appropriate Sourcing Document(s)
	Invite Bidders/Potential Offerors
	Receiving & Accepting Submissions
	Evaluate Submissions
	Select Supplier to be Awarded Contract
	Obtain Procurement's Recommendations for Award
	Obtain Internal Audit Review *(where required)*
	Obtain Legal Counsel Review *(where required)*
	Obtain Chief Information Officer Review *(where required)*
	Obtain Freedom of Information Office Review *(where required)*
	Conduct Negotiations *(when appropriate)*
	Recommend Contract Award - Executive Approval *(where required)*
	Obtain Contract Approval
VI. Award & Contract Formation	Inform Successful Bidder/Offeror
	Formalize Legal Aspects of the Contract
	Conduct Debriefing *(where required)*
Post-sourcing Phase	
VIII. Contract Fulfillment & Administration	Expediting & Follow-Up
	Delivery and Acceptance
	Quality Assurance
	Certification for Payment
	Payment
	Reporting & Information Exchange
VIII. Contract & Asset Management	Manage Corporate Supply Management Program & Operations
	Stakeholder Performance Reporting
	Evaluate Contract Fulfillment
IX. On-Going Supply Planning & Management *(These steps will cycle back to the first phase - Pre-Sourcing)*	Planning for Future Sourcing Requirements
	Global and Regional Market Research
	Industry Trending

Table 1. *The Procurement Life Cycle*

Methods of Solicitation

A minimum of 11 different sourcing methods have been discovered. Some are procedurally simple, while others are very complex. Procurement professionals have used at least one or more of the following sourcing methods:

- Small Dollar/Purchasing Card
- Emergency Purchases
- Sole Source
- Request for Quote (RFQ) (Telephone and Informal)
- Invitation for Bids (IFB)/Invitation to Tender (ITT)
- Request for Proposal (RFP)
- Request for Information (RFI) or Request for Expression of Interest (REI)
- Reverse Auction
- Invitation to Negotiate (ITN)
- Request for Supplier Qualification (RFSQu)
- Notice of Intent (NOI)
- Joint Solutions Procurement (JSP)
- Public-Private Partnerships (P3s)
- Strategic Alliances (SAs)

While this list of sourcing methods or strategies is not exhaustive for the public sector, it identifies the most common and includes some that are new to the sourcing arena.

Small Dollar/Purchasing Card

The small dollar purchase strategy is based on granting authority for an individual or organization to independently purchase goods or services within a pre-established dollar threshold, independent of authorization and formal purchasing processes. This strategy can save time and money by reducing the administrative burden caused by directing all purchasing requests through a central purchasing authority. The decentralization of the procurement process has increased the use of this sourcing strategy in the hopes of greater efficiency (MacManus, 1992). By nature of its existence, the procurement process is an expense to the organization; and, as a result, any selected strategy for small dollar purchases must consider reasonable administrative costs. Some questions to be asked when considering a small dollar purchase include:

- Can an alternate be used that is available on an existing contract?

- Is the request a seasonal item that should be placed on a schedule for future purchases?

- Is the user requesting the item frequently and combining purchases that could provide justification for a demand contract?

- Should the item be purchased locally for service needs?

- Is there only one source?

- Is there a long delivery time?

- Should more than the required minimum number of quotations be solicited for greater competition and value? (NIGP, 2004)

While the purchasing card (pCard) is merely an extension of the authority granted for small dollar purchases, the benefits received in reduced administrative burdens far outweigh the risks of the decentralization of procurement control. Studies have shown that the paper processing of small dollar purchases may cost between $12 and $14 per purchase order. The use of the pCard has been show to reduce the cost of processing in some cases to less than one cent (even with pCard finance charges and late fees included). Cost savings of pCard use will vary depending on the transaction fees and the anticipated transaction volume. Adequate training and expanded use of this method has further reduced the cost of pCard transactions. In addition, reporting documents provided by card issuers can help identify purchasing trends and monitor the information for strategic planning, audit, and financial reporting purposes; however, procurement card scandals have created severe political pressure that have resulted in more strict central controls. The savings from the cards is far greater than the "abuse "of a select few and the perception of widespread abuse placed pressure on the Federal Government to introduce reforms.

Emergency Purchases

NIGP's Public Procurement *Dictionary of Terms* defines an "emergency purchase" as:

> A purchase made due to an unexpected and urgent request where health and safety or the conservation of public resources is at risk. Usually formal competitive bidding procedures are waived. (NIGP, 2007)

In such situations, the agency must respond quickly to an immediate need. Often, decisions made under these circumstances are not as efficient or impartial as procurements that follow formal guidelines while maintaining adequate supplier lists; however, the use of term contracts can help ensure that even under emergency circumstances, the agency still receives goods at reasonable prices (MacManus, 1992). Procurement officials cannot avoid such acquisitions due to bona fide emergencies; but immediate need purchases should be minimized, as they can result in significant additional costs to the jurisdiction.

Sole Source Purchase

NIGP's Public Procurement Dictionary of Terms defines "sole source procurement" as

> A situation created due to the inability to obtain competition. May result because only one vendor or supplier possesses the unique ability or capability to meet the particular requirements of the solicitation. The purchasing authority may require a justification from the requesting agency explaining why this is the only source for the requirement. (NIGP, 2007)

Sole Source acquisitions, also known as directed contracts", do not equate to bad procurements. It is merely a different process with different options. While it is important for purchasing agents to be aggressive in limiting the use of this procurement method, they need to recognize that competitive bidding is not a suitable purchase method for these types of items. While similar products may exist, a particular product may be the only one that can satisfy the customer's requirement for parts or service compatibility, or other valid reasons. Justification for specifying and choosing such products is extremely important and needs to be clearly stipulated in these situations. For example, a manufacturer has established an exclusive sales arrangement with a dealer in the southern portion of the United States, which is the only dealership that maintains stock of distributor caps for the riding lawn mowers used by the Park Commission. The dealership, being the only supplier of a specific product, is considered a sole source and a directed contract is appropriate.

Narrowly defined

specifications

may impair the

competitive process...

The critical element in determining the legitimacy of the sole source or directed contract purchase is the nature of the requirement specifications. Narrowly defined specifications may impair the competitive process and may potentially give an unfair advantage to one particular supplier. There must be adequate justification to utilize the sole source or directed contract purchase option. (A Sample Sole Source Procurement Request is included as Appendix A.)

The following definition can be found on the Treasury Board of Canada Secretariat website:

Directed Contract (marché prescrit) - a contract awarded to a pre-selected contractor in circumstances where the contracting authority has justifiably set aside the requirement to solicit bids under the provision of one or more of the exceptions to competitive solicitation in Section 6 of the Government Contracts Regulations. Contracting authorities are strongly encouraged to provide public notification of these contracts through an Advance Contract Award Notice (ACAN) using the electronic bidding methodology. If this is done and if there are no valid challenges received to the ACAN within 15 days, the directed contract is deemed to be competitive and may be awarded using the higher electronic bidding contracting authority levels. (www.tbs-sct.gc.ca/pubs_pol/dcgpubs/Contracting/contractingpol_a_e.asp)

A "directed contract" occurs when an award is made to a supplier on a preferential basis and there are several others in the marketplace that offer the same product and or service, some at lower prices, and at better delivery and supply terms. Prior to making an award in these situations, a completed "Directed Contract" document is required to justify why the end-user or internal customer wants to award a contract without competition, and to other than the lowest available supplier (lowest responsive and responsible supplier). The directed contract document is used where a single source supplier is selected. In other words, there are more than one supplier available, but a single supplier is selected, other than the lowest priced and best fulfillment supply arrangements is recommended. (A Sample Directed Contract Procurement Request is shown as Appendix B.)

Request for Quotation (RFQ)

This method, also known as informal competitive bidding (ICB), is generally utilized without advertising the need for a procurement or requiring sealed proposals or bids to be submitted. This is an efficient way to gain comparative information from suppliers either by phone or in writing. This method can also be utilized if the expected dollar amount for the procurement is relatively small but exceeds the minimum threshold and requires some level of competitive pricing. A minimum of two or three quotes from responsible suppliers is typically sufficient. This can assure that the organization is paying a reasonable fee for the product and may introduce a minimal element of competition in the process.

Invitation for Bids (IFB)/Invitation to Tender (ITT)

Also known as competitive sealed bidding, this strategy is

> [The] preferred method for acquiring goods, some services and construction for public use in which award is made to the lowest responsive and responsible bidder, based solely on the response to criteria set forth in the IFB; does not include discussions or negotiations with bidders. (NIGP, 2007)

A common choice in the public sector, it is perceived to be the most impartial means of awarding public contracts. MacManus (1992) suggests that competitive sealed bids meet these three basic principles of public procurement:

- Openness is achieved by requiring public notice and public opening of bids.
- Fairness and efficiency are maintained by awarding contracts to the lowest responsive bidder.
- Competition is assured by increasing the number of suppliers interested in bidding on public projects.

Some questions to consider when deciding to use a competitive sealed bid include:

- Is the dollar value of the bid large enough to justify the expense incurred by both buyer and seller?
- Are the specifications explicit enough to provide a clear understanding of the product to be provided for estimation of cost by the supplier?
- Is there an adequate number of suppliers in the market to respond to the bid?
- Is there a supplier community that is qualified and interested in responding to the bid?
- Have allowances been made for sufficient time to complete the competitive sealed bid process?

An IFB should include the following information:

- a Notice of Letting or public advertising;

- standard clauses that would include: instructions and information to bidders concerning the bid submission requirements, time and date set for bid opening, a contact person, the address of the office at which bids are to be received, when the bid is due and the procedure for receiving and certifying bids, information about a bidder's conference or how supplier questions will be processed; deviations or waivers of technicalities in specifications; and any other special information;

- instructions to suppliers, which include a description of the required procurement, specifications, evaluation criteria, delivery or performance schedule, and inspection and acceptance requirements for the good or service to be acquired;

- contract terms and conditions, including warranty, bonding, or other security requirements, as applicable;

- statement of work and delivery timetable;

- a bid proposal form;

- directions for obtaining reference documents, if applicable;

- the acknowledgment by the bidder of the receipt of any amendments issued; and

- instructions for the submission of bid samples, descriptive literature, and technical data, which may require inspection or testing of a product before award, if required.

Clearly defined specifications result in greater savings potential.

If cost is not the only factor to be considered, it is best to consider a broader, more competitive procurement, such as a Request for Proposal (RFP) or Invitation to Negotiate (ITN). The IFB is not appropriate for large-scale competitive procurements. If an organization were to consider building an additional bridge to handle commuter traffic, an ITN or RFP would be a better sourcing strategy. It is important for the procurement official to be able to determine which competitive procurement option is the best vehicle for the situation.

Request for Proposal (RFP)

The Request for Proposal is a competitive procurement method that allows the reviewer or evaluator to consider factors other than price (supplier qualifications, experience, project approach, innovation, and creativity or value-added services) when making the decision to award. The RFP is such a complex procurement option that entire books are devoted to the topic. *Developing and Managing Requests for Proposals in the Public Sector*, 2nd Edition, by Khi V. Thai, Ph.D., Florida Atlantic University, is another in the NIGP LEAP series of texts. (NIGP, 2007) In order for the RFP to be used effectively, all elements must be clearly defined in order to provide the supplier with a total understanding of the product or service that is being requested. Most RFPs have, at a minimum, the following distinctive sections (Stocks, 2001).

- **Background/Overview** - includes the history of the project and the reason for issuing; contains contact information, project time lines, and other pertinent information.

- **Submittal Instruction** - defines the proposal format, number of copies required, answers to related questions, submission deadlines, bidder's conference details, and indicates the format and offeror's requirements for participation.

- **Terms and Conditions** - include all language normally incorporated into the contract, i.e., applicable standard clauses and special provisions, information on governing law, limitations of liability, remedies, and indemnifications.

- **Mandatory Requirements** - identify obligatory elements of the proposal. This section contains clearly defined, minimally acceptable limits of each requirement and should be measurable.

- **Scorable Mandatories** - provide obligatory requirements that have associated point values.

- **Desirables** - include functional or technical requirements over and above the mandatory requirements with associated point values.

- **Pricing** - includes a separate form to be completed by the supplier for submission of their pricing. It is generally opened following the evaluation of the functional and technical proposal.

- **Evaluation** - clearly defines the weighing factor for each requirement and the scoring methodology to be used.

One of the most difficult aspects of writing an RFP is providing good functional and technical specifications. Research by Pettijohn and Qiao (2000) indicates that suppliers add, on average, approximately 20% to most fixed price contracts because of uncertainty and risk caused by unclear specifications. The research also revealed that most public organizations consider their distributed specifications to be of a high quality and easy to comprehend. This incongruity of perceptions is costing public organizations millions of dollars and presents an opportunity to significantly reduce the cost of an acquisition on the part of the agency or jurisdiction. Organizations should be charged with strategically approaching project goals and working to fully identify and describe functionality and technical requirements. Clearly defined specifications result in greater savings potential.

Request for Information (RFI)/Request for Expression of Interest (REI)

This strategy is generally used during the information gathering and analysis stage of procurement. The organization collects relevant product information and availability data to determine the level of competition in the marketplace. The RFI or REI is appropriately used if there is a need for new or additional information concerning: (1) what type of product or service a supplier offers or (2) if a specific type of product or service is available in the marketplace. RFI's do not include any estimate of pricing for the specific solution and does not obligate either the entity or the supplier.

If an exceptional amount of data is required to develop a complex specification, it is a good idea to issue a RFI, as it will assist in the development of specifications. The RFI should include the following:

- the scope of the proposed procurement
- the organization's intent
- the time frame for the procurement and
- the functional requirements of the procurement.

Reverse Auction

This sourcing method allows the buyer to manage the procurement through the use of Web-based technology to achieve real-time, dynamic pricing from the supplier community. A commodity request is made via a public auction notice with the intent of allowing suppliers to compete for the opportunity to provide the requested good or service at the lowest possible cost to the buyer. As bids are submitted in real time, the price of an item decreases until the bidder offering the lowest price is awarded a contract.

Prior to 1997, federal purchasing regulations prohibited the use of reverse auctioning. The Federal Acquisition Regulation (FAR) was revised to allow agencies to participate in this type of procurement following its success in the private sector. Agencies have reported substantial savings, often in excess of 20%, for specific commodity purchases. With such dramatic pricing results, some suppliers have expressed reservations about participating in the process, as the consequence of the fact that the savings realized by this method generally reduce the profit margin of the vendor.

The Federal Government reports success with this procurement method.

> "The State Department recently said it had conducted 4,700 reverse auctions worth $169 million, with a savings of close to $18 million on what it had expected to pay for the items. At the beginning of the year, FedBid announced a contract with the General Services Administration for a similar five-year award to provide reverse auction services to that agency and others eligible to use GSA contracts." (Robinson, B, 2006)

State and local governments, likewise, have seen some substantial savings using this method. For example, both the state of Connecticut and the city of Washington, DC report high savings from energy auctions. In fact, auctions of very volatile, indexed commodities, such as natural gas and electricity, have proven to be very fertile ground for savings using the reverse auction method.

In Washington, DC, the Office of Contracting and Procurement, or OCP, and Office of Property Management (OPM) held a reverse auction on June 4, 2007 for the procurement of natural gas. OCP successfully aggregated 25 neighboring jurisdictions to participate, which allowed all participants the advantage of aggregation of over 41 million therms (a measure of natural gas). This was the largest aggregation the region had ever had for the procurement of natural gas.

The previous contract that the District of Columbia (DC) had for the natural gas supply only had one supplier respond, OCP had 4 suppliers participating in this reverse auction event. This level of participation-created competition proved very beneficial to all of the participating governments in the DC Region. Figure 3 below shows the actual event in the DC auction.

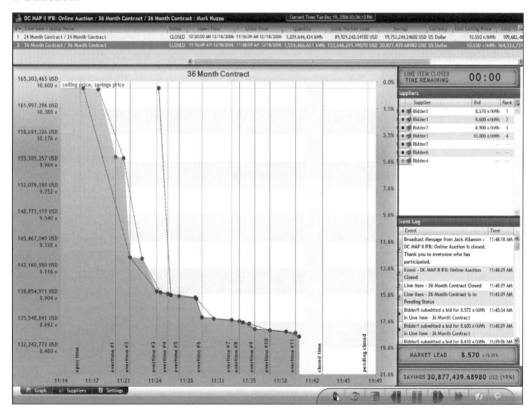

Figure 3. *Chart of Online Reverse Auction Conducted by Washington DC, OCP and OPM.*

In testimony delivered to the DC City Council on February 7, 2008, the CPO stated "With an online auction, buyers initiate the auction by sending out advance purchasing specifications to sellers that detail the buyer's coming needs. Suppliers compete against each other in web-based, real-time auctions, driving down the price in the process. Bidding is done on each requirement based on one or more contract durations, so that a buyer is able to determine whether a longer or shorter term contract is more cost effective. Online reverse auctions reduce purchasing costs, streamline procurement and increase savings when purchasing energy. Typically online reverse auctions reduce purchasing cycle time by 80% and save 30% or more in pricing."

As with any procurement strategy, success depends on the amount of preparation that is applied to the process. Leseur (2001) states that three elements have led to some of the skepticism surrounding reverse auctions.

- Those who provide online reverse auction services have recommended the use of the reverse auction for all types of acquisition. Procurement officials should analyze the types of categories that make for good auction candidates, as this method should not always be considered to be appropriate.

- Second, the organization often focuses only on the lowest cost without considering best and total value. Whether the auction can provide the best value at the lowest cost also depends on the preparation of the specifications.

- Finally, it is absolutely critical to attend to supplier screening and have good communications with the supplier community. Conducting auctions that result in faulty or no bid awards will eventually discourage the supplier community from participating and eliminate the viability of this strategy.

Faulty reverse auctions cause the supplier community to feel exploited and tend to undermine existing buyer-supplier relationships (Jop, 2000; Kwak, 2002). When performed effectively, though, the reverse auction can save money for public organizations and increase the competitiveness among the supplier community.

Evaluation of offers under this contracting method is simple. This procurement method is in essence competitive bidding on a very well-defined commodity or service, where only price matters in the award. The offered price is dynamic, meaning it changes in response to other offerors' pricing. This dynamic pricing environment allows other bidders to see what their competitors are providing as low price, and can react to that. Obviously, that sort of dynamic pricing allows the government to receive the lowest price on the spot market at that time on that date.

In addition to a very well-honed specification, it is often beneficial to pre-qualify bidders, mainly to eliminate possible disqualification of bids. Another reason to establish a finite bidder group is to allow for training the bidders on the auction application that will be used. Technology is what makes this procurement method work, and given that it is not commonly used, pre-training the bidders makes for a smoother auction event and a more successful outcome for the government buyer.

Invitation to Negotiate (ITN)

The Invitation to Negotiate is a competitive strategy differing from an IFB or RFP, both in content and objective, and requires distinct preliminary work in advance of the actual procurement such as negotiating factors, end results expected by the owner, negotiating give-aways, and considerations the owner is not prepared to relinquish. In pursuing an ITN, the procurement officer predetermines goals for a competitive negotiation that:

- state the non-negotiable elements of the requirements, terms, and risk elements
- state the mandatory framework for payments, performance mechanisms, and contract management and
- identify the functionality needed and desired while allowing sufficient flexibility for proposed innovation.

The ITN provides the basis for negotiation and is not a structured methodological approach, as defined by an IFB or RFP. The contents of an ITN establish parameters for a long and potentially expensive procurement process. The quality of the document content demonstrates the commitment and professionalism of the issuing organization and can impact the quality of the proposals received from the supplier community. A typical ITN will have the following components:

- **Overview** - a basic statement that outlines the purpose and vision for the procurement.
- **Relationship of Issuing Organization and Supplier** - an outline explaining the relationship between the organization and the supplier.
- **Scope** - outlines the nature of the services desired and the boundaries of the proposed engagement.
- **Requirement Specifications** - include any functional or technical requirements for the proposed project along with clearly defined mandatory elements allowing for supplier innovation and suggestions.
- **Performance Measurement and Payment Strategy** - the explanation of project success evaluation measures and how the remuneration is structured.
- **Implementation Plan** - a statement articulating the transition from the current to the new environment.
- **Supplier Responses** - outline the structure, format, and necessary components for the supplier proposals and includes basic response evaluation methodology.
- **Draft Contract** - a copy of a sample contract included for supplier review.
- **Supporting Information** - any additional documentation and information that will assist the supplier in understanding the nature of the desired acquisition.

By using an ITN, suppliers can propose an innovative approach without the restrictions or limitations of fixed requirements established well in advance of the procurement. A potential solution, offered by the supplier community, allows the organization to take advantage of innovative approaches. However, the issuing organization must be prepared to articulate specific functionality, provide a clear and exact description of the current environment, and devise an approach for evaluating supplier proposals.

Because suppliers can alter their proposals during the negotiation process and before presenting their Best and Final Offer (BAFO), the agencies must be aware of the potential for protests against them. Without adequate control over supplier communication and assurances of objectivity and fairness, the supplier community may protest the final decision. The procurement officer must establish a responsible evaluation team and determine which proposals best competitively meet the needs of the organization. FAR, Part 15, addresses both competitive and non-competitive negotiations. Competitive negotiations have, thus far, not been widely used but are gaining acceptance among public organizations. The ITN has been successfully used in many state government acquisitions.

Request for Supplier Qualification (RFSQu)

Similar to an RFP, an RFSQu extends a solicitation notice to known vendors and to others by invitation. An electronic bid notification service or system is often used for the announcement. Rather than making an award, bidders and proponents are pre-qualified based on the criteria contained in the solicitation notice. The respondents' names are then placed on a list for future solicitation opportunities as they arise during a specified period of time. Internal users or customers of the organization can then select any of the pre-qualified suppliers or service providers for contract award without the delay of a competitive sourcing process. Only those pre-qualified suppliers can be used for work described in the original solicitation notice. A subsequent request for similar work does not have to be posted for competition, thus saving the organization time, effort, and expense.

Notice of Intent (NOI)

A public notice issued to announce the intended award of an agreement to a certain supplier or service provider without a formal competitive sourcing exercise is called a Notice of Intent. This notice may be issued through a newspaper advertisement; business, trade or commerce journal; or by an electronic bid notification service or system. The provision of this notice requires that any bidder or proponent that wishes to participate in this work may object to the award. A bidder must provide substantiated evidence of contract performance capability and marketplace competitiveness. The NOI must indicate details of the work, the process for submitting objections, closing time for objections, and the location for objection filing. These types of solicitations are often used if a satisfactory relationship exists with a supplier or service provider and it is not in the organization's best interest to change providers. Organizations should consider the value attached to the continuity of work (consulting system development), training, cost of switching to an alternate firm, stage in the project life cycle, proprietary product, parts or components compatibility, etc., before ending a supplier relationship. (A sample NOI is included as Appendix C.)

Joint Solutions Procurement (JSP)

A Joint Solution Procurement is a multi-step sourcing process, and varies by jurisdiction and the nature of the specific acquisition. It is referred to as "joint" in that the supply community is directly involved and engaged in the establishment of the specification, potential project design, and deliverables prior to posting the solicitation for formal bids or proposals. These acquisitions normally involve pioneering technology where the specific product and/or service has never been acquired before in the intended state of use or installation. These acquisitions tend to be high value (multi-million dollars) and high risk. Therefore, if you get it wrong on the first go, you have no opportunity of recovering any value. Prime examples of this are the VENUS and NEPTUNE projects in current implementation stages on the west coast of Washington and British Columbia through the University of Victoria and several private sector and federal, state, and provincial partners. These projects involve the laying of fiber-optic cables beneath or on the ocean floor that are interconnected with villages of technological sensors and monitors. Data and photographs are fed back to a super computer via the fiber-optic cabling and sensors or monitoring devices affixed to the cables. This is state-of-the-art technology and has never been tried before in its current context. A Joint Solutions Procurement Model was used to acquire the products, technology, services, installation and maintenance of these networks.

The steps in this solicitation method are as follows:

1. A Request for Information or Request for Expression of Interest is issued. This document stipulates that only those respondent's to this RFI/REI are eligible to participate in any subsequent solicitation for the same or similar work on this or a directly related part of the project.

2. Proponent submissions are evaluated and considered based on their ability to meet the vision of the agency and project. Proponents deemed capable of meeting the perceived needs of the project are invited to make formal presentations, including sharing of technical details on a non-proprietary basis and the right of the agency to utilize concepts, technology, etc., in subsequent sourcing competition.

3. Should the agency proceed with the acquisition(s), a formal Request for Proposal is issued in accordance with #1 above. This RFP makes provision for short-

listing, formal presentations, site visits, prototype provisions, field testing, inspections of manufacturing plants, parent company guarantees where alliances and sibling firms are used, "Best and Final Offers" (BAFO), negotiations, and no-cost to the agency for development of the technology and product design.

Firms are instrumental in the overall design and success of implementation and participate in developing emerging technology at their cost with little or no risk to the agency. All firms are given an equal and open ability to participate in the final outcomes.

Some jurisdictions also post a DRAFT Request for Information or Request for Proposals on an electronic BID Board for potential offerors to submit their ideas, concepts and proposals on a non-exclusive and non-proprietary basis.

Public-Private Partnerships (P3)

A "Public-Private Partnership" (P3) is a form of acquisition and procurement arrangement between a public sector agency and a private sector supplier for the delivery of a project. This arrangement may include, but is not limited to, some combination of ownership, design, construction, financing, operation and/or maintenance of public capital assets and which typically relies on user fees or alternative sources of revenue to recover all or part of the related capital (debt servicing and return on equity if applicable), operation and capital maintenance costs. In most cases the supplier covers all up-front development costs and operating costs for a specified period of time, and after this time has elapsed, the facility or project reverts to the public sector agency. In all cases a formal Request for Proposal or Invitation to Tender/Invitation for Bid is issued to secure the contractor. Each P3 arrangement has unique characteristics and will depend on the nature of the project or acquisition.

Strategic Alliance (SA)

Strategic Alliance (SA) is an agreement between two or more organizations to cooperate in a specific business activity so that each benefits from the strengths of the other, and gains competitive advantage. (Business, 2002) (NIGP, 2007) It is mutually beneficial to both parties in that the public organization permits the private organization (supplier) marketing privileges in specified public sector publications, structures, events and/or venues.

Characteristics of a Strategic Alliance are:

- Value is provided by the external organization in cash, products and/or services, in-kind assistance, promotional items, etc.

- To provide value to the public sector organization through supply arrangements that include values that are over and above best-in-market pricing (point-of-purchase)

- Multi-year contracts, usually at least three, with options for renewals

- Higher value acquisitions, usually greater than $200,000 per year

- Value-added revenue supports public sector organization fundraising objectives

- Often results in a preferential agreement offering exclusivity (marketing rights), including preferred supplier status

- Exchange of value between the parties, usually marketing rights for the period, or recognition for contribution to the public sector organization

- Strategic Alliance Supplier requested and arranged specifically through a formal RFP or Tender

- Cannot be sole/single sourced to achieve the identified/expected results

- The user department's needs and specifications must be met before the value-added benefits are evaluated

- Internal user shall not bear any added cost or be in a "worse" situation with a Strategic Alliance supply arrangement than prior to the arrangement

- Point-of-Purchase (POP) prices (costs) to internal users take priority and must not be compromised to achieve a Strategic Alliance agreement

- There must be willingness by the Supplier Community to engage in a SA prior to competitive sourcing being undertaken

- There must be an internal user agreement and sign-off to proceed with a SA for the designated category of products and/or services.

- If there is no value-added offering from potential offerors, then it reverts to a standard supply relationship.

Solicitation Categories

Public sector procurements range from school laboratory microscopes to airport landing lights, from fire department ladders to "911" emergency communication systems. Yet, the majority of acquisitions primarily fall into the following categories:

- **Products:** defined as "anything purchased other than services or real property" (Council of State Governments, 1988).

- **Products and/or Services (Supply, Install, and Maintain):** a combination of goods and services in the same acquisition where the supplier of the good must also provide installation and/or some initial or ongoing support.

- **Professional Services/Other Services:** the "furnishing of labor, time, or effort by a contractor not involving the delivery of a specific end-product other than reports which are merely incidental to the required performance" (Council of State Governments, 1988).

- **Technology and Related Systems:** a combination of goods and professional services specifically related to the purchase of technology and information systems.

- **Construction, Infrastructure, and Facilities Management:** acquisitions that involve "the process of building, altering, or repairing a public structure or building or other improvements to any public real property" (Council of State Governments, 1988). There are three primary types of construction methods. They are: The traditional Design-Bid-Build; Construction Management as Agent; and Design-Build. Common variations of these three main types of construction methods are: Design-Build-Finance, Design-Build-Maintain, Design-Build-Own-Operate-Transfer, Design-Build-Own-Operate, and P3s. Each have their strengths, weaknesses, opportunities and threats and should be thoroughly investigated prior to commencement of the procurement solicitation.

- **Printing and Reprographics:** specialized service procurement category for printing and copying. This category now includes "Convergence" which integrates photocopiers, multi-functional printers, desktop printers, scanners, and facsimile devices.

- **Capital/Major Equipment:** major dollar value purchases of "personal property of a durable nature which retains its identity throughout its useful life" (Council of State Governments, 1988).

Each of these categories has its own characteristics with respect to the methods and strategies. Some sourcing strategies will work for one and others for another. These differences will be articulated throughout the book and within the ensuing discussion of the sourcing process.

eProcurement as a Strategy

Electronic procurement, or eProcurement, is the process of using electronic technologies for purchasing goods and services. It offers an opportunity for an organization to transition from a traditional paper-based process to a real-time electronic platform to improve customer service and reduce costs. It is a technology that has changed the way that procurement officers define their roles in procurement. Used appropriately, eProcurement provides information and streamlines the process, thus, allowing procurement professionals to concentrate on more strategic issues. Once over-burdened with the administrative details inherent in a predominantly paper-based process, organizations are released to examine issues that will dramatically change the way government must conduct its business. eProcurement covers a variety of options (Thai & Grimm, 2000), including:

- posting on the Internet the procurement manuals, forms, and policies used by public organizations and the supplier community;
- maintaining and updating approved supplier lists online;
- utilizing online catalogs to research and acquire approved commodities;
- providing online information pertaining to bid opportunities, supplier information, and bid tabulation results;
- providing notice to the supplier community of current bid opportunities and allowing online submission of bids;
- posting contract opportunities for historically underutilized supplier populations, such as small, minority, or women-owned firms;
- allowing for the e-signing of contracts;
- enabling existing procurement processes, such as Electronic Data Interchange (EDI).

Anticipated benefits of eProcurement may include:

- cost savings through reduced data entry errors in procurement systems;
- savings in cycle time within the procurement process;
- the ability to negotiate best value with suppliers;
- increased opportunities for streamlining and re-engineering business processes;
- improvement in monitoring supplier relationships; and
- fewer misunderstandings and errors between purchasing staff and departmental requestors.

eProcurement requires careful planning in order to integrate the systems, policies, processes, and human resources necessary to make eProcurement a viable tool. Mitchell (2000) outlines four steps that should be followed in order to help migrate successfully into an eProcurement environment:

1. Review the plans, strategies, technologies, and operating environment of the current procurement process in order to identify opportunities for improvement. It is important to find some areas of rapid improvement and "proof of concept" victories in order to build support for the initiative. He suggests asking questions such as:

- What do our customers want or expect from the purchasing function?
- What services should we provide and how are we positioned to provide those services relative to other organizations, both public and private?
- Do we have responsibilities for implementing programs that benefit under-utilized firms, such as small, or minority suppliers; and how can this strategy incorporate those responsibilities?
- How can the customers be provided with the right product at the right time, and is the supplier community willing and able to assist in this process?
- What are supplier expectations with respect to doing business with this organization?

2. Build a strong, realistic business case for moving into an eProcurement environment. Opportunities exist for rapid success in the form of cost savings and customer satisfaction from both internal and external customers if the solution is well planned and has the support of key stakeholders. The business case should focus on the expected results from the transition and not solely on the programs and initiatives that may be necessary to bring it to fruition. The goal of the business case is to present a picture of before and after results once accomplishing or implementing the strategy. The business case should present the total costs for transitioning to such a model as well as provide measurable and quantifiable objectives that may be met upon implementation. A "top-down" strategic view of the initiative in addition to a "bottom-up" operational analysis documenting the need with corresponding benefits and costs will enhance the explanation and rationalization.

3. Evaluate and select the appropriate software to implement an eProcurement solution. Choosing the wrong supplier can mean the difference between success and failure. Select a software solution that has robust specification capabilities, automatic links to supplier tools, multimedia capabilities, and uniform product descriptors. An organization should be able to start with a small system and increase its capacity and capabilities as their needs expand, in addition to being readily accessible by even low-end personal computers to ensure small business participation. The software should be easily customizable to meet the organization's needs and include audit trail capability. eProcurement software allows the organization to integrate different facets of eProcurement and requires a careful analysis of organizational needs matched against the strengths of different software packages before a final decision is made.

4. Keep a "people centric" perspective of the situation. The procurement professional, as well as the multitude of departmental users, must be thoroughly trained in the use of the new procurement options. The communication lines among the procurement offices, supplier community, and organization staff must remain open throughout all stages of the transitional project; and stakeholders should have significant involvement, beginning with planning through its implementation and evaluation.

eProcurement options can be incorporated into many of the stages of sourcing. Procurement officers who want to transform their current operations should be mindful of the tasks described in the remaining chapters and evaluate which of the tasks are candidates for use as an eProcurement option in their organization.

Green Procurement

Another aspect of public procurement that is gaining momentum is the topic of green procurement. Green procurement is a way of adding environmental considerations to the price and performance criteria public organizations use to make purchasing (transaction) decisions. Green procurement is a consideration of supply chain management and is known by a variety of names such as environmentally preferred purchasing (EPP), affirmative procurement, eco-procurement, and environmentally responsible purchasing. Green procurement attempts to identify and reduce environmental impact and to maximize resource efficiency.

Green procurement attempts to identify and reduce environmental impact and to maximize resource efficiency.

In the United States, green procurement was originally authorized under the Resource Conservation and Recovery Act (RCRA), which requires federal agencies to "give preference in their purchasing programs to products and practices that conserve and protect natural resources and the environment." Listed below are the major laws and regulations associated with green procurement.

- Executive Order (EO) 13101, "Greening the Government Through Waste Prevention, Recycling, and Federal Acquisition," was written to improve the program's use of recycled-content products and include other environmentally preferable products and services.

- The 2002 "Farm Bill" requires the purchase of bio-based products.

- The Energy Policy Act and EO 13123 require the purchase of energy efficient products and Alternative Fuel Vehicles (AFVs).

- The Federal Acquisition Regulations (FAR) Subparts 23.2, 23.4, 23.7 and 23.8 support the above requirements. Green procurement applies to commodity purchases, construction and service contracts, items bought from military base supply stores, items used for in-house construction and services, and everything else purchased by government personnel and contractors.

In Canada, the Treasury Board Ministers approved the Policy on Green Procurement, effective April 1, 2006, as presented by Public Works and Government Services Canada,

Environment Canada and Natural Resources Canada. The Policy on Green Procurement is designed to advance the protection of the environment and support sustainable development by integrating environmental performance considerations into the procurement decision-making process. The policy applies to all departments within the meaning of section 2 of the Financial Administration Act, unless specific acts or regulations override it. The policy was designed to:

1. Contribute to environmental objectives, such as:
   - reducing greenhouse gas emissions and air contaminants
   - improving energy and water efficiency
   - reducing ozone depleting substances
   - reducing waste and supporting reuse and recycling
   - reducing hazardous waste and
   - reducing toxic and hazardous chemicals and substances.

2. Result in more environmentally responsible planning, acquisition, use and disposal practices in the Federal Government.

3. Stimulate innovation and market development of, and demand for, environmentally preferred goods and services, making these available and mainstream for other sectors of society.

4. Support emerging environmental technologies.

The policy in Canada required that Deputy Heads incorporate environmental considerations into the procurement process consistent with the overall objectives of value for money in procurement and also complying with associated legislative, regulatory and policy obligations. Department management also set green procurement targets for their organizations as appropriate.

As a result of this and other legislation in other countries, green products or services generally must be considered as the first choice in all procurements. There are some green procurement rules that "mandate" the specific procurement of supplies/services while others "prefer or recommend" them. For example, when considering purchasing products and services in the following categories, procurement rules require purchasing green products:

- Office products (including electronic equipment)
- Printing services
- Fleet maintenance products
- Building construction, renovation and maintenance (including janitorial and landscape)
- Traffic control
- Park and recreation
- Appliances
- Lighting

Green procurement requirements apply to all acquisitions and purchases, for both supply and services, regardless of how purchases are made or the dollar value of the purchase.

Generally, the various legislation calls for procurement requesters to justify the reason for not procuring recycled or bio-based products in accordance with the requirements of green procurement programs. The justification must be in writing, and must be based upon the inability to acquire the product in a timely manner, at a reasonable price, or to satisfy the technical/performance requirements.

Many government organizations have revised procurement policies to include green procurement. Organizations practicing green procurement acquire products or services that have a lesser impact on health and the environment than other alternative products or services that accomplish the same purpose. Starting a green procurement program starts with the following actions:

- Develop a green procurement policy – Creating a statement that outlines the organizational objectives with respect to green procurement.
- Identify a leader. Having someone in charge creates the momentum for moving forward.
- Work individually with departments to set realistic goals. Create green teams to help provide expertise to departments as they start the change.
- Evaluate the goods you currently purchase. Ask current suppliers what green alternatives they have to replace current products.
- Evaluate performance and cost saving opportunities; easy alternatives are replacing new printer toner cartridges with recycled cartridges, retread tires instead of new ones, etc.
- Test performance based on acceptable criteria and cost savings. Determine if green products provide the performance and cost savings anticipated.
- Share your findings with other programs. Network with other jurisdictions to share information about green products and services.
- Collect and publish findings. Collect cost savings information and performance measures and publish them so that you can learn from your experience and the experience of others.

Implementing green procurement can start with small steps and build as the program gains traction in the organization. The top ways public organizations can implement green procurement policies are as follows:

- Review purchase specifications and contracts to determine if they contain environmental performance standards or requirements.
- Ask your existing suppliers about environmentally friendly alternatives and give them a try.
- Consider how to make your product or service "green" and what you'll need to purchase differently to make it happen.
- Create a suitable green products listing and use it when making purchases.
- Purchase and install energy efficient lighting in buildings.
- Evaluate your energy sources and consider changing to alternative-powered energy sources.

- Request vendors to provide supplies in reusable packaging that can be used for your products or returned to the supplier.
- Purchase appropriately sized lots to minimize waste. Purchase bulk where feasible but in small quantities for shelf life/dated materials.
- Buy recycled office consumable products, Energy Star certified office equipment, and reusable utensils, plates and cups.
- Buy and use less toxic cleaners and/or hire those who do.

Green procurement is one way government organizations can have a major effect on improving environmental quality and taking the lead in establishing environmental responsibility as good public policy.

References

Council of State Governments (1988). *State and local government purchasing* (3rd ed.). Lexington, KY: National Association of State Procurement Officials.

Harris, S. (2001). Bidding wars. *Government Executive, 33,* 45-46.

Jop, S. (2000). Going, going, gone. *Harvard Business Review, 78,* 30.

Kwak, M. (2002). Potential pitfalls of e-auctions. *Sloan Management Review, 43,* 18.

Leseur, A. (2001). Analyze, analyze. *Purchasing, 130,* 30-34.

MacManus, S. A. (1992). *Doing business with government.* New York: Paragon House.

Michels, W. L. (2001). Preparation is key in reverse auctions *CMP Media LLC, 1264,* 63.

Mitchell, K. (2000). Instituting eProcurement in the public sector *Public Management International City Management Association, 82,* 21-25.

National Institute of Governmental Purchasing, Inc. (NIGP) (2007). *Public procurement dictionary of terms.* Herndon, VA: NIGP.

National Institute of Governmental Purchasing, Inc. (NIGP) (2004). *Planning, Scheduling and Requirement Analysis.* Herndon, VA: NIGP.

Pettijohn, Carole and Qiao, Yuhua (2000). *Procuring Technology: Issues Faced by Public Organizations,* Journal of Public Budgeting, Accounting, and Financial Management 12 (2): 441-461.

Robinson, B. (2006). DHS moves forward with reverse auctions. Federal Computer Week, October 12, 2006.

Stocks, K. (2001). RFP 101. *The American City & County,* 16, 18-23.

Thai, K. V., & Grimm R. (2000). Government procurement: Past and current developments. *Journal of Public Budgeting, Accounting & Financial Management,* 12, 231-247.

Treasury Board of Canada (2006). Policy on Green Procurement.

United States Air Force (2005). Guide to Green Procurement.

Part II: Public Sourcing: Analysis Before Action

Chapter 3

Requirements Analysis

Gathering Information

The work of procurement officials begins in advance of the actual procurements. The planning process is the first step required of those directly involved in the procurement. The planning process is so critical to the purchasing function that the National Institute of Governmental Purchasing (NIGP) has dedicated an entire text within its foundation curriculum to the subject. Public procurement professionals are strongly encouraged to read *Planning, Scheduling, and Requirement Analysis* (2004), produced by NIGP, as this chapter will only briefly introduce this critical topic within the context of sourcing.

Procurement planning is a means of identifying trends, forecasting needs, and collecting procurement strategies to ensure that organizational resources are available to meet a particular need. This planning process involves individuals from the management, operational, and procurement departments to strategically assess departmental needs. The procurement official brings knowledge of current market conditions, technological advances, opportunities for procurement efficiencies, and procurement strategies that can assist the management team in evaluating the feasibility, cost-effectiveness, and timing of potential acquisitions.

In the past, purchasing was not included in planning activities because the department was viewed as merely an administrative service function that was only involved in the implementation of the planned process. This view has changed over the years, enabling organizations to reap the benefits of departmental expertise. Some organizations have even extended the role of the procurement official by eliciting their comments on budget requests related to major purchases for appropriateness and suitability.

Planning information is available from a variety of sources to assist procurement officials when forecasting agency needs. By requiring organizations to periodically submit reports that outline anticipated needs for the coming year, the procurement team is able to identify opportunities for volume purchases. An analysis of agency budget requests may pinpoint indicators for dollar volume savings and anticipated needs.

Some organizations have automated procurement management information systems, which, in addition to providing the ability to encumber funds as acquisitions are made, can provide information on the types of commodities purchased during prior fiscal years. By analyzing prior year's acquisitions, the procurement official can review a detailed accounting of the organization's procurement history. This is a valuable tool for conducting trend analysis and compiling past data to support future purchasing programs. Armed with historical information and future needs projections, the procurement official can perform cost-savings analyses to determine the most effective means of acquiring goods and services.

The Purchase Requisition (PR)

The procurement cycle begins with a purchase requisition (PR). Although it may be handled differently across organizations, the requisition process is designed to inform a procurement official of an internal customer department's need to acquire a particular good or service. General notification of the funding source certifying the availability of budget resources accompanies the requisition as well as an approval from the department's authorized signatory to procure the items requested.

Upon receiving a requisition, the procurement official must first review it for completeness, compliance to policy and standards, and to ensure that they completely understand what good or service is required. Often, this task requires engaging the requesting department in dialogue to further clarify functional or technical specifications with respect to the goods or services desired. While the procurement official may not be a technical expert, they may be able to offer suggestions about similar items, which are available on the market that may meet the need and result in cost savings to the department or offer improved delivery and serviceability to the user. Familiarity with the type of goods or services requested will allow adequate and correct information to be assembled in order for the procurement to proceed.

An official should understand the business of the requesting department well enough to prepare an outline of the documentation necessary to determine and implement the appropriate procurement strategy. Knowledge of standards and specifications related to the request is useful when the procurement official recommends mandatory, optional, and desirable requirement specifications. The following is a basic checklist for evaluating the purchase requisition:

- review for completeness and budget/approval authorizations
- review for clarity of the requisition
- evaluate the existing supply (if stocked)

- determine the potential to bundle items requisitioned with similar requisitions to achieve a volume discount and
- evaluate potential sources to acquire the needed goods and/or services.

Once the requisition is deemed to be complete, the task of determining whether to initiate the acquisition through selecting a strategy begins.

Strategic Sourcing

Strategic sourcing is a methodology and process that enables procurement officials to analyze what and how they acquire products and services, with the objectives of lowering costs to the organization, and improvements in supply fulfillment from the producer level to the end-user (supply chain). Other elements of strategic sourcing are to improve supplier performance, reduce waste, eliminate non-value-add activities and costs, and minimize risk. This methodology requires strategic planning of acquisitions, and development of policies and procedures that are not intrusive to programs and operations. Some guiding principles of strategic sourcing are: making acquisitions in a manner that reflect the greater good of the organization, cost-effective and efficient acquisition methods, manage suppliers for performance, and compliance with all statutes, regulatory provisions, and organizational policy and procedures. A fundamental tenant of strategic sourcing is continuous improvement and evaluation of methods and process to enhance effectiveness and efficiency.

Elements of strategic sourcing are to:

- Analyze the organization's spend patterns with suppliers based on a highest to lowest spend value on an annualized basis compared year-on-year.
- Focus on the highest spend values and on the commodities and categories that pose the greatest opportunity to reduce costs and improve returns to the organization.
- Continually asses the market in terms of suppliers, products, and opportunity to consolidate to drive value.
- Develop a sourcing strategy that addresses organizational needs, resources available, and timing of opportunities.
- Analyze organizational requirements to implement company-wide standardization programs to reduce product SKU's and cost.
- Engage in global sourcing through electronic means.
- Identify suppliers and service providers that excel in product quality, delivery, and performance.
- Manage supplier performance.

Identifying the Need and Requirements Definition

Procurement officials must continue to make decisions before finalizing a sourcing strategy. Primarily, the strategy rests on market issues and cost analyses that must be given some consideration prior to finalizing the decision.

Surveying the Market

When using the supplier source list, the procurement official should conduct a review of its contents in order to determine if the requisitioned goods or services can be provided in the necessary quantities and within the required time frames. This may entail surveying potential suppliers for basic availability and preliminary cost estimates. Supplier analysis is a technique used to evaluate a supplier's performance relative to stated deliverables, includes interviewing, value analysis, and ensures that a supplier has the ability to meet specifications and fulfillment requirements. These cost elements will be used in cost analyses and to help determine the recommended sourcing strategy. The market survey also produces information regarding alternative goods or services that might meet the requesting organization's needs. Conducting market surveys adds value to the process, because it will provide information that may prove to be useful when developing requirements definitions and functional and technical specifications for the solicitation document. Often, the market survey will uncover functionality or features that the requesting organization had not included in the original requisition, yet may be worth considering prior to finalizing the sourcing mechanisms.

...the market survey may uncover functionality or features that the requesting organization had not included in the original requisition...

Having completed the review of the supplier source list, the procurement official knows whether competition exists for the product or service. The jurisdiction must also consider to what degree they are interested in promoting economic development among historically under-utilized businesses (local preferences or set-asides). Many jurisdictions have procedures in place that establish a percentage of acquisitions to be targeted for particular groups, classes, or types of businesses. These procedures, also known as "set-asides," are generally designated for minority suppliers, women-owned businesses or "small" businesses (with assets or net worth under a specified threshold). Proponents of set-aside programs argue that the programs expand the supplier pool and give new businesses a chance to participate in the process, making the public procurement system equitable and more open to all. Opponents of such programs argue that they provide unfair advantage to a sub-population of the supplier community and, by their nature, violate the principles of fair and open competition, impartiality and efficiency. These opponents contend that all suppliers should be required to participate on a level footing. Giving a percentage of public business to minority-owned or small business without the element of competition may not be in the best interest of the jurisdiction, especially if more qualified firms are not considered or selected in order to adhere to set-aside guidelines.

Initial Cost Analyses

Determining the best method of sourcing may also depend on varying cost factors. The option to take advantage of economies of scale by bundling goods and services requests should always be considered. This process of combining requests may also be referred to as volume buying. Volume buying requires more planning and coordination to factor in additional transaction or processing costs as they relate to savings determination. Many acquisitions may not benefit from volume purchases. In some instances spot buying, as in small dollar or pCard procurements, will meet the need more effectively. Following is a discussion of varying cost analyses approaches.

Make or Buy Cost Analysis

Many cost analyses occur prior to the decision to acquire goods and services. A "make or buy" analysis will result in the decision to provide the good or service by using internal organizational resources or to contract out for similar support to meet the need. Costs are defined as resources expended at a pre-defined level and quality. When comparing the costs between public and private sector options, three principles should be considered.

- *All costs considered should be compared equally using the "apples to apples" approach.* All operating costs required of both private and public providers are not always considered. Exclusion of such data and hidden information may tend to favor private providers. The public organization's budget is used to determine all public costs and is then measured against the direct cost. Conversely, few of the indirect costs of the private provider are considered. Many privatization decisions have been mistakenly justified as a result of this omission.

- *Only the costs that differ between the providers should be evaluated.* Costs that are the same, regardless of who provides the service, are irrelevant and need not be included in the analysis. If evaluating the costs of providing services between two functional areas within the same organization, the management costs (indirect costs) would likely be exactly the same and need not be included in the cost analysis.

- *The costs for maintaining the same service levels and quality must be evaluated.* There can be no difference in the levels or quality under consideration in the cost analysis. Both private and public providers must work under similar constraints with similar populations. For example, comparisons cannot be made between private and public service providers if one sector is providing services to a lower risk population, because services to a high-risk population would be more expensive.

Cost comparisons should cover, at a minimum, three to five years of collected data to allow for the conversion or implementation costs spread over a reasonable period of time. All cash flow should be discounted to net present values to eliminate the element of changes in the value in money over time.

A simple four step approach to conduct "a make or buy analysis" involves:

1. **Defining the outputs (goods or services) to be analyzed:**
   The first step requires the creation of output specifications to describe the performance standard for the goods and/or services. The performance standard ensures that the same level of quality, measurement tools and reporting requirements are being evaluated. Output specifications should be designed to ensure that prospective suppliers are capable of developing more efficient ways of providing the same intended outcome. Poorly written specifications often lead to ambiguities in service provision. Knowledgeable staff and program managers should develop specifications.

2. **Determining the costs that would be saved from outside or external provision:**
   As mentioned earlier, a complete review of internal expenses should be considered when determining the total cost of the procurement. Figure 4 identifies potential areas for consideration.

	Identified Expenses	Associated Costs
Personnel	Salaries Benefits Other Allowances Training	
Operating and Maintenance	Material and Supplies Maintenance and Repair Travel Other	
Facility	Rent Utilities	
Capital	Assets Opportunity Costs	
Overhead	Administrative Overhead Program Support Overhead	
Conversion	One-Time Recurring	
Additional	Miscellaneous Costs Not in Other Categories	
Common Entity Services	In-House Service (i.e., legal services)	
	Total In-House Costs	$

Figure 4. *Potential internal expense areas for consideration.*

3. **Computing the cost of contracting from the private sector:**
   The third step requires an accounting of all costs associated with privatizing the product or service procurement. This list should include in-house costs incurred (e.g., contract management costs) as well as the costs by a private sector provider (using the same checklist in Figure 4). Figure 5 provides a checklist for determining these costs.

	Identified Expenses	Associated Costs
Contact Administration	Within Agency Within Outside Provider	
Conversion Costs	One Time Materials One Time Labor Additional One-Time Costs Recurring Costs	
Net Salvage Value	Transfer of Assets Disposal Charges	
Contract Performance Costs	Compliance Audits Miscellaneous Audits	
	Total Contract Costs	$

Figure 5. *Checklist for cost determination.*

4. **Comparing the difference in net cost and the final decision:**
   The final step requires reviewing the cost comparisons to ensure that all costs for each have been included at the same service and quality levels. Any intangible factors (costs that cannot be quantified in dollars) should be noted. Risk is considered to be an intangible factor. The cost of purchasing the service from an outside provider should then be compared to the savings retained if the service is provided in-house. If the cost of contracting the service is less than the savings, then moving the provision of goods and services to the private sector is warranted. If the two costs are nearly the same, a sensitivity analysis should be performed to determine the consideration of the costs relative to the assumptions. This additional information and any intangible factors could influence the final decision.

Leasing and Renting

The decision to lease or rent, rather than purchase goods, should be evaluated carefully and the following critical factors should be considered:

- purchase price versus the sum of the lease payments
- maintenance and service costs
- life expectancy of the equipment

- duration of need for the equipment
- obsolescence
- cash flow
- prevailing interest rates if the goods are going to be financed and
- funding source for the equipment.

The majority of goods, especially equipment, are purchased outright, but the option of leasing or renting can save the jurisdiction dollars and may provide the best solution. A lease or rental agreement is very similar to the contract used for purchasing goods or services. Lease agreements may contain particulars that could affect the decision. Available options at the time of expiration should be fully explained to the organizations and all costs to the jurisdiction should be itemized. If the jurisdiction decides to purchase the item at the end of the lease period, any payments made over the course of the agreement should be credited toward the purchase. Cancellation clauses and any penalties associated with early cancellation should be itemized prior to signing the agreement. Insurance responsibilities of both parties during the term of the lease or rental period should be clear. The procurement official should consider and determine the cost associated with owning versus renting the equipment in terms of the potential tax liabilities to the jurisdiction. The following is a four-step approach to assess the lease or buy decision.

1. Capture all up-front costs associated with the lease/rental agreement.

2. Determine the sum of all lease/rental payments discounting to net present value over the term of the lease and any other costs that occur during the lease period (e.g., insurance, maintenance, etc.).

3. Calculate the purchase price. (If payment is financed, calculate costs with interest discounted over the payment period.)

4. Compare costs over the planned period of use. Consider any trade-in value or cancellation penalties if newer equipment would be required prior to the end of the lease or finance period.

Requirements Definition

All procurements have requirements statements. Even the simplest acquisition begins with a statement of need; however, the rush to procure goods and services often precludes a careful requirements definition process. The requirements definition or requirements specification describes the specific capabilities and conditions that are to be fulfilled by the acquisition. As such, it will be the foundation of the final specification section in the solicitation document. Procurement officials should be able to answer four questions when developing the requirements definition statement.

What do we want to purchase? The answer should include a functional description of what is to be acquired. This relates to the outcome of the acquisition and describes what function the item serves, but not necessarily how it may perform the function. This flexibility allows for some level of innovation from the supplier community. Also included in the description should be specific requirements that allow for no flexibility on the part of the supplier. These details will form the basis of the mandatory specifications in the final solicitation document. Any other constraints, such as limitations due to resources, schedule, legal requirements, budget, etc., should also be included.

Who will be reviewing these requirements? Initially, the team requesting the acquisition (the user community) will review the requirements definition, but the internal management team may also be reviewing the requirements definition as part of the approval process. Depending on the number of levels of approval required, there may be others reviewing the requirements statement. The supplier community may also have access to the requirements definition as part of the scope/ specifications section in the solicitation document. It is important that requirements definitions be written clearly for every intended audience to eliminate vague and ambiguous information.

Developing good requirement definitions ...can provide the framework for the sourcing document.

Why do we need to procure the goods or services? The third question addresses the reasons behind the acquisition. Answering this question will provide the basis for "selling" the need to the approval authorities. It will be the basis of the solicitation document to facilitate supplier understanding of the requirements and to help frame performance expectations in the eventual contract. Any pertinent background for the acquisition should be included as part of this answer to enable the audience to understand why this acquisition is important.

How will we structure the requirements definition? A well-developed requirements definition includes an introduction that describes the purpose of the document and its intended audience. It should describe the background for the acquisition and explain the need. A clear and concise description of functional and technical, mandatory, and flexible requirements should be included, along with any additional information (diagrams, technical documents, organizational information, etc.) that may be helpful in preparing the solicitation document.

Developing good requirement definitions involves more than just answering these four questions. It can provide the framework for the sourcing document.

Requirements Characteristics

While it is difficult to define requirements characteristics for all categories of procurements, it is possible to classify several generic characteristics of requirements definitions. First, requirements are either primary or derived. A primary requirement is an unambiguous provision or specification that can be contractually upheld, e.g., the system will be able to support 2,500 concurrent users. A derived requirement is one generated apart from, but is related to, a primary requirement. Using the same example, if the requirement states that the system response time must be no more than 10 seconds, the derived characteristic is also unambiguous and may also be contractually applicable. Primary requirements tend to define the scope of the acquisition, and changes to primary requirements usually require a contract amendment. Derived requirements are more flexible as long as a change to the derived requirement is still within the scope of its primary requirement.

A second characteristic is the requirements application. These characteristics stipulate product parameters and program parameters. The product parameter is a requirement that relates to the specific good or service to be acquired and is either qualitative or quantitative in nature. Examine the following statement: "The training program's pass rate should be no less than 95% for qualified candidates." This product parameter is quantitative because it identifies measurable performance expectations. A qualitative parameter has no measurable requirements. Consider this statement: "Included in the training program will be an examination component." This parameter does not measure the performance of the product required. Program parameters are activities associated with creating or supplying the product and may involve contractor relationships. Program parameters are often evident in documents involving intellectual property rights or warranties. Program parameters are one of three types:

- **Task** - The task component identifies what is being provided as a result of the acquisition, e.g., "Performing an Electronic Document Management Technology Assessment."

- **Compliance evaluation** - The compliance evaluation program parameter identifies how the organization will measure successful completion of the program, e.g., "Trainees should be able to increase their pre-test programmatic policy knowledge test score by 20% following completion of the training module.

- **Regulatory** - The regulatory parameters contain all other administrative and contractual elements, for example, e.g., "The source code for all software shall be furnished to and become the property of the government."

A third characteristic indicates the compliance level of the requirement. Requirements may be determined to be mandatory for guidance, or for informational purposes. The supplier must provide a mandatory requirement. If it is omitted from the submitted response, the bid will be deemed non-responsive. (A non-responsive bid does not conform to the mandatory or essential requirements of the Invitation for Bids.) A requirements statement of this type includes the word "shall" to denote the obligatory nature of the requirement. Unachievable mandatory requirements generally require a contract change or waiver and should not be undertaken without great consideration. Changing mandatory requirements after supplier submittals have been received could place the organization at risk for litigation. Guidance requirements are mentioned within the desired requirement but are not mandatory. Failure to provide guidance requirements will not constitute non-responsiveness on the part of the supplier but are merely additional features or functionality that would be favorably evaluated if included in the procurement. Informational requirements help clarify the meaning or context of mandatory or guidance requirements. These statements are used to ensure that the potential supplier understands the reasoning behind requirements or to establish expectations on the part of the purchasing organization.

The fourth and final characteristic is priority. Establishing the order of preference for a requirement assists the supplier in understanding which requirements are the most important to the customer or the sequence in which requirements should be implemented.

Figure 6 is a checklist for procurement officials to use in reviewing requirement definitions for the essential elements that characterize effective requirements.

Category	Characteristic
Type	Primary Derived
Application	**Product Parameter** Qualitative Quantitative **Program Parameter** Task Compliance Evaluation Regulatory
Compliance Level	Mandatory Guidance Information
Priority	Program and Company Dependent

Figure 6. *Requirement characteristics.*

Requirements Relationships

The characteristics of a requirement provide information about the nature of the acquisition. Requirement relationships enable the supplier to understand how the requirements are related or grouped and help determine the interdependence and interaction of the specific details. By establishing requirement relationships, one can establish an importance hierarchy and identify related component parts. A relationship hierarchy might be constructed around the elements, components, or interfaces contained in a product. Relationships of higher level to lower level requirements, assignment of specifications or standards to individual requirements, or individual compliance methods pertaining to a group or groups of requirements may also be considered. By determining requirement relationships in advance, meaningful evaluation methods can be developed that will ensure compliance with all contractual elements.

Requirements Descriptions

Often, requirements definitions include specifications that prescribe a solution rather than state a need. A requirements definition describes what is needed by the organization, not how it is to be provided. Prescribing design implementation features are different from requirements definitions. Subtly prescribing the solution can have negative implications. The organization may be forcing a particular design strategy when other, more innovative approaches could be available. By prescribing implementation features, the organization may be lulled into thinking that all requirements have been covered; but, in fact, important features have been omitted. Such confusion is most often found in complex acquisitions that may involve requests for bundled goods and services.

When creating requirements, the question of "what" should supersede the question of "how" the need is to be met. To prevent specifying a design or implementation solution, alternative means of providing the requirement should be determined. If there are no alternatives, it is likely that the requirement is a design implementation instead of a requirement and should be re-evaluated to state the needed functionality.

Requirements Quality

The quality component of the requirements definition is also to be considered. The quality of the requirements definition is the crossing point between the definition process and the interpretation process. The definition process occurs when the conceptual intent of the acquisition is transformed into a written needs statement. The interpretation process occurs when the written needs statement is transformed into a series of more detailed requirements that enable potential suppliers to understand and interpret the nature of the proposed acquisition.

Requirements quality is composed of three elements. Requirements quality provides all of the program-specific information needed to derive or propose a solution. A requirement is complete if it enables the potential supplier to identify the options available for satisfying the requirement, if they can then select the most appropriate option and eventually validate that the option selected will, in fact, satisfy the stated need. Requirements quality must leave nothing to interpretation. A quality requirement is one that will be interpreted in the same manner by any reviewer. Poorly written or constructed requirements statements will result in a variety of interpretations and should be eliminated. Assumptions made regarding supplier knowledge and the organization's business procedures may compromise the requirement quality. A quality requirement definition provides enough information for the potential supplier to determine whether or not the scope of the requirement has been met. A requirement that states that the proposed solution "shall be of high quality" does not set measurable boundaries for meeting the requirement. This ambiguity of scope often results in significantly higher costs to the requesting organization.

The ability to construct effective requirements definitions is one of the most critical elements of public sourcing. Without having an accurate translation of the requesting organization's needs and expectations, it is nearly impossible for the supplier community to understand and provide acceptable solutions.

Determinants of Cost - Manufacturer and Supplier Pricing Considerations

Purchasing agents should be aware of, and take into account, the many factors or cost influences that manufacturers and suppliers may incorporate into their final prices. Fearon, Dobler, and Killian in "The Purchasing Handbook" identified a number of these cost influences that may have a material and significant impact on pricing and delivery:

- Supplier cost
- Competition
- Product differentiation
- Quality and specifications
- Packaging requirement
- Payment terms
- Service and technical support
- Buyer creativity

- Supply and demand
- Profit (Variable Margin Pricing)
- Quantity
- Transportation
- Just-In-Time delivery
- Potential obsolescence
- Contract length
- Acquisition options

Other factors may include:

- Finance costs (lease vs. outright purchase vs. rent-to-own, buyout options vs. consignment)
- Global markets during civil disobedience and political unrest
- 24x7x365
- Seasonal availability
- Weather conditions
- Marketing board price adjustments
- Environmental stewardship and sustainability

- Discounts
- Perishable products
- Natural disasters
- Fuel and environmental fees

Reference

Fearon, H.E., Dobler, D.W., & Killen, K.K. (1993). *The purchasing handbook* (5th ed.). New York: McGraw-Hill Companies, Inc.

National Institute of Governmental Purchasing, Inc. (NIGP) (2004). *Planning, scheduling, and requirement analysis*. Herndon, VA: NIGP.

Chapter 4

Sourcing Suppliers

As trends and procurement needs are made known, the next major activity involves locating suppliers who can supply the needed goods and/or services. This activity determines whether competition exists in the acquisition of goods and services. Given the importance of competition to the procurement process, this is a critical step. If the proposed acquisition is to be procured using a competitive procurement strategy, a sufficient number of potential suppliers that will likely be able to participate in the procurement must exist in the market. To do so, procurement officials assemble a source list of potential suppliers.

Many organizations maintain extensive lists of potential suppliers classified by the particular goods or services that may be needed. Often, though, it is difficult to identify potential suppliers due to the technical or functional requirements identified in the requisition. When the requirements for the procurement seem to be unique, the procurement official must make an effort to determine if there are adequate numbers of available potential suppliers. A common benchmark for organizations is to identify, at a minimum, three potential suppliers for any given acquisition. Potential suppliers may be found in published directories, from industry sources, sales literature, word of mouth recommendations, electronic bid notification boards and supplier URL's for access through the Internet. The following source lists provide a starting point for locating suitable suppliers:

Publication sources:

- Chicago Buyers Guide
- Sweets Catalog
- Conover-Mast Purchasing Directory
- ThomasRegister® of American Manufacturers
- Regional Chamber of Commerce directories
- Trade Directories of the World, Croner Publications, Inc.
- Manufacturers' catalogs and sales literature
- MacRae's Blue Book
- Made in Europe
- BCBid, MERX, Ebay

Industry sources:

- Industry associations
- Trade papers or journal advertisements
- National and regional association publications and Websites
- Specialized industry buyers guides

- Trade associations
- Professional associations

Professional source services:

- Microfilm libraries
- Computer-based data retrieval services
- Consumer or technical review or evaluation resources
- Internet-based product subscription services

- Inquiry services

Additional sources:

- Classified telephone directories
- Trade and product shows
- The requesting organization
- Manufacturers' catalogs or product literature
- Other procurement officials/supplier lists from other organizations

- Internet product searches
- Salespeople

An established and well-maintained source list allows for accurate and efficient determination of competition existing in the marketplace. Such a list can enable the procurement department to avoid unproductive and wasteful solicitations.

Creating and Maintaining Supplier Lists

In order to provide competition, an adequate number of suppliers should be competing for public contracts. An up-to-date supplier list will ensure that potential bidders can be notified of current procurement documents. Organizations that want to create a supplier list can do so by allowing suppliers to register their products under certain grouping or commodity codes that identify the type of goods or services that the firm is capable of supplying. The National Institute of Government Purchasing released the first version of the NIGP Code in 1984. The Code is available as a 3-digit class code, a 5-digit class-item code, a 7-digit class-item-group code, and a detailed 11-digit code. The Code is maintained and supported by Periscope, an Austin-based company. NIGP has developed an electronic version of one of the most widely used commodity/service code lists available to member organizations. The list is updated dynamically as new codes are needed. Information about subscribing to this service can be found at http://www.nigp.com. A sample of how the codes are organized is shown in Figure 7. Another common grouping system used in both Canada and the United States is the Goods and Services Index developed by the U.S. military.

Code Structure	Sample Code	Sample Description
3-digit (Class) Code	620	Office Supplies: Erasers, Inks, Leads, Pens, Pencils, etc.
5-digit (Class-Item) Code	620-80	Pens (General Writing Types): Ball Point Nylon Tip, etc.
7-digit (Class-Item-Group) Code	620-80-21	Pens, Ball Point, Retractable, Refillable, All Plastic Barrel w/metal Pocket Chip
11-digit (Class-Item-Group-Detail) Code	620-80-21-035-4	Fine Point, Black Ink, 12/Box
	620-80-21-045-3	Fine Point, Black Ink, 12/Box
	620-80-21-065-1	Fine Point, Blue Ink, 12/Box
	620-80-21-075-0	Fine Point, Red Ink, 12/Box
	620-80-21-095-8	Medium Point, Black Ink, 12/Box
	620-80-21-105-5	Medium Point, Blue Ink, 12/Box

Figure 7 - *Samples of the NIGP Commodity/Service Code.*
Source: www.nigp.com

A supplier list can be created in one of two ways. The first allows any supplier to register for the supplier list based on the products and services they offer. In this situation, the supplier provides basic company information, such as the name, address, and contact person and a list of the commodity codes for the goods and/or services they provide. The second method is to pre-qualify suppliers based on a number of criteria before including them on an approved supplier list. Pre-qualification of suppliers enables the procurement professional to narrow the number of potential suppliers participating in the acquisition by ensuring that only qualified suppliers are sent procurement notifications. The type of information gathered when pre-qualifying a supplier includes all of the previously mentioned information but also may include any of the following items as well:

- size of the company
- financial reports
- internal procedures
- references
- resumes of individuals participating in projects
- supplier preference certification (minority/women-owned, small business).
- past experience with the organization
- management staff information
- bonding capacity
- locations and facilities of the company

While not all factors are appropriate for all commodity types, many are useful in determining the qualifications of potential suppliers.

Allowing all suppliers to register based on the products and services they provide has both advantages and disadvantages. By allowing all suppliers to register without any pre-qualification, the goal of equity in the procurement process is satisfied. This may create a large and unmanageable number of potential suppliers registered for a certain type of product or service.

Providing notification to everyone on the list may prove to be costly for the organization. An excessive number of supplier submittals may prevent the timely evaluation of submissions and eventually delay the contract award.

...electronic bulletin boards and Web pages [and] the ability to solicit and receive supplier proposals online has created additional avenues to improve the efficiency and effectiveness of the procurement office.

Different strategies for reducing the number of suppliers exist. Company size or geographic location may be used to reduce supplier participation. This is not permitted in some jurisdictions if federal funds are being used to pay for the acquisition. Another approach may be to rotate suppliers invited to participate, allowing for all interested parties to have an opportunity over a period of time. While these strategies result in fewer supplier submissions, they may create the perception of preferential treatment and potentially expose the procurement office to criticism and allegations of supplier bias.

Pre-qualification of vendors can have advantages. Certified suppliers, registered and approved to do business in the jurisdiction, can accelerate the selection process. Pre-qualification allows the procurement official to conduct solicitations efficiently and effectively by preventing unnecessary solicitation costs and receiving competitive, responsive solicitations from suppliers. Often, pre-qualification eliminates new or small businesses in favor of older established firms and implies a maintenance commitment to ensure that the bidder's list reflects the most current financial and technical status of the suppliers.

A pre-qualified source list maintenance program involves multiple tasks. New suppliers must be added to the list as they are discovered, to foster increased competition. The commodity/ service codes must be maintained in order to ensure that supplier capabilities are updated. Commodity/service codes can be broadly or discretely defined, as illustrated in Figure 7. The more narrow or discrete the commodity code, the more accurately the supplier can be categorized. The narrower the set of codes, the more work there is involved in maintaining the codes and the respective suppliers.

Removing suppliers from the list because they no longer exist, fail to submit proposals, and/ or have demonstrated poor performance may be time-consuming. Removal of a supplier based on poor performance should be done with adequate due process provisions in place and clearly defined procedures for supplier reinstatement. Detailed records with respect to supplier performance must be maintained. Repeated failure to bid or failure to bid responsively is justification for removal of a supplier from the source list provided records are retained in the supplier file. Failure to meet specified delivery deadlines, to meet specifications, and/or poor quality should be well documented, if the supplier is removed from the list. Unfortunately, this type of documentation is rarely maintained; and, as a result, few jurisdictions actually remove suppliers from the list for reasons of poor performance. If the organization is going to effectively use source lists, such maintenance can be time-consuming.

Many organizations have abandoned the use of pre-qualified supplier lists and have turned to post-qualification efforts or alternative methods of soliciting bid responses. Increasingly, the use of site visits, benchmarking or rigorous reference checks have all been used to perform due diligence and qualify the bidder before awarding the contract.

Alternative methods of soliciting bidders include public advertising and electronic postings. Posting sourcing opportunities in newspapers and official government publications has become the primary source for eliciting supplier proposals for many organizations. As a result, many rules and regulations have been promulgated with respect to the format, notice period, and process for notification of procurement opportunities. With the advent of Internet-based technologies, such as electronic bulletin boards and Web pages, the ability to solicit and receive supplier proposals online has created additional avenues to improve the efficiency and effectiveness of the procurement office.

Determining the Appropriate Sourcing Strategy

The sourcing strategies previously identified fall into two categories: competitive strategies and non-competitive (or limited competitive) sourcing strategies. Competitive strategies include: Invitation for Bids (IFB), Reverse Auction, Request for Proposal (RFP), Invitation to Negotiate (ITN), Request for Quotation (RFQ), and Request for Information/Expression of Interest (RFI/REI). Limited or non-competitive strategies include: Small Dollar, Procurement Card Purchases, Emergency Purchases, and Sole Source or Directed Contract Purchases.

Competitive strategies are generally preferred by most public organizations and are statutorily required by many jurisdictions if the dollar value of the acquisition exceeds a designated dollar threshold. Close attention should be paid to the requirements and specifications outlined in the requisition. Free and open competition is encouraged by ensuring that:

- Requirements or technical specifications favoring one supplier are not used in order to avoid competition.

- The requesting organization has not engaged in communications or assistance from one supplier that would give the supplier an unfair advantage (e.g., a supplier assisting in the development of technical specifications).

- The requirements do not place unnecessary restrictions on supplier qualifications.

- The proposed contract does not allow unlimited contract extensions, multiple awards, or major post-bid contract changes that significantly change the nature of the solicitation.

While the competitive solicitation should be the preferred means of acquiring goods and services, there are times when a non-competitive or limited competition strategy is in order. The requirement for competitive acquisitions may be waived as a result of any number of special situations.

- The required good or service is available from only one supplier or the product is proprietary to a specific piece of equipment or application.

- An emergency situation necessitates a much faster acquisition than the competitive process would allow.

- The dollar value of the acquisition is too small to justify the expense of a competitive solicitation.

- The product or service can be purchased from another governmental organization or a public purchasing cooperative (e.g., prison industries, other agency, etc.).

It is the responsibility of the procurement official to review the procurement request and determine if the situation warrants a waiver from the requirement to issue a competitive solicitation.

When deciding on which sourcing strategy is the most appropriate for a given procurement, several factors come into consideration. Often, a combination of factors and the degree to which each has an impact will affect which strategy should be pursued. In addition to thinking about the model's parameters, procurement officials should ask the following questions before deciding on any particular sourcing strategy:

- *Are there multiple suppliers of the requested goods or services?* This is the first element in determining whether competitive or non-competitive strategies should be explored.

- *What is the delegated authority level and the value of the procurement?* Decentralization of the procurement process has enabled the delegation of purchasing authority to functional areas within the organization rather than the need to process all procurements through a centralized purchasing department. Along with the delegation of purchasing authority, purchasing departments have issued policies and guidelines with respect to the types of purchases allowed, the dollar threshold, and the sourcing strategies appropriate for the category of procurement. Some jurisdictions require the use of a competitive strategy if the value of the acquisition exceeds $10,000. Some jurisdictions have slightly higher or lower thresholds. With the advent of the Internet, many organizations are choosing to post their procurement guidelines on the Web to ensure that all departments having delegated approval authority for acquisitions, follow standardized procedures, and use standard forms and templates with boilerplate language.

- *How much risk and uncertainty is involved in the procurement?* The model in chapter 1 identified sourcing strategies based on the level of risk uncertainty involved in the procurement. There may be uncertainty with respect to the eventual cost of the procurement and to the actual functionality required or even the supplier's ability to deliver the required goods or services. Risk or uncertainty may be based on the visibility or the importance of the acquisition with respect to the organization's ability to perform its mission. With high risk and high levels of uncertainty, it is important to gather as much information as possible prior to selecting the appropriate strategy and to select a strategy wherein the supplier must clearly identify how the risks and uncertainty will be handled throughout the procurement and implementation processes.

- *Is the requesting organization able to provide the exact specifications for the item(s) needed, or is there some flexibility and subjectivity allowed the suppliers in proposing how to provide the requested item(s)?* Many acquisitions are quite simple, as the organization knows exactly what is needed and can provide detailed technical requirement specifications for the item(s) to be purchased. Whether purchasing office supplies or computer workstations, the exact specifications can be determined; and suppliers can be found that are capable of providing the required items exactly as ordered. This being true, the appropriate sourcing strategy selected depends on the delegated authority levels, the timing, and the cost of the anticipated procurement. If exact specifications can be determined, the lowest cost approach is generally followed. There are times when an organization needs to purchase a combination of goods and services appropriate for a variety of solutions. In these situations, it is more appropriate to gather information about the needed functionality and expected outcomes. The selection of the appropriate strategy allows the requesting organization to evaluate supplier proposals. Cost is only one of many criteria used to determine which proposal should be selected.

- *How quickly does the requesting organization need the goods or services?* Only in the case of a justifiable emergency can timing be used to forego what should, under any other circumstance, be a competitive procurement. In the event of an emergency, though, the procurement official can choose the strategy that will result in the most immediate acquisition of the necessary item(s).

Electronic Sourcing (eSourcing)

Electronic sourcing is the process of conducting competitive sourcing on-line by communicating an organization's sourcing opportunities on electronic Bid Boards in a manner than enables bidders and potential offerors to complete their responses on-line and submit their bids, proposals or quotations in a secure environment via electronic technology. All suppliers and potential bidders or respondents have access to the same information, at the same time, and in the same format. Potential respondents can access and respond to specific opportunities of interest utilizing assigned security passwords and ID numbers.

Electronic sourcing saves considerable time and effort, reduces overhead costs (mail/paper/ handling), and in many instances improves fulfillment of delivery schedules. Communication of Addenda and correspondence is quick, accurate and traceable to the source.

Electronic sourcing (eSourcing), also known as electronic commerce (eCommerce), is the integration of electronic data interchange, electronic funds transfer, and similar techniques into a comprehensive electronic-based system of procurement functions; could include the posting of IFBs and RFPs on electronic bulletin boards, the receipt of bids via electronic data interchange, notification of award by email, and payment via electronic funds transfer. (NIGP, 2007) Some examples of electronic sourcing bid boards are the Commerce Business Daily (CBD) administered by the U.S. Department of Commerce, MERX administered by the Government of Canada, and BcBid administered by the Province of British Columbia in Canada. Organizations may also have their own internal electronic solicitation notice board where they may also post the successful bidders or potential offerors to their respective solicitation opportunities.

Security issues during the advent of electronic sourcing appear to have been resolved through the use and application of user IDs and passwords for authorized user access to receive and post solicitation opportunities and responses.

Reference

National Institute of Governmental Purchasing, Inc. (NIGP) (2007). *Public procurement dictionary of terms*. Herndon, VA: NIGP.

Chapter 5

Specifications and Standards

Specifications

O nce an agency user has identified that a "need" exists to make an acquisition, the next step is to define "what" must be purchased. The key to quality acquisitions is the specification. Price, delivery, ability to measure performance and ultimately, the supplier or service provider selected will depend entirely on the ability of the end-user to accurately and concisely describe the product or service required.

The importance of specification development is so critical to the planning process that the National Institute of Governmental Purchasing (NIGP) has dedicated an entire book to the subject of procurement Planning, Sourcing and Requirement Analysis (2004). This book addresses such topics as specification development and management, sources, content, and specification types. The types of specifications are reiterated in this chapter because these variations are the hallmarks for developing a solid technical specification. Public procurement professionals are encouraged to review and refer to both books to develop a broader understanding of the relationship between planning and specifications.

Purchasing agents, acting on behalf of their internal customers, rely extensively on the information provided in their purchase requisitions. Purchasers cannot make any assumptions about what is needed, delivery expectations, or the anticipated quantities needed. The completeness and detail represented in the description of each product or service is paramount to a successful acquisition. Suppliers and potential offerors heavily rely on the ability of the purchaser to properly describe what is being purchased and corresponding terms and conditions. Similarly, suppliers cannot and should not assume what is being purchased but, rather, should clarify, quantify, and qualify each acquisition prior to submitting a bid on the tender or proposal.

Particular attention must be placed on specifications and standards for long-term agreement contracts. The term of the agreement will impact the ability of the organization to administer it. Specifications must be reasonable and not overly restrictive. Stating requirements that are not needed may result in increased costs and lead to a supply arrangement with a firm that does not offer a "best-value" procurement. Without comprehensive and concise specifications, potential suppliers and proponents may not offer the optimum product or service at the best price.

Some organizations retain external expertise to assist in specification development. Often purchasers resort to professional contacts that may be able to identify products and services or to obtain template specifications. There are a number of organizations, such as Frasers Directory, Canadian Standards Association (CSA), National Institute of Standards and Technology (NIST), American National Standards Institute (ANSI), or Buyers Laboratory, that offer assistance and information in developing specifications.

End-users generally know what they want and where the items might be available. Often, they do not know how to prepare the specifications or how to clearly describe what they want. The responsibility to adequately communicate specifications rests with the purchaser or owner. Purchasers, because they act as agents on behalf of the individual or entity, are bound to acquire precisely what is requisitioned and, therefore, may not change the physical or performance characteristics of the products or services being requested without collaboration involving the individual or entity. As part of the mandate of most purchasing agencies, the purchaser has the obligation and right to question the adequacy of a specification and delay the process until such time as they are satisfied that they will be able to reasonably source the requirement. Supplier selection and final award approval are the responsibilities of the purchasing agency. The ultimate selection of the supplier or proponent will depend exclusively on the ability of the purchasing agency to interpret and select what the end-user needs.

Accordingly, it is of vital importance that products and services required through an external solicitation process are accurately described. These are commonly referred to as "specifications" and "standards." Specifications and standards are tools available to purchasers that assist in the identification of specific end-use requirements and are intended to ensure that the product and services acquired will accommodate the desired end result and perform in accordance with expectations.

The use of quality specifications achieves fairness, equity, and transparency and provide for maximum competition resulting in reduced cost. Over-specifying "design" or "performance" specifications may frequently lead to increased capital and operating costs. Developing and designing relevant specifications requires considerable skill and training. Purchasers must be knowledgeable in all aspects of specification development and management when carrying out their responsibilities. Organizations such as NIGP offer specialized training for procurement professionals through various seminars and distance learning options.

Organizations that do not provide adequate specifications within their bid/tender, quotation, or proposal invitations expose themselves to a potentially long and protracted acquisition process. Making an acquisition without adequate clarity and understanding may result in disputes with internal customers and/or suppliers where there was an improper interpretation. In high-value—highly visible or politically sensitive projects where a real or perceived inequity exists—litigation may often be initiated. If this happens, there are usually no winners. The results are costly for all parties, and long-term supplier-purchaser relationships become strained. It is paramount to the sourcing process that organizations approach each acquisition with the most comprehensive, accurate, and concise information and specifications possible.

It is paramount to the sourcing process that organizations approach each acquisition with the most comprehensive, accurate, and concise information and specifications possible.

This court case illustrates this point: P&L Communications v. Library of Parliament (2001) CITT No. 57. The CITT (Canadian International Trade Tribunal), in a response to a complaint about unfair treatment with respect to a Request for Proposal (RFP) for an electronic news monitoring service issued by the Library of Parliament ruled, that, in part, the RFP relied extensively on trade names as a proxy for performance specifications when recognized open standards existed. Microsoft was the trade name used; and, as such, the RFP favored Microsoft-based solutions over the other bidders (The Legal Edge, 2001-2002).

General Definition

NIGP defines "specification" as:

> A precise description of the physical or functional characteristics of a product, good or construction item. A description of goods as opposed to a description of services. A description of what the purchaser seeks to buy and what a bidder must be responsive to in order to be considered for award of a contract. Specifications generally fall under the following categories: design, performance, combination (design and performance), brand name or approved equal, qualified products list and samples. May also be known as a purchasing description. (NIGP, 2007)

A specification also describes the desired outcomes or performance, technical requirements, intended use, manufacturing processes, size or units of measure, or packaging requirements. A description of a product and/or service may not be a specification, and purchasers are cautioned to ensure that all the attributes are present. The following attributes should be included in a comprehensive and concise specification:

- general description of the product or service
- numerical expression of appropriate units and limitations
- specific make or model
- "equal to" a specific brand, make, or model
- item characteristics (size, shape, weight, etc.)
- component characteristics (chemicals, ingredients, etc.)
- material composition
- assembly or construction composition
- output characteristics and performance
- engineering drawings and assembly methods
- test methodically
- industry standards
- standard grades
- prototype sample
- brand name
- port specifications
- tolerance and
- appearance and finishes.

It should be noted that a specification does not include terms and conditions, special conditions, instructions to bidders or proponents, warranty, or delivery terms. These are outlined in the formal Invitation to Tender/Invitation for Bids, Request for Quotation or Request for Proposal, or the final agreement.

Specifications are primarily used to compare offers of products or services to stated requirements, establishing compliance to the "responsive" and "responsible" provisions of public procurement solicitation requirements. Care should be taken not to restrict the competitive nature of a solicitation with specifications that overtly restrict competing suppliers. Specifications may also be represented in the form of an industry standard. Manufacturers have created standards for particular items. Such standards can serve as requirement specifications within an acquisition. For example, an industry standard for a particular container can be specified, and the dispensing devices for this product will become "the standard" if this size of container is specified.

Purpose of Specifications

The primary purpose of a specification is to enable bidders or proponents to know precisely what is being purchased and to assist the end-user in unequivocally defining or describing their requirements. Often, the end-user has obtained unsolicited information on the product or service, may have seen or experienced its use, or may have seen the product or service in professional or technical journals or supplier brochures.

Specifications are intended to:

- describe and articulate minimum requirements
- identify performance, quality, and operational characteristics
- enable suppliers and service providers to compare their products and services against stated requirements and offer tenders, bids, quotations, or proposals on a comparable or equal basis
- enable the purchasing agent and organization to evaluate solicitation responses and
- maximize competition in the marketplace.

Characteristics of well-prepared and meaningful specifications will:

- accurately, clearly, and concisely describe the product or service
- be relevant to the application or use
- avoid ambiguity
- describe the process and use
- allow for measurement, performance testing, and acceptance or rejection upon delivery or installation
- provide for maximum acceptable tolerances enabling maximum competition
- identify brand, make, and model for comparisons as to an "approved equal" or "exceed"
- maximize competition at the manufacturing and distribution levels
- minimize extraneous costs
- allow for alternatives within reasonable and acceptable tolerance levels
- be written in terminology understood by the target market
- identify physical, functional, and quality characteristics, such as design, size, and weight and
- identify physical characteristics, such as speed, power, output, or grade of component.

Types of Specifications

Specification types can be as different as the things they describe. When contemplating which type to use under the specific situational requirements, one must evaluate the results expected and which type is most applicable. These variations are also identified in NIGP's Planning, Scheduling, and Requirement Analysis textbook (2004). The following most common types will be defined with sample appropriate applications:

- Design
- Combination (design and performance)
- Regulatory and testing agency
- Industry standards (generic)
- Material and manufacturing method
- Part drawing and part specification
- Qualified Products List (QPL) and samples.
- Performance
- Brand name or approved equal
- Restrictive (propriety products)
- Market grades
- Tolerances
- Finishes

Design Specifications

The agency or its consultants establish and describe the requirements in terms of how the item to be procured is constructed or manufactured and then write a design specification. The design specification details physical characteristics, appearance, connectivity, size, weight, and dimensions and often explains the specific materials to be used and assembly methods that must be employed. Design specifications often restrict competition or are proprietary to one manufacturer's product and/or service and reflect the manner in which the product is to be manufactured or constructed. Detailed engineering drawings or blueprints along with comprehensive descriptive building, installation, and testing processes generally accompany design specifications. These specifications result in the most accurate supply arrangement and compliance to tolerances and design characteristics.

When engaging design specifications...the organization must recognize and accept that it is ultimately responsible for costs associated with compliance.

Design specifications are frequently used in contracting for the construction of infrastructure projects and highly technical or specialized public works projects. Design specifications are often expensive to prepare and may be written in a manner that limits competition resulting in potentially higher purchase costs. For design "specs" to be effective, they must make provisions for tolerances and the ability to provide for alternates or variations from minimally acceptable standards for similar products or services. Design specifications that do not reflect the latest technological advancements will limit competition and, if written to incorporate precise dated requirements, may limit innovation.

When engaging design specifications in a procurement initiative, the organization must recognize and accept that it is ultimately responsible for costs associated with compliance. If a product is defined by a "design" specification and that product fails to meet the need, the organization is responsible for the costs. Similarly, the organization will incur all costs associated with the inspection and testing for compliance; and, therefore, the use of these types of specifications should only be used if the risks and costs for compliance can be supported. For example, a police department might request a firm to design and construct a prototype robot with remote control operation to be used in the removal of suspicious packages from buildings and public areas. The firm would design the robot per the police department's specifically defined requirements. It would then be constructed and tested. The police department would bear all the costs and expenses associated with this acquisition.

Performance Specifications

Performance specifications, or functional specifications, serve to describe what and how the product and/or service must execute the desired operation in order to achieve a specific result or outcome. Well-developed performance specifications translate into quality. If the specification is inadequate or does not describe the output, the quality of the end product or service may not meet the functional requirements. Inherent in any performance specification is the need to identify and describe capabilities and expectations that the product or service must satisfy.

Output tests, production performance measurement criteria, and methodology need to be developed and applied to ensure compliance to stated requirements. Performance specifications should make provisions for some tolerances, enabling suppliers to offer the maximum number of solutions and allowing for some degree of flexibility in the responses. When a performance specification is employed in a public solicitation, the onus and responsibility to meet stated requirements rests solely on the supplier. They not only have to offer a solution to meet the performance requirements; they must show conclusive evidence that the product or service actually meets stated requirements. Irrespective of the conciseness and comprehensiveness of a performance specification, the selection of the wrong supplier may result in a less than ideal outcome.

Consider the performance specifications for a photocopier requiring specific output volumes with specified quality standards. Another application of performance specifications may be in the acquisition of a "street sweeper" to be purchased by the city. The city requires this piece of equipment to be outfitted with floating brushes because many of the road surfaces are uneven. The proposed design must be very specific and incorporate this particular performance feature.

Combination Specifications

A combination specification incorporates the features and functionality of a "design" specification with the "performance" specification. It may also include a combination of commercial standards, brand names, or any indicators previously assessed for a Qualified Products List (QPL). In the case of the street sweeper procurement, in addition to the specific design characteristics, the combination specification could also stipulate that the equipment must lift a minimum of 95% of the road grit and that the grit be deposited in a holding tank. On a rough and uneven terrain, this would be most difficult; however, if this is the requirement, it could be expected and measured in the operational performance of the delivered street sweeper.

Brand Name or Approved Equal

This type of specification identifies a product manufactured by a specific firm and includes make, model, and specific product information. Specifying a product or service by brand/make/model is risky. It presumes that the individual stating the brand name as the base specification is knowledgeable of the market and believes there is no better product or service available within the market at better value. By using brand as a base, the organization may be overlooking alternative products of lower cost that can provide better functionality and quality from superior suppliers in terms of service, reliability, and customer relations. It also relies on the reputation and integrity of the manufacturer, distributor, or dealer. Often, a product that contains a brand name is established through labeling and becomes an industry standard; as the manufacturer establishes the product in the marketplace as a preferred item. Purchasers should be aware to only evaluate a branded product against industry standards and performance expectations.

Purchasers will frequently offer a brand, make, or model to identify the minimum acceptable product and will include the term "or approved equal." This allows and requires the supplier to offer any product they deem to meet "or equal" the capabilities (physical and performance characteristics) and places the onus on the supplier to prove product equivalency. The purchaser reserves the right to determine equivalency where brand, make, model, or equal is offered as a replacement for a design or performance specification. The alternative suggested product must be exactly the same as the brand, make, or model used or better. Brand, make, or model types of specifications should be limited to those situations where the purchaser is limited by time to develop a written design or performance specification. Purchasers must take care in their sourcing documents to indicate that the brand, make, or model shown is for reference and comparison purposes only and are not to be interpreted as the preferred product.

The Federal Acquisition Regulation (FAR) requires that all brand name specifications provide justification when solicitations include brand name. In addition, a memo in April 2006, required that any acquisitions over $25,000 that include a brand name have all documents, including justification, posted to the Government Point of Entry system at http://www.fedbizopps.gov as well as the E-Buy system at http://www.ebuy.gsa.gov. These measures are in keeping with the GAO's preference that agencies limit their use of brand name specifications. (Office of Management and Budget, 2006)

Qualified Products List (QPL) and Samples

Products and services are evaluated in advance of a solicitation through comprehensive laboratory or application testing, work-in-progress inspections, and product trials designed to ensure compliance with specifications or commercial standards. Once the respective product and service have been approved, the supplier and their approved products are placed on a QPL. These products are often referred to as approved brands and placed on an "Approved Brands List" (ABL) or an "Approved Products List" (APL) (NIGP, 2007).

If a required product or service appears on an organization's QPL, ABL, or APL, only those firms who can supply the specified product are eligible to compete and submit a bid, quote or proposal. Usually products on such lists are identified by brand, make, and model, SKU, UPC, and customarily have Canadian Standards Association (CSA) or Underwriters Laboratories (UL) certification. Highway paint is an example of a product that would appear on an organization's list. The product would be pre-qualified through sample application and vigorous testing, and only those that satisfactorily exceeded the test criteria and conditions would be placed on the QPL.

It is a good practice to "acceptance test" new or revised products prior to purchase or inclusion on the list. Testing for quality prior to solicitation may mitigate the risk of accepting an inferior product or product that does not meet actual requirements. When testing is used in the sourcing process, potential suppliers and their manufacturers should be invited to provide sufficient products at their expense for testing and future compliance monitoring. Organizations often use external professional laboratories to perform tests and provide an independent, impartial opinion as to compliance. In these instances, the purchaser must reserve the right to utilize compliance testing reports from a third party.

With the use of a QPL, an organization can identify, in advance of an acquisition, which products meet the intended end use or application. If a product has been pre-tested and acceptable suppliers have been identified, the process is simplified. The purchaser will need to verify price, delivery, and any other specific requirements. The QPL is updated as the required specifications change or if a firm introduces a comparable product that meets the specification that had previously passed inspection or testing. A QPL minimizes the difficulties associated with firms offering a product to evaluate during the solicitation process and having to determine whether or not the product meets specifications without testing.

The same sourcing rules apply when establishing a QPL for any product or service. The process must be open to other products, be open to competition, and be fair and transparent. Suppliers must not be restrained or restricted from having their respective products evaluated and tested. If a product is deemed unacceptable for inclusion on the list, the supplier must be informed of the decision and given an opportunity to remedy any deficiencies.

Even though an organization may have a QPL, it is incumbent upon them to regularly and periodically request that the industry have their products pre-qualified. This allows for continuous identification and recognition of new and innovative products entering the market.

Organizations using a QPL are encouraged to obtain and retain samples or prototypes along with written specifications or descriptive literature for each product approved for the list. This allows the organization to match what was originally requested or specified to what was delivered, installed, or applied. It also accommodates laboratory testing. For example, this approach could be valuable when selecting highway paving asphalt bases. The chemical characteristics would be laboratory tested, and the approved samples would be compared to the delivered product. This should all be documented and filed for future reference and use in the event of a dispute at a later date if the product fails. In one jurisdiction, an asphalt sample was taken from each tanker, labeled as to delivery data, and delivery firm (truck); the organization was able to identify on which stretch of highway the asphalt was applied. Documentation of each delivery enabled the organization to enforce its contract and ensure the stipulated quality was delivered.

Prior to issuing an order for the product, the purchaser should verify with the supplier that the product has not been modified from the sample on the approved QPL. Often, manufacturers modify their products to reflect innovation and ingredient changes without informing the purchasing organization. In some situations, these modifications fundamentally change the specification to such an extent that the originally intended requirement can no longer be met. The responsibility for insuring that a product on the QPL meets the stated initial requirements rests with the purchaser and their respective inspections or testing agencies.

Regulatory and Testing Agency

Certain products must meet regulatory approval and testing for compliance. These products must be labeled with a certification stamp. Two well-known types of certifications are offered by the Underwriters Laboratories (UL) and the Canadian Standards Association (CSA). Frequently, purchasers will require that the product must be approved by UL or CSA. Organizations may outsource the testing process to professional and certified laboratories. If the product does not contain the required certification or label, it does not meet the intended requirements. Occupational Safety and Health or Workers' Compensation Board Legislation and Regulations normally specify these requirements. Additional information about product labeling can be obtained from the certifying organization's Website.

Restrictive Specifications—Proprietary Products

Some acquisitions may require a sole source or directed contract process. Restrictive or proprietary specifications are applied if a product is unique to a specific application and is manufactured by only one firm. If only one supplier is authorized to sell and distribute the specific product or component, the same requirements may apply. Any new product must be compatible with the originally purchased product and/or equipment. To purchase a generic or substitute, even if it was deemed equal, would void guarantee or warranty provisions of the originally purchased product. Restrictive specifications may be required in the acquisition of replacement parts for a particular photocopier make and model or chemical cleaner ingredients, for example.

Industry Standards—Generic Products

Industry standards may also be considered as a type of specification resulting from the manufacture of generic products, Acetylsalicylic Acid (ASA), commonly known as aspirin, distilled or bottled water, and IBM-compatible products are good examples. These products are generic in nature and have become industry standards. Purchasers may make reference to generic names in their sourcing documents and processes.

Market Grades

Organizations such as The Chicago Board of Trade, New York Mercantile Exchange, Minneapolis Grain Exchange, and Kansas City Board of Trade apply standards for product measurement. Such products may include grains, cattle, lumber, oil and gas, coffee, sugar, cotton, orange juice, and metals. Commodities are rated and compared to predetermined international benchmarks based on evaluations and inspections and are affected by the general market supply and demand. Reliance is placed on suppliers to authenticate quality or grade, which ultimately determines the price required of commodity-type products acquired from reputable suppliers. When in doubt as to the grade of quality, enlisting the services of an impartial, reputable inspector or testing agency will benefit the organization.

Material and Manufacturing Method

Material specifications are applicable if explicit products, materials, ingredients, and components are specified to effect a pre-determined result, or if the product may involve a blend of chemicals, ingredients, and manufacturing protocols. They may also be used if a mixture of ingredients in a specific order or manner is required. In these circumstances, the purchaser assumes the risk of manufacturing cost and product performance, as the manufacturer has no discretion on ingredients, assembly, or manufacturing processes. When employing this type of specification, the manufacturer is obligated to follow very precise processes defined by the purchaser.

The organization establishes the specific materials to be used in the manufacturing process and precisely how the ingredients, parts, or components must be assembled along with tolerances and performance criteria. Responsibility for performance rests with the buying organization, as the manufacturer is compelled to use the materials and employ the process specified. This type of specification is commonly used in the manufacture of specialized chemicals and military products. This is very costly and carries a high degree of risk to the purchaser. Development of specifications, tooling for manufacturing, inspection for quality and compliance during the manufacturing process, and testing for compliance are costs that the purchaser will bear, as the manufacturer will pass these along in the final price paid.

Care must be taken in selecting a manufacturer or supplier who can produce the product in compliance with stated specifications. In these sourcing situations, a more sophisticated type of sourcing, supplier evaluation, and selection process will be required.

Tolerances

The NIGP's Public Procurement Dictionary of Terms defines "tolerance" as a "specified allowance for variation in weight or other designated measurement; the range of allowable deviation within which an item or service is classified as acceptable." (NIGP, 2007) Purchasers should be very specific as to tolerances allowed and only engage restrictive tolerances where the nature of the item must be compatible with fit or operate in accordance with specific Original Equipment Manufacturer (OEM) supplied items. Overly restrictive tolerances will limit competition and could result in a product that does not meet best-value criteria.

Part Drawing and Part Specification

If a product is specifically illustrated in terms of physical characteristics and dimensions, it may require more detail within the specification. The part or item must be described in such minute and literal terms as to virtually paint a picture of the item. Drawings and blueprints usually have a copyright and cannot be given to other suppliers without written permission from the copyright holder.

Finishes

Requests for a specific look, feel or aesthetic appearance will require the inclusion of finishes specifications. Fulfillment of such requests will incur a higher price for the final product, as their incorporation will require special manufacturing and tooling. Often, samples are required prior to final production and are used for comparison and matching.

Standards

Commercial standards are formulated through successive acquisition of similar or the same type of products over a period of time and are a direct result of organizations having a recurring need for the same products and services. A standard sets out specific conditions to be fulfilled, functions to be performed, applications to be achieved and/or physical characteristics described for a comparable item. They become the formal product standard accepted by an organization for a stipulated future procurement period.

Manufacturing methods, assembly, or fabrication processes and use of specific ingredients or components in terms of quality, features, or applications often are the basis for establishing a certain product or service as a standard. Similar or like items bearing the same characteristics, regardless of manufacturer or process, inevitably become the standard. Typical recurring needs may be for plastic two-liter soda bottles, or small plastic containers with snap-on lids. An industry or manufacturer's standard has the benefit and advantage of mass production and supply availability on relatively short notice.

Standardization Program

Standardization is the methodology and process used in the manufacture of a product that establishes the physical and functional characteristics of that product. It becomes the norm or chosen preference of one brand, make, or model over another and reflects a uniform or common appearance or application of functionality. Effectively applied standardization will result in cost reduction to an organization and lead to effective maintenance, training, integration, reallocation, and economy of scale when making future purchases. Included in any standardization effort are the testing methods for measuring compliance to the stipulated standard. Overstated standards will inevitably lead to increased and unnecessary costs.

Standardization focuses on agreement of designs, sizes, shapes, colors, quality, material composition, chemical properties, performance characteristics, and assembly methods. Purchasers and internal users often confuse a standardization program with a simplification program. A simplification program involves screening the inventory of the entity in order to determine which items should either be eliminated or replaced with more popular items. Its intent is to intentionally reduce the number and variety of inventory items and eliminate duplication. A good standardization program within an organization results in:

- fewer varieties of items in larger quantities being purchased
- lower cost due to volume increases on fewer variety of items
- fewer varieties of items to purchase resulting in fewer specifications and less time needed to prepare for sourcing
- reduced inventory of more items
- better inventory control and
- reduced operational and administrative costs.

With the rapid globalization of markets, the need for universal or international standards is essential to leverage cost and product availability. The competitive environment of global markets is forcing manufacturers to develop standards for certain products, which, by their nature, establishes standardization of products. Two good examples can be seen in the manufacturing of latex medical gloves where production standards in Mexico and off-shore countries must be comparable to European and North American manufacturing standards; and similarly with plastic 18.9-liter bottled water containers where Asian manufacturer's must have the same standards of manufacturing and production as do North American producers.

Several prominent international organizations exist that develop and support international standards and can provide assistance in the procurement process.

- Underwriters Laboratories (UL)
- Canadian Standards Association (CSA)
- Canadian General Standards Board (CGSB)
- American National Standards Institute (ANSI)
- International Organization for Standardization (ISO)
- International Electro-technical Commission (IEC)
- Pan American Standards Commission (COPANT)
- American Society of Test Materials (ASTM)
- Organization for the Advancement of Structured Information Standards (OASIS)

Standards Committee

The effectiveness of a standards or standardization program will depend on the value the organization places on the benefits achievable under such a program. Some organizations assign responsibility to individuals or departments with expertise in administering such programs. A Standards Committee is governed by policy and reports to a senior executive. This group has responsibility for the following key functions and activities:

- Developing standards through a simplification process for designated products and services
- Establishing specifications
- Formulating policy, procedures, and guidelines for administering the standards developed
- Monitoring maintenance and updates
- Receiving unsolicited offers and product introductions for review, evaluation, and consideration
- Approving products for the Qualified Products List
- Evaluating exception requests to established standards
- Reviewing items to determine which items should be incorporated into a standards program
- Reviewing and evaluating other organizations' standards programs and establishing benchmark criteria
- Inviting suppliers to participate on a regular basis in providing input as to comparison, quality, reliability, and cost.

As an example, a leading university has established furniture standards for office chairs, filing cabinets, bulletin boards, and systems stations. A committee has been established to identify, evaluate, and select products or components that will meet the University's overall requirements. In addition, this committee develops specifications for competitive sourcing along with product trials and testing. The committee consists of representatives from Occupational Safety and Health, Facilities Management, Purchasing Services, and Project Planning. End-users, manufacturers, and other key internal stakeholders often participate on this committee, particularly when large acquisitions are made. A major benefit of using a committee in this particular case is that the furniture purchased is interchangeable among operating units and will allow for a consistent-looking office landscape. It will also provide maximum flexibility to transfer items between operating units. A Standards Committee is an effective way to minimize the proliferation of similar items being purchased.

Sources of Standards

Throughout North America and internationally, a variety of professional standards organizations have evolved to develop and maintain specifications and standards for reference and use by others, wherein they benefit from the trials and tests performed in past use. Some of these organizations are as follows (NIGP, 2007):

- American National Standards Institute (ANSI)
- American Society for Quality Control (ASQC)
- American Society for Testing and Materials (ASTM)
- Canadian General Standards Board (CGSB)
- Canadian Standards Association (CSA)
- Federal Bureau of Specifications (FBS)
- International Organization for Standardization (ISO)
- National Bureau of Standards (NBS)
- National Institute of Standards and Technology (NIST)
- National Lumber Manufacturers Association (NLMA)
- Society for Automotive Engineers (SAE)
- Society of Mechanical Engineers (SME)

Requirements Analysis

An organization can determine its specific product and service needs relative to the intended operational applications by performing a value analysis. This comprehensive review, assessment, and evaluation of products and services must be completed to eliminate or remove products that are not suited to the application. The analysis will also focus on products and services that best meet the intended need at "best-value" for the organization. Specifications are formulated and written to reflect specific needs enabling all potential suppliers to offer their most suitable product and service.

"Best value" has been defined as

> . . . a measure that is established through a process that determines the value of products and/or services acquired through a competitive process that results in

supply arrangements at the most effective life-cycle cost, in the correct quantities, at the right quality, and from the most responsible and responsive supplier, proponent or firm. (University of Victoria, 2003)

The NIGP's Public Procurement Dictionary of Terms states:

An assessment of the return which can be achieved based on the total life cycle cost of the item; may include an analysis of the functionality of the item; can use cost/benefit analysis to define the best combinations of quality, services, time, and cost considerations over the useful life of the acquired item. A procurement method that emphasizes value over price. The best value might not be the lowest cost. Generally achieved through the Request for Proposal (RFP) method. (NIGP, 2007)

When performing a requirements analysis, an assessment of real value to stated requirements is performed. By way of reference or example, a slightly higher amount may be paid for an alternate equal product; but, if the life expectancy and/or serviceability of the item during its life cycle is extended, the result is better value.

Requirements analysis is the responsibility of everyone in the supply acquisition process. End-users and suppliers should be included in the process to identify products deemed suitable for the intended application as well as the evaluation and analysis process. Suppliers and their competitors can be valuable resources when establishing compliance to stated and expected requirements. Sales and customer service representatives dedicate considerable time and effort in assessing competitors' products. This information is of the most value during the analysis process.

Establishing Mandatory and/or Optional Sourcing Criteria

The key to acquiring the best-suited product or service, at the best-value or life cycle cost is the "specification." The sourcing documents must consider and make provision for evaluation, analysis, and ranking of the submissions in terms of compliance and meeting the terms and conditions stipulated.

When mandatory, desirable and optional criteria are applied in conjunction with the solicitation scope of work, deliverables, terms, and conditions, an organization will be able to achieve a smooth and successful sourcing exercise, irrespective of the nature of the acquisition.

References

The Legal Edge, 40 (2001-2002, December-January).

Office of Management and Budget, Executive Office of the President, *Memorandum April 2006*

National Institute of Governmental Purchasing, Inc. (NIGP) (1996). *Public procurement dictionary of terms.* Herndon, VA: NIGP.

National Institute of Governmental Purchasing, Inc. (NIGP) (2007). *Developing and managing requests for proposals in the public sector.* Herndon, VA: NIGP.

National Institute of Governmental Purchasing, Inc. (NIGP) (2004). *Planning, scheduling, and requirement analysis.* Herndon, VA: NIGP.

University of Victoria (2003). Policy on strategic alliances. In *University of Victoria policy manual* (Policy Number 1792). British Columbia, Canada: Office of the University Secretary.

Chapter 6

Authorization and Approvals

Introduction

Throughout the solicitation process, there are approval points and authority levels required for a variety of operational, organizational, and financial control purposes. Some approval levels exist to monitor spending authority against operational budgets, while others are established to control the value and types of purchases. Still others exist for technical compliance to standards or business functions or applications. Illustrated later in this chapter are the various types of authority that exist in one form or another in most public sector organizations. This chapter will focus on the wide range of approval levels and address the specific purposes and requirements of each at the various stages of the procurement cycle. An overview of the process is included at the end of this chapter as Figure 10.

The end-user and the purchasing organization conduct basic reviews and required approvals during the solicitation process. Figure 8 indicates who may be asked to conduct basic reviews or make approvals during the solicitation process. Other approvals or authorizations may also be required where specific acquisitions do not comply with an organization's policy or where the acquisition would result in fundamental public procurement practices being brought into question. This chapter will address the requirements for each of the review, approval, and authorization levels throughout the life cycle of a sourcing exercise. These will vary by organization and will depend on the policy and cultural climate of each organization. It will also depend on whether the organization has a centralized or decentralized procurement agency and the role, responsibility, and authority of that agency.

Solicitation Process	End-User	Supervisor Manager	Purchasing Organization
The decision to make an acquisition	X		
The review and approval of specific requirements for value, cost, and nature of acquisition	X	X	
The formality of a Purchase Requisition (PR)—transfer of agent status to centralized purchasing unit	X	X	X
The review and approval of specifications and sourcing document	X		X
The evaluation, acceptance, and approval of tenders, bids, quotations, or proposal			X
The approval of samples	X		
The approval of Work-In-Progress	X		X
The approval of delivery and receipt certification as per purchase order or contract	X		
The approval of contract award	X		
The approval of purchase order or contract (execution of documents)			X
The approval for compliance to purchase order	X		
The approval of payment			X
The approval of sole source or directed contract			X
The approval where an award is recommended to other than low compliant bid, quote or proposal			X
Approval to acquire a product or service from a firm outside of a specified trading area			X
Technical approval	X		X
Other approvals as may be required by each organization depending on their regulatory or legislated requirements		X	X
Non-standard product acquisition approval	X	X	X

Figure 8. *Areas of responsibility during the solicitation process*

Identification of Need

The internal customer, or end-user, is responsible for determining whether or not a product or service is needed to perform operational or administrative business. The end-user must document the specific requirements for subsequent process and approval within the organization's stipulated policy, process procedures, and practice.

Establishing Specific Requirements

Together, the end-user and the organization will begin the evaluation and decision-making process that will result in the establishment of specific requirements. Once agreed upon, the authorized officials must approve the specific requirements. For example, if an organization requires a delivery vehicle to move items from point A to B, the type of vehicle required will depend on the nature of the operational requirements. Options may include: a pick-up truck, high cube van, regular van, deck truck (1-5 ton), body truck (1-5 ton), etc. While making these choices, the organization has already begun to make decisions about limitations, capital, and operational costs. This is only one aspect of an approval or authorization.

Budget Commitment Approval

Once the decision is made to continue with an acquisition, funding sources must be checked and verified. Some acquisitions have previously been identified within the organization's approved budget. In other instances, the organization may need to seek special funding approval, requiring a formal application through the executive arm of the organization. If funding is available, the organization will be required to code and cost the item(s) against the appropriate "cost center." A cost center is an organizational or operational unit tasked with specific operational and program responsibilities and is granted sufficient budget funding to carry out those responsibilities.

Formalizing the Acquisition

Upon identifying the need, the establishment of specific requirements, and the determination to move forward with an acquisition, the next step is to formalize the request for acquisition. How this is done and the process to be used is dependent on whether the organization operates within a "centralized" or "decentralized" structure.

In a "decentralized" structure, end-users are often permitted to source, evaluate, and commit to external third parties (suppliers) directly if the nature and value of the acquisition meets certain pre-determined criteria. In a centralized procurement operating environment, the end-user may be required to complete a formal Purchase Requisition, Work Order, Materials and Service Request, or any other formal documentation issued by the organization to initiate a purchase.

In a "combination" environment, the organization may permit the end-user to handle all of the process elements or aspects of the purchase, with compliance to policy and open to formal reviews and audits on a "without notice" basis. The end-user must follow the same rules, processes, and practices as the central procurement entity. The organization may also allow end-users to make acquisitions from external suppliers up to a certain dollar value, except where specifications are governed by policy or where they are required to process their requirements through Central Purchasing. Cellular phones, for example, often fall under this stipulation.

Generating a Purchase Requisition—"Law of Agency"

When an organization has specific provisions in its policy for the requirement of a purchase requisition or some other formal comparable document, the purchase request document should be complete, concise, and as accurate as possible. If individuals with spending and/or commitment authority sign or authorize the purchase request document, they are ostensibly granting another person the authority to act on their behalf to source and purchase the products and/or services as precisely specified within the stated dollar value established within the documents and in accordance with the terms, conditions, and specifications provided. Normally, the purchasing agent cannot exceed that authority which was passed on to them without prior acknowledgement, clearance, and approval of the granting authority (unless certain thresholds are established). The Law of Agency provides that a principal can appoint an agent to act on its behalf; and, when the agent acts, it is the principal, not the agent, who is bound by the action.

Purchasing Organization Authority

Once a completed and authorized purchase requisition or comparable document is received for processing, the organization is obligated to review the specifications for appropriateness and ensure that the specification does not limit competition. Upon receipt, the organization should review the documentation for:

- cost and correct cost center accounting information
- proper expenditures or spending authority
- restrictions imposed by terms and conditions; mandatory, optional, desirable requirements, delivery terms, etc. and
- solicitation process feasibility.

The organization's policy, procedures, practices, and processes will predicate each procurement organization's authority. The next stage includes "sourcing the requirements" through an open, fair, transparent, and competitive process. The sourcing documents are created and approved by the purchasing agent for processing. Each organization has unique sourcing requirements, and these must be incorporated into the Invitation to Tender/Bids (ITT/ IFB), Request for Proposal (RFP), Request for Quotation (RFQ), Request for Information/

Expression of Interest (RFI/REI), and any others. Once the sourcing document has been prepared and is ready for release to the marketplace, the end-user must be given an opportunity to review and approve the document with respect to their expectations and operational requirements. The purchasing agent should obtain a signed-off copy and retain it in their files. Going to market for bids, quotations, or proposals with specifications and documentation that do not reflect the nature and precise requirements of the operational organization could lead to public embarrassment, extended delay in delivery, acquiring an incorrect product, or increased costs incurred by having to conduct the process the second time.

Selection of Supplier or Contractor and Approval of Award

At the designated closing time and date for each procurement or as soon as possible thereafter, the purchasing agent must open, review and evaluate bids, quotations, and proposals for compliance with specifications stipulated in the sourcing documents. Only those that meet all terms and conditions are approved for inclusion in the detailed review, analysis, and evaluation for award purposes. In the case of RFP's, evaluation is performed for "best-value", and in the case of RFQ's and IFB/ITT's evaluation is performed for "good-value" (where all fulfillment terms are met for quality, delivery, etc.).

In a competitive bid or tender, the lowest responsive and responsible bid or tender is identified. This task is performed and approved by the purchasing agent representing the organization. Some organizations choose to utilize a "technical evaluation" committee or team, while others choose to use external expert consulting, engineering, or professional organizations to conduct the review, evaluation, and analysis that may include a written award recommendation. This is particularly effective if an organization does not have skilled or qualified resources to conduct these reviews, as in the case of purchasing public art for a community. The purchasing agent will then be required to assess the recommendation and supporting documentations and forward an approval or non-approval of the transaction.

The decision to proceed must fall within the authority established for each respective purchasing agent. If the transaction falls outside of the purchasing agent's authority or is inconsistent with the authority granted through the "Law of Agency," they will be required to secure the required approvals and signatures. When all parties involved in the acquisition have provided input, review, and approval, the purchasing agent is then in the position to award contracts through execution of a purchase order or long/short form formal agreement.

Assessing and Establishing Delegated Authority

Normally, an organization's executive will establish a formal delegation of authority and spending limits for specific organization officers. In some organizations, authority to commit expenditures to a specific operational budget may be delegated to the department secretary and/or front-line workers. For others, delegated spending authority is usually reserved for those at a supervisory level or higher. Spending limit thresholds are set at lower values to ensure proper control of expenditures.

Generally, the levels established are appropriate to the need for expenditure and the skills or expertise of the individual occupying the position. As an individual's position increases within the organization, the value of spending limits and the nature or types of purchases an individual can authorize also increases. The agency executive often participates in establishing the values, types of expenditures, and the methods of procurement that certain individuals can authorize. Procurement professionals can only delegate authority under particular circumstances and to accomplish particular tasks. The following are types of delegated authority common to the procurement process.

Delegated Authority is granted through legislation or by an organization's governing body to specific individuals, to exercise certain rights, within specific terms of reference or guidelines. These individuals may be granted rights to sub-delegate within policy limitations.

Spending Authority (also known as expenditure authority) is the permission granted by an organization to an individual, which allows them to spend funds up to pre-established limits against an operating or program account or budget. Often, spending authority may have restrictions based on certain types of expenditures, such as automobiles, technology over a stated value, dangerous goods, etc. Spending authority levels, like delegated authority, may vary by position within the organization and by the skills or expertise of the individual occupying the respective position.

Commitment Authority (with external third parties) is the permission granted to an individual to commit funds to an external third party. This authority is usually granted on an "at-arms-length" basis to a purchasing agent or individuals within a procurement organization acting as agents on behalf of internal users. These individuals normally have "Agent" authority.

Receiving, Certification and Acceptance Authority is permission granted to an individual within an organization who is specifically tasked with the role and responsibility to receive, inspect, test, and validate delivery or provision of goods and services in accordance with the contract. Normally, an individual who has spending or commitment authority for the same transaction does not hold certification and acceptance authority.

Payment Authority is permission granted to an individual in order to disburse funds and make payments (issue checks) against a contract or purchase order when certification and acceptance of work has been obtained. This function is normally performed within the Finance Department of an organization. It is incumbent upon the grantor to review the legality of payments and to exercise all appropriate financial controls.

Approval in Principle is applicable when an individual, operation, or business unit proposes a certain program or operation through a business case or other document. The approving authority (usually Board, Cabinet, Council, Executive Committee, etc.) provides authorization in principle for proceeding to the next stage of the implementation plan. Additional approval is required prior to any formal action to be taken with program delivery.

When approval in principle is granted, usually definite conditions are placed upon the program or operations managers that must be met prior to proceeding. Some instances may require information to be provided. Some may require a policy or procedural amendment, and still others may require funding allocation. Approval in principle may be granted for any number of reasons, and the parties of the transaction must meet each detailed condition. Approval in Principle is sometimes linked to the supplier's ability to meet certain conditions and/or organization's operational requirements. For example, an approval to award a 23-year contract would be contingent upon the supplier providing some pre-determined beneficial value to the organization. If the supplier meets these obligations, then the contract is advanced. If they do not, the contract does not proceed without the approving body being consulted for direction.

Other Forms of Authority

Express Authority: That authority that is explicitly given in direct language, rather than inferred from conduct.

Implied Authority: Authority that is not defined expressly, but is only determined by inferences and reasonable deductions arising out of the conduct of the principal toward the agent and the agent's actions.

Inherent Authority: Authority based on a government's sovereignty, to enter into contracts, although not explicitly authorized. (NIGP, 2007)

Determining Approval Levels

M ost organizations have established approval levels in terms of spending limits per transaction and for each category of purchase. As indicated previously, these levels may depend upon the position in the organization and the skills and expertise of the individual occupying the respective position. For example, construction contracts may carry different levels and values than those approved for conventional products and service. Professional services and technology acquisitions may have still different approval levels and spending limits. Those approving pCard acquisitions may have unique value thresholds from those utilizing conventional purchase order or formal contract procedures. Such values and thresholds are established through formal policy. Where approvals are specifically delegated in a decentralized procurement environment, the purchasing department often will function in an advisory role and is tasked with post transaction review and compliance audits. In a decentralized procurement environment, the purchasing department is relied upon to provide training assistance and guidance to end-users.

Solicitation Approvals

Electronic Authorization

The Internet has provided tools for organizations to engage in eProcurement and eCommerce using real-time technology. This innovation has been instrumental in making purchasing organizations more effective and efficient. Organizations that are taking advantage of this technology are experiencing significant benefits in the process; in output improvements, seeing a reduction in operating costs, offering more timely service, and acquiring accurate, up-to-date information that enhances decision making.

Nevertheless, there are inherent and significant risks associated with using electronic technology. Agencies can solicit bids, quotes, or proposals. They can electronically transmit information to a supplier, place orders, and accompany payment with pCard transactions or set up billing and payment through electronic data interchange (EDI) on the World Wide Web. Organizations that engage in electronic solicitations and receive electronic responses need to have documented guidelines, specific policy, procedures, and authorities in place to accommodate these unique types of acquisitions. Stated policy must make provisions for the organization to have authority to use electronic commerce for sending and receiving and to accept the date and time logged onto the electronic transmission document as the legal date/time for purposes of compliance relative to closing date/time provided in solicitation documents. The purchasing organization must clearly state within the sourcing documents that the bidder/firm/respondent is solely responsible for ensuring their responses are received on time. The organization should not be held responsible for the inadvertent release of any information, nor should it take responsibility for information that may be misdirected.

With the use of this new authority, the purchasing agent should also review, evaluate, and authorize only those acquisition transactions that are suitable for eProcurement and/or eCommerce technology. For example, a response that specifically requires illustrated brochures, technical drawings, or samples as part of a response may not be appropriate for electronic submission. In 2000, President Clinton signed the Electronics Signatures in Global and National Commerce Act (or eSign) making contracts sealed by computer as binding as those signed in pen and ink. This act has helped to accelerate the use of eProcurement in the United States at all levels of government. (NIGP, 2007)

Security requirements for electronic and Internet-type product and/or service acquisitions can be accommodated by providing personalized account numbers or by using identification numbers or passwords provided by the supplier and linked electronically to an organization and/or a specific individual within the organization who is authorized to use the respective service and make online acquisitions. An organization, through its formal approval policy, can enable the use of electronic solicitations under specified terms and conditions articulated in the sourcing documents or by separate agreement with their suppliers.

For example, the individual authorized to use a Boise Cascade, Grand & Toy, or W. W. Grainger electronic catalog ordering system would need a specific "user account number" (for the organization), a unique ID number, and a specific password before they could place an online order. Access to the catalog and generation of an order could only be established if these three numbers can be verified and the respective supplier has identified the registered user in the system. Further controls or authorizations might be required for specific transactions, thresholds, or types of purchases (i.e., equipment, furniture, chemical, etc.). These parameters or conditions can also be pre-established and linked directly to the access account, ID, or password. Some organizations already permit the use of pCards for online requisitions with suppliers or merchants and have experienced measurable savings.

Electronic procurement and commerce, through the use of the Internet, EDI, or Enterprise Resource Planning Software (ERP) systems, is becoming more popular. As jurisdictions and agencies overcome issues surrounding security, they are more likely to authorize a respective purchasing organization to use the technology.

Other Authorizations

Authorization does not only involve internal processes and procedures but can relate to the actual acquisition. Authorization and approval of products and services is equally important to the procurement process. Authorization may take advantage of submitted supplier samples by approving the requested work as it progresses through to completion, delivery approval, or end-user compliance approval.

- **Samples**. Many acquisitions require the comparison of current products to future acquisitions. With advancements in manufacturing processes and product innovations, many new products (replicas of prior products) take on new characteristics, qualities, and visual esthetics. Therefore, organizations wish to compare "what was" to "what is" for consistency, compatibility, and visual appearance. Purchasing agents often require suppliers to provide samples for review, testing, inspection, and field trial. End-users, testing agencies (on behalf of the organization), laboratories, and other professionals often engage in the validation and testing of a product or service for compliance with specifications and standards. The end-user makes the final recommendation, with approval often provided by the organization's purchasing agent.

- **Work-In-Progress**. Organizations often include within the solicitation documents or agreements provisions for work-in-progress inspections at certain stages in the manufacturing process. These inspections are intended to ensure that the manufacturer is using the specified ingredients, assembly protocols, and quality control practices. Authorization and approval at this stage is required to proceed to subsequent phases of the manufacturing and assembly process. A work-in-progress inspection and approval, for example, might be used in the manufacture, assembly, and packaging of a knockdown video lottery stand. The manufacturer is required to manufacture the parts (top surface, sides, back, bottom, doors, etc.) using specified plywood, glues, selected veneers, and fastening devices. Prior to packaging, and on inspection, a random sample is tested for manufacturing quality, stability when assembled, and strength (weight load) after assembly. Once these tests are completed and the manufacturer's processes are approved, the supplier is given authorization to continue with packaging in anticipation of future delivery.

- **Delivery and Receipt Certification**. Within an organization, the designated receiver within an organization is required to accept the delivery, inspect for damages, and verify shipment installation in accordance with contract terms and conditions and specifications. The individual must document the transaction, note any deficiencies or damages, and indicate approval for acceptance by signing the transport/delivery firm's bill of lading or delivery vouchers. Where an inspection cannot take place during the time the delivery agency is on site, the receiver is required to note that the delivery is "Subject to Inspection" for a designated period of time. This should be included as one of the terms and conditions within the original sourcing documents. The delivery must be consistent with the purchase order or agreement. Otherwise, it should not be accepted which should be properly noted on the documents.

- **Compliance to Specifications and/or Standards**. Another approval and authorization takes place if the end-user accepts the products from the receiver, the delivery, or transportation firm directly. When deliveries are made directly to the end-user, they are required to perform the delivery and receipt certification process noted in the preceding section. The end-user is required to certify that the products and/or installation have been provided in compliance with the specifications in the original sourcing documents and are operating or performing as intended. Should compliance certification not be made at this point, the end-user must document the reasons and immediately inform the purchasing agency of the non-compliance. If the products or installation comply with all aspects of the agreement, the end-user can authorize approval for acceptance and subsequent payment of invoices.

Payment Authorization

Normally, suppliers are directed to forward invoices to the organization's Accounts Payable Department for processing. Often, the invoice is sent directly to the delivery location or is included in the delivery itself. Organizations have specific policies and procedures for handling and processing invoices for payment. These requirements address, and are intended to comply with, the "segregation of duties" principles that are considered to be "Generally Accepted Accounting Principles" (GAAP). These principles require that an individual other than the requestor should, where practical and feasible, receive and certify the receipt of the products. Further, an individual other than the one who ordered and received the product should perform the matching process and authorize payment. Further, an individual, other than any of the above, should make the payment (issue the check). The precise methods will vary by organization, depending upon their policy, procedures and practices, including methods of payment (check, purchasing card, cash, voucher reimbursement, etc.). No matter the process, a transaction should only be approved and processed for payment when all of the terms and conditions of supply have been met. Occasionally, progress payments, prepayment, or deposits are required with a purchase order or agreement. Only payments that comply with these conditions should be authorized by the end-user or designated payment authority.

Sole Source Authorization

As discussed earlier in this book, every public sector organization has or should have formal policies and procedures to deal with internal end-users that request that an award be made on the basis of a "sole" source or "directed contract".

Approval and authorization for an award to be made on a "sole" source or basis resides with the organization's most senior purchasing agent. In some organizations, authorization and approval to purchase from a sole source or supplier rests with an even higher authority, such as a Vice-President, Deputy Minister, City Council, or Cabinet. Being given authority is often dependent on the nature of the purchase, economic development initiatives, preferred supplier partner, or political and cultural environments.

In some organizations, the end-user, principal investigator, researcher, engineer, or architect have pre-established a product, supplier, or manufacturer based on the specific needs, applications, or performance parameters and only that product and/or service can be engaged to suit the intended purposes. It is, therefore, incumbent upon this individual to adequately document and support a "sole" source justification and prepare an appropriate recommendation for acceptance, review, and approval by the designated higher level.

Other than Low-Compliant Bid/Quote/Proposal

As with a sole source or directed contract acquisition, many end-users and their represen-tatives specify products and/or services for which they have a preference. This may not result in a "good value" or "best value" procurement at the source solicitation stage of the process. The end-user may request that the award be made to a supplier who is not the low compliant bidder/respondent, resulting in overall increased life-cycle cost. The purchasing agent is then required to evaluate and either approve the request or make a recommendation for denial to a higher authority.

When considering such an acquisition, significant attention should be paid to the potential risk to the organization. A low-compliant firm may launch a dispute or legal challenge to the award. In the event a legal challenge is delivered by the accusing supplier through litiga-tion, there may be significant delay in the delivery/installation of the product/project and, subsequently, an award for damages and lost profit to the supplier. To accommodate the consideration of an "other than low-compliant bid, quote, or proposal," an organization must have policies, procedures and practices in place, including a formal mechanism to receive, consider, approve, and document such a request.

When considering a request of this nature, the organization must treat all submissions objec-tively, applying consistent and fair evaluation criteria and methodologies in an open, fair, and transparent environment. This process is often disputed and challenged in a court of law. Without adequately supported and justifiable practices, an organization's public reputation may be brought into question, if or when the supply community suspects unfair practices.

Consider the situation faced by the Hamilton-Wentworth Region in the mid 1990s. The council put pressure on the professional purchasing staff to award a road-building contract to the Dufferin Construction Company despite the fact that George Wimpley Canada Ltd. had tendered the low bid by $19,000. The decision to award the contract to a higher bidder was based upon criteria imposed after the bids had been secured and opened. George Wimpley sued the region for $950,000 in damages. The ruling indicated that conditions cannot be imposed after the fact. In this particular case, the council wanted the contractor to hire local labor. This was not a justified action in the eyes of the court, and the supplier was awarded damages. Accordingly, organizations must have a formalized process for receipt, evalua-tion, recommendation, and approval for other than Low-Compliant Bid/Quote/Proposal acquisitions.

Local Preference/Regional Restrictions

An often disputed and challenged acquisition is the "local preference" or "regional restric-tions" purchase. Each organization at the federal, state, provincial, municipal, civic, edu-cation, special boards, or agency level may have certain provisions within their procurement and supply management policies and procedures for handling acquisitions where local preferences are an issue. Local preference laws are known to increase costs by the very nature of their non-competitiveness and, therefore should be discouraged as a public procurement practice.

Local preference laws are known to increase costs by the very nature of their non-competitiveness...

When an acquisition is made that favors a local supplier or manufacturer without competition, the organization should ensure that it has formal policies and procedures in place to govern these acquisitions. Many organizations use the principle of "where all factors are considered and are deemed equal, preference will be given to local suppliers." This provision is written into the terms and conditions and specifications of many sourcing documents. Organizations need to have formal policies, procedures, and practices in place to receive, evaluate, recommend, and approve local preference acquisitions. For example, the City of XYZ, in the state of XYZ, is interested in purchasing a specific type of truck. A General Motors (GM) half-ton is specified for acquisition, including warranties. Several dealerships have submitted quote responses to an RFQ. A non-local dealer has delivered the low-compliant quote by more than $500. The end-user recommends that a local dealership be awarded the contract because they have provided excellent service on past purchases of GM vehicles. As all new vehicles carry a factory warranty and vehicles can be serviced at any GM dealership, the non-local firm should be awarded the contract. Application of local preference laws is this particular situation is not warranted.

Technical Reviews and Approvals

Some organizations have established "standards" through a standardization program and developed a formal "technical approval" process and mechanism to take advantage of economies of scale through volume purchases. End-users requesting certain types of equipment (i.e., computers or overhead projectors) or furnishings (i.e., desks, chairs, file cabinets, system furniture, or whiteboards) are required to comply with the organization's established standards. Within the terms of the agreement, suppliers are often required to stock a sufficient supply of requested products. Some items requested by an end-user require technical review and approval. For example, if an end-user wanted to purchase a computer that was not on an approved standards program, they would be required to secure technical review and approval from the designated internal support organization prior to purchase.

The purchasing organization normally monitors these requests and manages acquisitions falling within this class of acquisition in a centralized procurement environment. This may also apply to furniture and wall-mounted fixtures that require a review by Facilities Management. Furniture acquisitions require specific reviews for compliance to occupational health and safety standards as well as local, state, or federal/provincial Workers' Compensation regulations and legislation. In Canada, Master Standing Offer (MSO) agreements can be established on a fixed term basis to accommodate the acquisition on an "if-and-as-required" basis. Organizations, regardless of the level, should formulate policies, procedures, and guidelines for the acceptance, review, evaluation, recommendation, and approval of acquisitions where standards are in place and products and/or services are requested that are not included within the stated standards. Purchasing agents and their respective organizations significantly rely on these standards, as they can assist in processing transactions in a customer service, user-friendly manner.

Policy and Procedure Compliance

Most organizations establish purchasing policies and procedures for all types of acquisitions that prescribe specific processes for each category or type of acquisition. Depending on the nature or sensitivity of the acquisition, specific approvals in advance of solicitation must be followed. Organizations place responsibility for procurement or supply management policy and procedure compliance within the purchasing and/or supply management portfolio, which also establishes requirements and processes that should be followed where violations occur. To be effective in monitoring and enforcing acquisitions for compliance to policy and procedure, the agency executive must provide support to the purchasing agent or senior procurement official and their staff in carrying out their roles and responsibilities. The purchasing agent or senior procurement official must be able to exercise discretion as to reviews, audits, and investigations, and must be able to request supporting information, as needed, and block or approve transactions that are outside of approved limits.

The U.S. Department of Commerce, through their Commerce Business Daily (CBD) service, provides access to a listing of products or services wanted for or offered by the U.S. Government. This service also provides up-to-date procurement information either electronically or in hard copy for particular situations (NIGP, 2007). For example:

- proposed procurements in excess of specified dollar values
- contract awards greater than $25,000
- procurement opportunities for various levels of governmental entities
- surplus asset opportunities and sales
- non-U.S. standards that may affect U.S. exports and
- special notice board.

Canadian public sector procurement organizations have a variety of organizations they can use when seeking information on sourcing requirements and for posting purchase opportunities. Suppliers can access purchase and surplus sale opportunities through MERX, an Internet-based electronic tendering system designed to increase competition and is available to federal, provincial, municipal, academic, health, and special governmental agency markets within Canada. Organizations post opportunities at no cost; however, suppliers pay a variable fee when they wish to access, download, or receive a hard copy of a solicitation document. This service also provides a product/service matching option that directs specific solicitation opportunities to a supplier who has requested notification in specific categories.

See Figure 9 below for an overview of approval levels that occur at various stages of the procurement cycle.

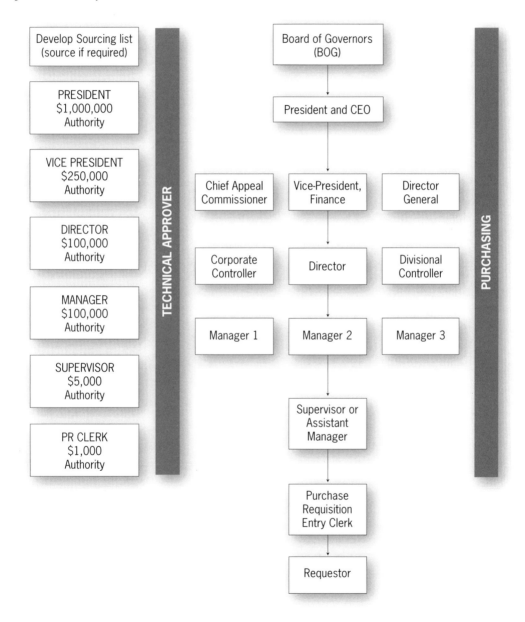

Figure 9 - *Financial approvals and commitment controls.*

References

National Institute of Governmental Purchasing, Inc. (NIGP) (2007). *Developing and managing requests for proposals in public procurement*, 2nd edition. Herndon, VA: NIGP.

National Institute of Governmental Purchasing, Inc. (NIGP) (2007). *Introduction to public procurement*, 2nd edition. Herndon, VA: NIGP.

National Institute of Governmental Purchasing, Inc. (NIGP) (2007). *Public procurement dictionary of terms*. Herndon, VA: NIGP.

University of Victoria (1997). Policy for signing authority. In *University of Victoria policy manual* (Policy Number 1002). British Columbia, Canada: Office of the University Secretary.

Part III

Assembling the
Sourcing Document

Preface

At the time of the decision to obtain competitive bids, quotations, or proposals for a specific product or service, the public entity will need to establish a formal (written) sourcing document. This may be in the form of an Invitation to Bid (ITB), Call for Bids (CFB) or Invitation to Tender (ITT), Request for Quotation (RFQ), Request for Proposal (RFP), Request for Expression of Interest (REI), Request for Information (RFI), or Request for Qualifications (RFQu).

The latter three methods usually result in a formal ITB or RFP. In many jurisdictions, low-value acquisitions are not conducted through a formal process. Quotes are obtained through phone calls, via fax, through email, or by face-to-face contact with a supplier representative. The method of source selection depends on the complexity, risk, value, delivery requirements, potential for competition, geographic location, or known number of qualified suppliers.

The sourcing document formally conveys the "Scope of Work," nature of the project, expectations and deliverables, as well as reflects the public entity's specific legal, technical, administrative, and operational requirements for the successful bidder. Second only to the specifications, the sourcing document is the most important component of the contract. It should carefully, concisely, and completely articulate the Scope of Work and how the successful bidders will be expected to perform the contract obligations. The sourcing document should also clarify any items that are considered to be "out of scope."

Once a public entity has proposed a public sourcing document and is ready to release it to the marketplace, it should be reviewed and approved by the end-user to ensure that the document accurately reflects the scope of work, deliverables, expectations and performance measures. An incomplete or inaccurate sourcing document can result in its withdrawal, cancellation and, eventual re-issuance; or, at a minimum, addenda may have to be issued to modify the requirements of the solicitation.

The content of a sourcing document will vary significantly and will depend on the nature and category of the acquisition (i.e., products, services, technology, construction, printing, etc.), the political and cultural environment of the public entity, and the policy or legislative agenda of the jurisdiction. The sourcing exercise may be carried out in a short three- or four-page document or may require as many as several hundred pages. As an example, a highly complex construction project valued in the millions of dollars would require a very detailed multi-page sourcing document. The solicitation document provides instructions to the potential suppliers, details on the background and specific project requirements, deliverables, how the supplier will carry out the work, evaluation criteria, and selection methodology, including timing of completion and performance measurement.

Each agency structures their sourcing document categories to suit their own unique requirements. How the document is formatted is not critical, but the attention to detail, its clarity, conciseness and consistency to public domain procurement practices is of primary importance. The National Institute of Governmental Purchasing's (NIGP) Specification Library and Standard Forms and Documents Library (www.nigp.org) contain source documents in varying formats and content that serve as prime examples of differentiating sourcing requirements of governmental entities. Generally speaking, a public sourcing document should include the following major categories:

- Instructions to Bidders
- General Terms and Conditions
- Special Terms and Conditions
- Technical Specifications or Statement/Scope of Work
- Bid Proposal Form (Response Form)
- Appendices

The next five chapters will provide an in-depth review of each of these sections.

Chapter 7

The Sourcing Document: Instructions and General Terms/Conditions

Instructions to Bidders

The first section of a solicitation document provides basic instructions to bidders that describe the administrative requirements of a solicitation along with specific guidance on all aspects of the solicitation. It often highlights the mandatory, optional, and desirable elements of the response. It identifies the obligations and requirements of the bidder and clarifies the intent, flexibility, and obligation.

There is no single, universal, standard format for instructions because every jurisdiction has varying policy and legal requirements and document submission response formats. Bidders should be cautioned to carefully read and follow the procedures required within the solicitation. The document should clearly indicate that any deviations from the stated instructions, terms, conditions, or submission requirements might be grounds for rejection or disqualification of responses. If alternatives or substitutions are permitted, these exceptions should be clearly articulated in this section. Details on any constraint or condition that would affect or impact a bidder's ability to comply with the delivery of the products and/or services should be included.

Schedule and Calendar of Activities

For highly complex procurements that require a lengthy solicitation process, it may be wise to publish a schedule and calendar of activities that provide guidance, to both internal stakeholders and the bidders, in the timely preparation of documents. This schedule provides details on the process cycle, decision making, and award timing. It also provides information to bidders on the mandatory, critical, or optional requirements of the solicitation. Key calendar events may include:

- solicitation issue date
- last date questions can be submitted
- date of pre-response meeting
- date of site visit
- date by which all addenda are to be issued to bidders or proponents
- date and time response submissions are due and opened
- date for evaluations to be completed
- date for oral presentations
- date for award of contract and execution of an agreement
- date work is to commence and
- scheduled completion date of work (by phase if a longer period).

Any changes to the published schedule of events requested by any bidder or internal user would require a formal (written) request for change, followed by addenda to the documents formally modifying the original milestones or dates. This would have to be organized and produced by the issuing public entity.

Closing Date and Time

All solicitations require a fixed closing date and time so that response submissions can be evaluated in a timely manner and also to ensure, from a legal perspective, that responses are handled in an open, fair, transparent, and equitable manner. This section indicates the closing date, time, and location of where the submissions must be delivered and received. The purchasing agent should clearly indicate that the public entity's time clock would be the determining clock for authentication of date and time. The solicitation document should state that bidders have the sole responsibility to deliver their responses and have the documents stamped prior to the specified closing date and time. Some public entities have an electronic or digital time clock for the purpose of certifying the exact date and time the response submission was received. To ensure accuracy, Greenwich Mean Time may be used to obtain and maintain the exact time for a particular region (www.greenwichmeantime.com).

To accommodate mail, courier, and hand-delivered responses, the street and location address must be specified in this section including building name, room number, and floor. If a jurisdiction accepts responses by facsimile or email, the correct number and address must be shown in this section. The document should specify that the public entity will not be responsible for busy fax machines that may result in a late, incomplete, or illegible submission. Likewise, if the public entity accepts submissions by email, this section must indicate that the public entity will not be held responsible for late responses due to failure of electronic communications. The time and date imprint on these documents can serve as the time clock for receipt and acceptance. This section should indicate that the public entity would not be responsible for the security of the bidders' responses from others, if it is transmitted electronically.

Public Entity's Contact Information for Inquiries

Bidders rely on the information contained in the solicitation document and expect that they will have the same access as all others to additional information and responses to inquiries. It is important that only one individual be identified within this section of the sourcing document to field all questions, clarify any issues, and respond formally to all known bidders or proponents. Typically, the purchasing agent assigned the responsibility of the solicitation fills this role. The individual should be identified with a full name, address, telephone and fax numbers, and email address along with their title and department name. All questions should be submitted in writing to prevent any possibility of a claim of misunderstanding or misinterpretation. This is especially important if a question or clarification relates to a deliverable that may impact performance or work fulfillment.

The section should clearly state the requirements and procedures for the submission of questions and clarification. In some jurisdictions, inquiries relating to the solicitation process, terms, conditions, and legal aspects are filtered through the purchasing agent, while the technical or operational aspects are directed to the internal user representative. This should be clearly explained in this section.

All bidders must be given the same information, at the same time, and in the same form or format. To do otherwise will expose the public entity to a potential dispute from a bidder who may feel that they have not been treated fairly or equally. Such accusations may cause a delay on the project work and possible litigation if a bidder believes and can prove that the award was made inappropriately.

Terms and Definitions

If a public entity uses specific terms, or makes reference to terms, each of these should be defined and clearly described in this initial section. These terms should reflect the language and meaning that is normally used in the respective industry. NIGP's Public Procurement *Dictionary of Terms* is an excellent guide for relevant terms. A public entity may also maintain a separate and unique listing of terms and definitions to be used in their sourcing documents and agreements. If this listing is maintained, the entity should make it available to bidders.

Inquiries Prior to Pre-response Conference

Prior to a bidder's meeting or conference, questions may arise requiring clarification and/or follow-up. Accordingly, this section should include a statement indicating that questions directed to anyone other than the designated purchasing agent and statements made by anyone other than the designated representative shall be deemed as an unofficial response and non-binding on the public entity. It is critical to the success of the solicitation to inform all bidders of the questions and the responses at the same time to avoid claims of unfair process. Technology can be used to improve the communication process. The acceptance of electronically submitted questions with an electronic posting of answers will improve the public entity's ability to provide accurate information in a timely manner. A public entity can use their Website, fax, or email to expedite the dissemination of information.

...questions and responses should be issued in the form of an addendum.

In some situations where questions or clarification are requested, the public entity's purchasing agent may be required to engage the internal end-user for the correct response. Purchasing agents are encouraged to obtain all responses in writing for future reference and follow-up, if necessary. In the event that bidders raise questions and a response is made, these should be issued in the form of an addendum.

Bidders Conferences

Posted solicitation notices may make provision for a "bidders conference," if required. The date, time, and specific location of this conference should be indicated in the Calendar or Schedule of Events section. The bidders conference is intended to be an exchange of information between the purchasing public entity and all bidders, and at the same time to discuss details of the solicitation, including scope, deliverables, and expectations. Any previous questions advanced by a bidder or proponent may also be answered at this meeting. Although a pre-response submission conference is often not mandatory, bidders should be encouraged to attend.

Bidders conferences are not normally held for routine acquisitions but, rather, are reserved for technical, complex, or sensitive acquisitions and are normally facilitated by the public entity's purchasing agent, end-user, and/or retained specialists or consultants. The bidders conference is held several days after the closing date for submitting questions (if this formal process is utilized) and very early in the solicitation process. Bidders use this event to clarify any information they may need to submit a responsive and responsible bid or proposal. All attendees at the bidders conference should be required to sign in with their names, firms they represent, telephone and fax numbers, and email addresses. Questions should be recorded; and, if possible, the proceedings should be electronically recorded. If attendance at the bidders conference is not mandatory, the questions and their responses should be distributed to those who registered yet did not attend. Addenda are normally issued and distributed with all questions and answers, to all registered bidders/proponents that have received the original bid solicitation for the agency.

Bidder Conference Calls

Occasionally, a bidder may not be able to attend a bidders meeting or conference due to logistics. Public entities should consider options available to bidders, which allow for his attendance via the Internet or by means of a conference call. The recording agent of the meeting or conference should also document all individuals linked to the conference call.

Communications Guidelines

The instructions should clearly state that from the time of the release of the solicitation until an award has been made, bidders shall not communicate with anyone from the public entity except as specifically provided within the documents. Also, provision should be made in this section to allow the public entity's representative to contact a bidder after response submissions and prior to award for the purposes of clarification of any matter related to the solicitation. Often clarification is required on intent, content, verification of data, or specific details. Therefore, contact is essential.

Issuing Addenda Due to Changes and Extensions

Due to circumstances beyond the control of the public entity, there may be situations where it is essential that changes be made to the original solicitation document's terms, conditions, specifications, deliverables, or timing. These may occur for one or more of the following reasons:

- changes to terms or conditions
- clarification or modifications to specifications
- quantity changes
- delivery location changes
- extension of time for response submissions and
- site meeting or bidder/proponent conference.

Accordingly, the instructions must include a provision that enables the public entity to issue changes through addendums.

Any change required to the solicitation documents prior to the stated closing date must allow sufficient time for bidders to reconsider and modify their responses. Modifications to sourcing documents must be communicated to all known and/or potential bidders or proponents through addenda. Generally, the only individual authorized to issue an addenda is the purchasing agent or designated agency representative that posted the original solicitation document. Addenda must not be issued in person, verbally, or by the telephone, as this will give rise to misinterpretation and potentially involve a dispute. Written addenda are the only means available to maintain an equal playing field. Typically, an addendum can be one of two types:

- An informational addendum that provides additional data which is non-material in scope or
- A formal addendum that does materially change the solicitation document (e.g., bid specifications, quantities, closing dates and times, etc.).

While both types of addenda must be distributed to all prospective bidders, the formal addendum typically must be signed by the bidder's authorized representative and returned with the bid proposal as a condition of responsiveness.

Since addenda are the only means of verifying, clarifying, or changing information within a solicitation document, this section should clearly state that addenda issued by the purchasing agent will be binding on the public entity and that any information provided by other than the purchasing agent or their designate in no way modifies the solicitation document. It is important that the contact information section state that only the individual identified as responsible for issuing the original sourcing document is authorized to represent the public entity for clarification and issuing amendments.

Site Visit and Examination

Frequently, site visits are required to provide the bidder with an actual perspective of the site conditions and nature of the work. If a site visit is required, the conditions must be provided within the solicitation document. Details should include designated dates and times and whether or not all prospective bidders will be in attendance simultaneously.

Oral Presentations

In some solicitations, there may be a requirement for oral presentations to be made by certain bidders. The oral presentations are typically requested of the top three or four ranked responses under consideration. Oral presentations are conducted in order for the bidder to highlight any aspects of their response that should be called to the attention of the Project and/or Steering Committee. It is an opportunity for the bidder to enhance the merits of their response and may include slide shows or illustrative presentations. The scheduled date, time, length, and requirements of the bidder's presentation must be clearly outlined in this section.

Receipt and Confirmation Form

With the increased use of the Internet and Web-based technology in the solicitation process, public entities must include in their solicitation documents provisions for receipt and confirmation that a bidder obtained or received a solicitation document and subsequently will be submitting a response. This is crucial to the public entity if there are changes in any aspect of the solicitation. This announcement, on the part of the bidder, will ensure that all bidders have the same information provided to them. As noted earlier in this chapter, failure to provide all bidders with exactly the same information at the same time may lead to a dispute or challenge of any subsequent award. This form may be included as an addendum requiring a signature.

Withdrawal Conditions

Public entities may make provisions for the withdrawal of a response under certain circumstances. The bidder may be unable to perform the contract if awarded due to an unexpected state of affairs. However, the ability of the bidder to withdraw a response is almost always limited to "prior to closing date and time." Withdrawal of a response after the closing date and time, particularly if the submission is low compliant, would suggest that the bidder or proponent made an error and does not wish to honor their response submission. Most jurisdictions do not allow for the withdrawal of responses after the closing date and time. This section of the solicitation document must clearly state the conditions under which response submissions may be withdrawn.

Copies of Response Documents

Often, a team of evaluators is involved in reviewing and recommending an award decision; and, therefore, several copies of the response submissions are required. This section of the solicitation document should indicate the number of copies required for inclusion in the response package. This often is considered a mandatory requirement if detailed drawings, plans or illustrative brochures are required to be included with the response.

Notification of Award

Some public entities notify all bidders as to whom the contract was awarded. Some may announce by letter, others via telephone or fax, while others post the awards on their internal or external Web services. The public entity should state the form and format of the award, i.e., formal agreement, purchase order, master standing offer, or short form service agreement. There is no mandatory or formal requirement to provide such notice to those who were not awarded the contract, but total notification is a good business practice and a courtesy to the supply community.

General Terms and Conditions

The General Terms and Conditions, commonly known as the boilerplate, typically apply to all solicitations issued by the public entity without regard to the product or service. As a rule, they are developed by the Procurement Department to align with the entity's statutes, regulations, and practices and remain static until these statutes, regulations, and practices are modified. For larger public entities, several variations of general terms and conditions are developed for classifications of procurements such as goods, services, and equipment; however, this diversification is not necessary unless it aids the public entity in developing its solicitation documents.

Essentially, general terms and conditions provide an indication of what will be required when the public entity executes an agreement with the selected supplier. Through the submission of a proposal, the bidder acknowledges that it has read, understands, and agrees to be bound by and fulfill the requirements and terms and conditions of the solicitation, unless exceptions are expressly made in writing. The following section identifies general terms and conditions that could be considered by a public entity.

Although this chapter will identify common general terms, the reader is cautioned to understand that each term needs to be applicable to the public entity's procurement regulations and corporate culture. One size does not fit all. Additionally, a public entity may decide to include one of the general terms listed below, which is unique to each solicitation, in the Special Conditions section. The movement of terms between general and special terms and conditions is quite acceptable. Most important, it is highly recommended that all terms and conditions (general and special) be reviewed and approved by legal counsel for compliance with applicable laws.

Statutory and Legal Terms

Governing Law and Compliance

The issuing public entity should cite the legislation, statute, or policy that provides it the authority to issue the solicitation request. The prevailing law that will apply in the event of a "statement of claim" is filed through the courts. The general terms should indicate how the bidder would be required to comply with all legislation and regulations of the public entity's jurisdiction and how these requirements will be necessary as a condition of contract award.

Workers' Compensation

All requirements for Workers' Compensation coverage and the obligation of the public entity and/or the bidders should be identified and enumerated.

Occupational Safety and Health–Infractions and Compliance

Similarly, all occupation, safety, and health requirements of the public entity and subsequent conditions applicable to all bidders should be identified in this section. The public entity should request bidders to provide information on any and all infractions committed during a specific post period and certification from the appropriate regulatory body as to compliance and documentation as to their current "in good standing" status.

Workplace Hazards

...each term needs to be applicable to the public entity's procurement regulations and corporate culture. One size does not fit all.

The public entity should be familiar with and include provisions that address any applicable Occupational Safety in Health and Workers' Compensation legislation that obligates public entities and suppliers to engage work and material handling practices that are designed to safeguard the health and safety of their employees and work environments. A Workplace Hazardous Material Information System (WHMIS) is available to assist public entities, manufacturers, suppliers, and workers in identifying these hazardous materials, how to handle each, and provide safeguards, along with related disposal and reporting methods. If required by statute, public entities must include a clause within their solicitation document that clearly articulates the specific legislative and regulatory requirements when handling WHMIS-labeled products.

Ownership and Intellectual Property

If the public entity wishes to retain ownership of intellectual property, or assign it away, these provisions should be detailed. If specific restrictions are to be placed on the use of information available and in the possession of the bidder during the term of an agreement, such restrictions should be included.

Disclosure, Confidentiality, and Public Information

Ownership rights of the public entity to all response submissions and contents of all documents submitted may be subject to the Freedom of Information and Protection of Privacy Act and Regulations, as enforced by the public entity. A disclaimer as to the public entity's limitations should also be included. A clause indicating the bidder's obligations and responsibilities to ensure that a complete and comprehensive response is submitted should be inserted for clarity. As it relates to the evaluation process, some public entities do not disclose evaluation information unless a request is filed under the Freedom of Information or Protection of Privacy legislation and regulation; and, therefore, they must clarify their obligations in this section. A public entity may also require the bidder or proponent to execute a "Non-Disclosure and Confidentiality Agreement." This may be documented in an addendum.

Indemnity

Public entities should include an indemnification and "save harmless" clause to protect its members, officers, employees, agents, volunteers, and independent contractors against any and all claims, demands, losses, damages, costs, and expenses that may arise from an agreement resulting from a solicitation. This is a common inclusion in many standard terms and conditions documents.

Personal Harassment

Should the public entity require its bidders to comply with the public entity's personal or workplace harassment policy, this should be clearly indicated in the General Terms. The implications of non-compliance should also be enumerated.

Infringement

The General Terms should state the public entity's requirements and position on any infringement on patents, copyrights, trademarks, and intellectual property rights. The consequences for violation, including costs of defending a claim and indemnification from an action of claim by a third party, must be outlined.

Administrative Terms

Acceptance

The General Terms should state that it is the responsibility of a bidder to strictly comply with the provisions of a solicitation document and that deviations or failure to comply will/may result in disqualification of a response/submission. It is within the rights of the public entity to not accept the lowest bid or any response, or to award in whole or part, or to reject all or any responses. As such, this statement must be indicated in this section.

Rejection of Responses

The General Terms should describe under what conditions a response submission would be rejected. Bids may not be accepted, for example, because they have been declared late, they offer the lowest price but not the "best value," or serviceability may have to be provided by a non-local operation.

Force Majeure

This clause generally will waive liability of either party to an agreement if the failure, delay, performance, or observation of obligations is beyond either party's direct control, such as fire, storm, flood, earthquake, war, sabotage, labor disruption, or any other act of God. The solicitation document should make provision for this eventuality.

Non-Waiver

In the event that the public entity fails to insist on strict performance or compliance to specifications, terms, or conditions, the inclusion of a non-waiver clause in the solicitation document will indicate that the public entity shall not have their rights to/or remedies at law waived.

Funding

If the public entity has any doubts as to funding availability and a particular acquisition is contingent upon funding approval, the public entity should include a clause alerting the bidders as to this possibility; giving the public entity the right not to purchase or award a contract if funding proves to be unavailable.

Financial Conditions

Where the public entity has a requirement to ensure an award is made to only financially stable firms, the public entity should indicate its expectations for presentation and evaluation of financial statements, annual reports, or any other security or bonding documents. Bidders should be informed that they have the sole responsibility and obligation for costs associated with provision of these documents.

Non-Collusion

This clause requires that the bidder certify that such person, firm, association or corporation submitting a bid has not, either directly or indirectly, entered into any agreement, participated in any collusion, or otherwise taken any action in restraint of free competitive bidding in connection with such contract by executing a "Statement of Non-Collusion and Affidavit." This document ensures that the response submission is genuine and is not made in conjunction with or on behalf of another party. It also should stipulate that the bidder was not directly or indirectly induced or solicited by any other bidder and that the bidder has not in any manner secured an advantage over any other bidder. Some sourcing documents contain this statement in the form of an addendum that is to be signed and returned with the submission.

Amendments and Withdrawals

The public entity's position and handling of amendments and withdrawal of response submissions prior to closing date and time, after closing date and time, but prior to award and after award notification, should be clearly noted. The public entity's right to amend and/or withdraw any solicitation at any time during the solicitation and award process should be indicated.

Error in Response

A public entity's obligations for handling errors and omissions within a response submission and the obligations of the bidders to submit complete responses should be identified. Even though the public entity has made considerable effort to ensure accuracy of the information within the solicitation document, the statement should reflect that the information is supplied solely as a guideline and is not necessarily comprehensive or exhaustive. Such a claim should not relieve bidders from carrying out their own reviews and forming their own conclusions relative to the solicitation request.

Error in Pricing

Errors in pricing may prevent a bid from being accepted. The public entity should clarify how errors in pricing are to be handled. The statement should include policy on the bid acceptance or rejection. If different policies regarding conflicts or arithmetical errors exist, these, too, should be included.

Dispute Resolution

In Canada under the Agreement on Internal Trade (AIT), public entities are required to establish a dispute resolution mechanism and inform bidders how they may proceed to file a dispute of a solicitation process or award. In the United States, each jurisdiction formulates a dispute resolution process based on their legislative and policy requirements. Public entities should detail their dispute resolution guidelines and process.

Disqualification

A public entity has the right to disqualify responses that are incomplete, deceptive, frivolous, not signed, or conditional. Responses that contain arithmetical errors, or do not comply with mandatory formats, or contain irregularities may also be rejected. The public entity should indicate the conditions that will lead to the disqualification of a bidder's response.

Termination for Convenience

Rarely, but on occasion, a public entity may be required to prematurely terminate a solicitation process prior to award or after award and prior to completion. The public entity should make provision for early termination without penalty in the event it is required to do so by serving an agreed-upon notice. The public entity should exercise its right to early termination resulting from cancellation of funds, a change in priorities, or cancellation of a program. An explanation of the process for notification should be included. All provisions of particular options and agreement termination, extension, and/or fulfillment of obligations should be detailed in this section. Notice of termination, time consideration, rights, manner in which termination is served, and actions resulting for failure to comply should be provided.

Performance and Default

The public entity should indicate its rights to monitor performance, certification, and any subsequent recourse available in the event of default or non-performance. Should penalties in the form of costs or disqualification for a specified period be applicable, these, too, should be clearly stated. The General Terms should clarify the rights of the public entity in the event of default by a bidder, including the public entity's rights and remedies concerning the failure of the bidder.

Purchase Order/Agreement Number on Invoice

If the public entity requires the supplier to include a purchase order or contract number on invoices, this should be indicated. The public entity may require this information in order to track payments for commitments and to accommodate efficient processing.

Reference

National Institute of Governmental Purchasing (NIGP) (2007). *Public procurement dictionary of terms*. Herndon, VA: NIGP.

Chapter 8

The Sourcing Document: Special Terms and Conditions

Special Terms and Conditions apply to a specific solicitation issued by the public entity. In many cases, the text of each special condition is developed over time, approved by the entity's legal counsel, and maintained in a database of terms for future retrieval. In this way, the text language carries the same consistent message of the public entity. By using a database of special terms, the purchasing agent simply needs to identify which special terms apply to the specific solicitation being assembled.

Like the General Terms and Conditions, the Special Terms and Conditions outline what is specifically required when the public entity executes an agreement with the selected supplier. Through the submission of a proposal, the bidder acknowledges that it has read, understands, and agrees to be bound by and fulfill the requirements and terms and conditions of the solicitation, unless exceptions are expressly made in writing.

As mentioned in the previous chapter, it must be understood that each term needs to be applicable to the public entity's procurement regulations and corporate culture. Each term also needs to be reviewed and approved by legal counsel for compliance with applicable laws. One size does not fit all. Additionally, a public entity may decide to include one of the special terms discussed either in the General Terms and Conditions or the Statement of Work. The placement of terms between the general and special terms is a decision made by the purchasing agent assembling the solicitation document.

Pricing

Since pricing is a critical component of the evaluation process and is typically the sole determination for awarding quotes and bids to the lowest responsive, responsible bidder, significant consideration must be given to the pricing terms selected by the public entity.

Developing and Managing RFPs in the Public Sector, 2nd edition, produced by the National Institute of Governmental Purchasing (2007), provides details on the options to be considered in selecting the best pricing alternatives based on the type of solicitation.

Essentially, there are two major types of pricing and several variations to these two major groupings—fixed price and cost reimbursement.

Fixed Price

Fixed pricing is appropriate when it is possible to accurately predict the costs and when it is reasonable to ask the supplier to assume responsibility for all costs. Fixed-price contracts are generally used when an organization can clearly specify what it wants to buy and there are no uncertainties anticipated during the performance of the assignment.

In fixed-price contracts, the supplier is responsible for managing all costs, regardless of whether they exceed or fall below the total contract price. The supplier usually agrees to complete the work before being paid (though work can be broken down into stages of contract performance or, in the case of maintenance contracts, the supplier can be paid in full at the beginning of the contract). The total amount of predetermined payment cannot be exceeded and reflects the end result of the contract effort.

For fixed-price contracts, the supplier accepts most, if not all, of the cost risk. The agency should not interfere in the way the project is managed. The supplier is to be allowed to make major decisions regarding the use of resources and the control of the work. This means less contract administration and monitoring by the public entity.

Variations of Fixed-Price Contracts

There are several types of fixed-price contracts, and the extent of administrative activity may vary. The following are the four most commonly used fixed-price types, with brief descriptions of their respective characteristics.

Fixed Firm Price

The fixed firm price contract is the most commonly used type of contract because the pricing remains constant for the duration of the contract period. Under this scenario, the supplier assumes full responsibility and risk for completing the project or purchase. The total cost is specified when the contract is awarded and is based on the initial specifications or Statement of Work. There are no adjustments to price based on changes in the marketplace and/or the supplier's performance. This type of pricing provides the greatest incentive for effective cost control because the supplier keeps any savings realized.

Fixed Price with Escalation (Fixed Price with Economic Price Adjustment)

A fixed price with escalation contract provides for upward or downward adjustment of price based on certain contingencies that are specified in the contract. This type of pricing is used when there is concern about the stability of the market and labor conditions during a period when production is to take place and when it is possible to identify contingencies. Pricing adjustments are made according to provisions included in the contract providing a basis for price escalation or decrease. (The base is often a specific index of wage rates or raw materials costs.)

The supplier and the public agency share the risks and potential benefits. The supplier is protected against unusual price increases, but the public agency will save money if costs decrease. If the contingencies specified in the contract do not occur, the contract is the equivalent of a fixed firm-price contract. The primary performance risk is still on the supplier, and the supplier's profit will not change as a result of any cost increases or decreases. Contract administration concerns for this type of pricing include:

- making sure that price changes are handled properly
- verifying the validity of all requests for increased compensation and
- making sure that the public agency receives the benefits of any price reductions.

Fixed Price with Incentive

A fixed price incentive contract provides for adjustment of profit and establishment of a final price through the use of a formula that compares the total actual costs to initial target costs. This type of pricing is used when achievable cost and performance goals exist beyond the target or minimum acceptable levels established by the contract, and the goals may be achieved by giving the supplier a profit incentive. If final costs are above the targets and/or performance is below the target, the supplier's profit is reduced. If final costs are below the target and/or performance is above the target, the supplier's profit is increased.

This type of performance-based contract is often used for contracted service contracts for the purpose of rewarding high quality performance. An example is a custodial services contract where performance goals are established, such as scoring "excellent" on 95% of the weekly customer inspection reports. If the supplier exceeds the goals, a predetermined "incentive" is paid.

Fixed Price with Redetermination

A fixed price with redetermination contract is used when a realistic price can be determined for initial periods but not for subsequent periods. A contract for the development of a prototype is an example. The supplier has the cost risk for the initial determination and the public entity for the redetermination.

Cost Reimbursement

C ost reimbursement is used when there is uncertainty and a variety of unknown potential cost risks and when it is unreasonable to ask a supplier to assume these risks alone. In cost-reimbursement contracts, the specification or statement of work may be less definitive, and the focus of contract administration is largely concerned with establishing the precise methods and manner of performance as the work progresses. The supplier is reimbursed for all allowable costs incurred during performance and commits to making a best effort to complete all work. The total amount to be paid to the supplier is not fixed at the outset, but it is highly recommended that a ceiling cost be established. The initial ceiling cost can be increased by contract modification if circumstances warrant. Payment is for the supplier's effort and is paid upon incremental receipt of that effort. In cost-reimbursement contracts, the public entity is assuming most, if not all, the risk and responsibility and, therefore, has a keen interest in the use of resources and the way in which work is proceeding.

In cost-reimbursement contracts, the public entity is assuming most, if not all, the risk and responsibility...

Cost reimbursement contracts occur when the parties are unable to assess the full costs to perform the work prior to the commencement of the work. Examples of this are the repairs to a piece of equipment that need to be disassembled and may or may not require certain potentially expensive parts. Another example is if repairs to a building or structure are required, some demolition has to take place, and the full extent of the work cannot be determined until after de-construction. In these instances a cost-reimbursement arrangement would be appropriate.

Variations to Cost Reimbursement Contracts

There are a variety of cost-reimbursement-type contracts that are appropriate under any of the following circumstances:

- When the uncertainties of a contract effort cannot be estimated reasonably.
- When a supplier's cost accounting system is adequate for accurately determining the exact costs that apply to that contract.
- When an organization is confident that personnel assigned to monitor performance will be able to determine whether the supplier is using inefficient or wasteful methods.

Cost Plus Fixed Fee

In a cost plus fixed fee contract, the supplier is reimbursed for all reasonable, allocable, and allowable costs. The supplier receives a fixed fee (profit) amount negotiated at the time of award. There are two types of cost plus fixed fee contracts: completion form and term form. A completion form cost contract identifies a specific task or goal and specifies an end product. The supplier is normally required to complete and deliver the specified end product within the estimated cost. A term form cost contract commits the supplier to a specified level of effort based on the general "statement of work" for a specified period of time.

Cost Plus Incentive Fee

A cost plus incentive fee contract is used when a formula can provide an incentive for effective management. Targeted cost minimums/maximums and fee adjustment formulas are established at the outset. The supplier receives reimbursement for costs as in a cost-plus-fixed-fee contract, but the fee is determined after the contract is completed according to a formula comparing actual to target costs as in fixed-price incentive contracts.

Cost Sharing

A cost sharing contract is used when it is impossible to estimate costs firmly and there is a high probability that the supplier will receive a substantial present or future commercial benefit. This type of contract may be used in research and development contracts.

Time and Materials

Time and materials contracts are used only when no other type of pricing is suitable. This type of pricing provides the supplier a fixed rate for each hour of labor plus the cost of materials. (If no materials are involved, this is referred to as "labor hour" contract.) A contract ceiling price is negotiated at the outset of a contract.

Method of Award

As a rule, the public entity must define how the contract will be awarded based on several options. Three primary options are listed below, but this is not an exhaustive listing of options available to the public entity.

- **Award Item-by-Item**. Awards may be made to multiple suppliers because each item is awarded on the basis of the lowest unit price. This method offers the best pricing to the public entity but requires significant contract administration if multiple suppliers are selected for award.

- **Award by Group**. Awards may be made to multiple suppliers based on the lowest aggregate price for all items within a specific group. The public entity may group items by classification, category, or geographic zone in its best interest. This method allows the public entity to target each grouping to a specific supplier for contract management purposes but may also limit competition and therefore, increase pricing.

- **Award in the Aggregate**. An award is made to the lowest responsive, responsible bidder based on the aggregate pricing for all items. While this allows the public entity to enter into a contract with a single supplier, this method does not provide the best available pricing and may be overly restrictive, unless multiple bidders are able to supply all of the items contained in the solicitation document.

There are other variations to these types of awards that the public entity should consider when selecting the best method to meet its needs. Two prominent methods to consider are achieving best value through total cost bidding as well as multi-step bidding that allows the entity to assess technical compliance before revealing pricing.

Life Cycle Cost Based on Bids Submitted

Life cycle costing (LCC) is defined in the NIGP Public Procurement Dictionary of Terms as:

> The total cost of ownership over the life span of the asset. A procurement technique that takes into account operating, maintenance, the time value of money, disposal and other associated costs of ownership as well as the residual value of the item. (NIGP, 2007)

LCC is often utilized as a method of award when significant acquisition of equipment, infrastructure, construction, or technology is being solicited. If the public entity plans to use life cycle costing as the element for awarding the contract, this must be communicated to the bidders through the solicitation document, since the bidder must identify several of these costs in its bid proposal.

If the public entity utilizes LCC as the method of award, the purchasing agent will be required to prepare a comparative analysis of all response submissions, options, and alternatives offered by a bidder. All elements of cost and/or beneficial value must be taken into consideration when determining best value, including:

- initial cost of acquisition
- life cycle maintenance costs
- training and orientation costs
- payment terms
- depreciation or capital cost allowances
- residual value
- installation costs
- start-up costs
- finance costs
- duty and taxes
- disposal costs
- storage or holding costs
- operating costs, such as fuel, power, gas, water, labor, parts, etc.
- licensing/regulatory costs where applicable.

Multi-step Bidding

The Multi-Step Bidding method is most commonly used for highly technical and complex procurements processed under a formal Invitation for Bids/Invitation to Tender solicitation. In this case, the public entity instructs the bidder to place its proposal in two distinctly marked, sealed envelopes. In one envelope, the bidder provides its technical information to include its offered solution in compliance with the specifications and its capabilities to perform under the contractual terms as a responsible, responsive bidder. In a second envelope, the bidder provides its pricing.

When bids are received and opened, the public entity only opens the envelopes with the technical proposals and evaluates these proposals based on compliance with both technical merits and capabilities. As a result of this evaluation, a short list of bidders who meet the mandatory solicitation requirements is created. Once this step is completed, the pricing proposals are opened to determine the responsive, responsible bid proposals offering the best pricing.

Privilege Clause/Best Interest

For some jurisdictions, the purchasing laws or statutes do not require that the contract be awarded to the lowest responsible, responsive bidder. In Canada, the public entity may wish to include a privilege clause in the Special Conditions section if the public entity does not wish to be legally obligated to award a contract to the lowest bidder. The *privilege clause* provides the owner with powers to exclude, select and award tenders or proposals if/when the owner explicitly states these powers in the terms and conditions (rules) of the respective solicitation. According to Paul Emanuelli, a Toronto-based lawyer and author of the textbook "Government Procurement", the *Privilege Clause* is "A legal provision inserted into a tender call that reserves the purchasing institution's right to depart from typical practice in exceptional circumstances to, among other things, bypass the low bidder or cancel the tendering process. Such provisions have historically been subject to a fairness review by the courts and therefore typically do not give purchasing institutions an unfettered discretion." (Emanuelli, 2008)

The *privilege clause* provides the owner with the ability to not be legally required to award a contract to the lowest proponent or bidder; provides the owner with the right to reject all proposals or bids/tenders at their sole discretion without being legally liable to any or all of the proponents or bidders. This clause is defined in the NIGP Public Procurement Dictionary of Terms as:

> A clause traditionally used in Canadian tenders which says "the lowest or any tender will not necessarily be accepted". A "privilege clause" provides the tendering authority with broad discretion in relation to the acceptance or rejection of tenders. It usually reserves to the owner the discretion to accept or reject the lowest, or any, tender. It does not displace the overarching duty of procedural good faith that the Courts have found is an implied term of the bid contract (contract A). (NIGP, 2007, revised 2008)

The U.S. uses a similar term known as *Best Interest.* In one jurisdiction it is referred to as "Rights of County" and states that "The County reserves the right to accept or reject all or any part of any bid, waive informalities and award the contract to the lowest responsive and responsible bidder to best serve the interest of the County." *Best interest* is defined in the NIGP Public Procurement Dictionary of Terms as:

> A term which grants the chief procurement officer the discretion to take the most advantageous action on behalf of the entity they represent usually in the absence of law or regulation. (NIGP, 2007)

The clauses allow the public entity to be able to accept any or none of the response submissions at their option providing the language of their solicitation document is clear, is not contradictory, and makes provisions for these privileges. There are many variations of the privilege/best interest clause that usually reflect the public entity's policy and legal requirements. Purchasing agents and public entities should be cautioned that the clause does not legally protect them if the public entity engages in unfair, discriminatory, dishonest, or misleading and improper processes or motives. However, if the public entity's officials make an award to other than the low-compliant proponent and this decision is consistent with the provisions of the solicitation document and can be justified on their merits, then the public entity will be protected by a *privilege or best interest clause.*

Risk Management

Insurance

Care must be taken to ensure that all types of applicable insurance to be provided by the bidder are identified (comprehensive, general liability, automobile liability, error and omission, and travel-per-occasion) for the term or post contract.

Bid Deposit, Bond, and Security

Bid bonds and bid surety are often requested in high risk, high value, and highly sensitive requisitions. A bid deposit, bond, or surety ensures that if a bidder's offer is accepted by the public entity, the bidder is obligated and will be able to enter into a formal agreement and will not withdraw its response prior to evaluation and award. It should be a reasonable amount (typically 5% of a total bid) based on the risk and nature of the acquisition in terms of its technical aspects or sensitivity. A bid bond takes the form of a surety bond, irrevocable letter of credit, a bank note or draft, a certified or cashier's check, money order, bearer bond, or an insurance certificate from a registered bonding company. Under normal practices, the bid surety submitted by every bidder is retained by the public entity until the evaluation process has been completed and contact award has been determined.

Performance and Payment Bond

The performance and payment bond serves two purposes. The first is to indemnify or protect the public entity for a certain percentage of the value of a contract in the event of default on the part of the supplier, or the supplier in performance of the work covered under the contract. The public entity can only encroach on the portion of the bond equal to the value of the costs it incurs to remedy defective work and complete the contract. The second purpose of a performance and payment bond serves to guarantee that all suppliers and sub-suppliers are paid for labor and materials furnished to the prime supplier for use on the project and work described in the solicitation document, and agreement and detailed in the bond. Clear and concise explanation of the bond should be included in the Special Conditions section.

Financial

Liquidated Damages

If the public entity decides that it wishes to enforce liquidated damages, the entity should indicate its rights in the event that the bidder breaches its agreement. The inclusion of a statement regarding reimbursement losses or direct damages due to the breach and/or a specified daily penalty (if applicable) due to delay of completion of work is essential. All conditions pertaining to a breach in terms of liquidated damages should also be included.

A liquidated damages clause is intended to motivate the supplier to deliver on time by assessing less severe monetary damages for each day of delay. The entity's legal right to assess liquidated damages is stated in the U.C.C. Section 2-718(1). Fixed amount liquidated damages clauses are included in construction contracts but may be applicable to some supply and service contracts. In general, a fixed liquidated damages clause should be included when there is an expectation to incur damages if performance is delinquent, and where it is difficult or impossible to prove the amount of damages actually incurred.

The assessment of fixed liquidated damages is subject to some limitations. The most important of these is that the fixed amount must be reasonable. Reasonableness is situational; but, where liquidated damages are construed to be a penalty, the clause is not enforceable. The reasonableness criterion demands a best effort estimate on a case-by-case basis. Many organizations routinely set fixed liquidated damages unreasonably low. In cases when the public entity sets a fixed cost for liquidated damages, and if delay costs more money than the fixed liquidated damage amount, the entity is not entitled to recover actual damages where fixed liquidated damages provisions are included in the contract. As public entities consider the utilization of liquidated damages, it is important to remember that liquidated damages may impact such issues as pricing, competition, and the cost and difficulty of contract administration.

Prompt Payment

Should a bidder offer a discount for prompt payment, the solicitation should indicate whether the public entity would consider this factor to determine the overall best value to the entity when making its final award decision.

Volume Discounts

Some bidders offer better pricing based on specified volumes of business being attained during the contract period. The solicitation should indicate whether the public entity would consider volume discounts to determine the overall value to the entity when making its final award decision.

Invoicing and Payment

A detailed description of all requirements for payments, invoices, products or services receipts, late payment charges, interest, method of payment (electronic fund transfers, or checks), and net terms should be identified and included in the solicitation.

Holdbacks

In most jurisdictions where supply, installation, and service are required during a warranty period, particularly in construction projects, there is a regulatory requirement for statutory holdbacks to be retained for a specified number of days. This requirement is in place to protect sub-suppliers from a prime supplier in the event they have not been paid for work and materials as the sub-supplier provided for the project. The public entity should require their applicable regulatory requirements and include adequate provisions in their sourcing document.

Taxes

There are a variety of taxes that may apply, depending on the jurisdiction and its specific legislation and regulations. For example, in Canada, there is a Federal Goods and Services Sales Tax (GST), a Provincial Sales Tax (PST); and, in Eastern Canada, there is a Harmonized Sales Tax (HST). In the United States, each state, city, and municipality assesses varying rates and has different formulas for assessment and collection of taxes. Public entities should use this section to clearly describe all taxes that are applicable to the acquisition and the specific obligations of the bidder.

Bid Deposit—Plans and/or Drawings

Plans and drawings, primarily used in construction projects, are costly to reproduce. Public entities may assess a plan/drawing bid deposit, which is refundable upon return of the plans unmarked (in original condition). These plans may then be used during the construction phase by the various sub-trades. If a plan or drawing deposit is applied and is to be refunded, the terms should be included in the sourcing document.

Purchase Order or Agreement Number on Shipment

The Special Conditions section should stipulate that all shipments must be legibly imprinted with the public entity's purchase order or agreement number on packages, bill of ladings, or courier vouchers. The conditions should also stipulate that if shipments are not received in this manner, they might be refused.

Shipping and Delivery

*C*ontract Administration, 2nd edition, produced by NIGP (2007) discusses the importance of selecting the correct delivery method as a condition for managing the contract after award. Some of the terms identified in the book are worth mentioning here because they should be included in the Special Conditions section.

Definite Delivery

Definite delivery terms are utilized when a specific requirement quantity and delivery date have been established. This is the most common type of delivery requirement. Common examples include one-time purchase orders and capital outlays.

Indefinite Delivery

Indefinite delivery terms are suitable for commodity purchases because the products purchased are standard throughout the industry, with numerous vendors. All of the indefinite delivery types of clauses should be used only with fixed firm price or fixed price with escalation pricing contracts. There are three variations of indefinite delivery contracts:

- **Indefinite delivery with a definite quantity** occurs when a quantity of supplies or services is specified, but the time of delivery is flexible. This type of delivery requirement is used where requirements are definite or have a short lead-time.

- **Indefinite quantity and delivery** is used to establish a minimum and maximum quantity that can be ordered within a definite delivery period. This contract requirement is flexible in terms of both quantity and delivery schedule.

- **Requirement delivery** is used when the public entity agrees to purchase all requirements for a certain period of time from the supplier. Under this scenario, the quantity of items and the number of deliveries is unspecified; thereby, differentiating it from a definite type of contract, since specific quantities have not been established.

F.O.B.—Delivery and Transportation

Various Free on Board (F.O.B.) terms may apply to the specific solicitation. Public entities should specify which of the F.O.B. terms are applicable. There are two essential components to the F.O.B. terms. The first component of the term determines when the title to goods is passed from the seller to the buyer. The second component determines responsibility for payment for the shipment.

Regarding title, *F.O.B. Origin* means that the title changes hands from the supplier to the public entity at the origin of the shipment. In this scenario, the public entity owns the goods in transit, assumes responsibility for carrier selection, and files any claims for damages incurred during this period. *F.O.B. Destination* means that the title changes hands from the supplier to the public entity at the destination of the shipment; and the supplier owns the goods in transit, assumes responsibility for carrier selection, and files any claims for damages incurred during this period.

Regarding the payment for the shipment, there are several variations. *Freight Collect* means that the public entity pays for the shipping costs as the buyer. *Freight Allowed* means that the supplier pays for the shipping costs as the seller; however, if the public entity has already paid the freight costs since it selected the carrier under a F.O.B. Origin arrangement, the public entity is entitled to seek reimbursement from the supplier for these costs. *Freight Prepaid and Allowed* means that the supplier pays for the shipping costs as the seller. *Freight Prepaid and Added* means that the supplier pays for the shipping costs as the seller but is entitled to add the cost of freight to its invoice that is submitted to the public entity.

Figure 10 demonstrates how these title and shipping terms work together to create levels of responsibility.

Freight Terms	Public Entity takes Title of Goods	Public Entity Responsibilities as Buyer	Supplier Responsibilities as Seller
F.O.B. Point of Origin, Freight Collect	At point of origin or factory	Pays freight Bears freight Owns goods in transit Must file claims for loss, damage or overcharges	
F.O.B. Point of Origin, Freight Prepaid and Allowed	At point of origin or factory	Owns goods in transit Files claims	Pays freight Bears freight
F.O.B. Point of Origin, Freight Prepaid and Added	At point of origin or factory	Bears freight Owns goods in transit	Pays freight and Adds freight to invoice
F.O.B Destination, Freight Collect	At destination	Pays freight Bears freight	Owns goods in transit Files Claims
F.O.B. Destination, Freight Prepaid and Added	At destination	Bears freight	Pays freight Adds freight to invoice Owns goods in transit
F.O.B. Destination, Freight Prepaid and Allowed	At destination		Pays freight Bears freight Owns goods in transit Files claims

Figure 10 - *F.O.B. shipping terms.*

The majority of public entities prefer to use F.O.B. Destination because this shifts the burden of locating effective carriers to the supplier, and the entity does not have to concern itself with the details of transportation investigations. Since the supplier has agreed to pay the freight charges, the public buyer does not have to worry about costs of transportation. In the event that problems arise from shipping damage, the public buyer is not responsible for the time-consuming negotiation with the carrier that often ensues.

Proactive buyers should focus on two shipping issues. The first issue is the control of routing a shipment. F.O.B. Destination gives the supplier the right to route the shipment as economically as possible. An example of routing is a buyer on the West Coast who purchases a product that is shipped from the East Coast. Chicago, St. Louis, Denver, Dallas/Ft. Worth and Salt Lake City are major distribution hubs for many common carriers. The shipment could be unloaded and reloaded up to five times before it reaches the West Coast. This exposes the shipment to external and concealed damages and loss.

The second issue for the buyer is that the firm from whom the product was purchased has probably negotiated a freight rate with the common carrier that is lower than that charged the West Coast buyer. The firm does not have to pass shipping cost savings on to the buyer. The almost exclusive use of F.O.B. Destination is viewed negatively by most purchasing professionals. A solution to the issue is to solicit a base bid of F.O.B. Destination and an alternate bid of F.O.B. Shipping Point. Costs can be compared objectively, and the proactive professional purchaser can make an informed buying decision.

International Commercial Terms (INCOTERMS)

Purchasing agents should be aware that shipments originating in European countries may be covered by the INCOTERMS provisions of shipping rules rather than North American rules. One of the provisions of INCOTERMS is where and when title passes to the Purchaser.

> **INCOTERMS:** An abbreviation for International Commercial Terms. They are published by the International Chamber of Commerce (ICC) and are internationally recognized terms for moving goods. These terms define the responsibilities and risks of both the buyer and seller including while the merchandise is in transit. INCOTERMS apply to goods that cross national borders.

The goal of the INCOTERMS is to alleviate or reduce confusion over interpretations of shipping terms...

The purpose of each INCOTERM is to clarify how functions, costs and risks are split between the buyer and seller in connection with the delivery of the goods as required by the sales contract. Delivery, risks and costs are known as the critical points. Each term clearly specifies the responsibilities of the seller and the buyer. The terms range from a situation in which everything is fundamentally the responsibility of the buyer to the other extreme where everything is fundamentally the responsibility of the seller.

The goal of the INCOTERMS is to alleviate or reduce confusion over interpretations of shipping terms, by outlining exactly who is obligated to take control of and/or insure goods at a particular point in the shipping process.

INCOTERMS address and answer the following common shipment considerations:

- **Costs:** who is responsible for the expenses involved in a shipment at a given point in the shipment's journey?
- **Control:** who owns the goods at a given point in the journey?
- **Liability:** who is responsible for paying damage to goods at a given point in a shipment's transit?

More information may be viewed at the following URL: www.irishexporters.ie/printer_incoterms.shtml

Customs and Brokerage

When products, equipment, and technology are imported or exported across international borders, duties and tariffs are applied by the respective countries. These are handled through Customs and Brokerage firms established for the specific purpose of receiving, clearing customs, application of the duties, tariffs and taxes, and delivery to the public entity or receiving entity. There are numerous Customs and Brokerage firms operating worldwide, and each public entity contracts with different firms, normally through a competitive process, to provide this service. Public entities should identify the firm the bidder is required to use by including all relevant contact information and stipulating which forms must be completed for compliance.

Delivery and Installation

Often, public entities are required to provide off-loading facilities and equipment for heavy items or movement to restricted locations or heights. Where there is a requirement for specialized receiving, suppliers and transport agencies should be required to provide adequate notice of delivery so that the public entity can make the appropriate arrangements. All other conditions for delivery, including partial shipments, various delivery locations, time of delivery, delivery after time of order, etc., should be specified.

Returns and Refunds

The public entity should request that bidders state their return, refund and restocking charge policy in their response submissions. The Special Conditions section should indicate the public entity's expectations and rights related to returns and refunds. In Canada, for example, under the Sale of Goods Act, a purchaser has four days to request a return of a product in an unused condition or under warranty provision where the item is defective or inoperable. In the United States, these provisions are specified in the Uniform Commercial Code.

Over Shipment and Errors in Shipment

The public entity should indicate its obligations and the bidder's responsibility for over/under shipment and/or errors in shipments. It is known in the printing industry that printers notoriously produce in excess of the offered quantity and will ship this excess and charge the public entity for the over-shipped quantities. The public entity should indicate in the sourcing document how it would deal with any over-shipments or over-billings.

Recycling and Packaging

Sustainability in terms of environmentally sound acquisition practices, including specification of products that are environmentally friendly, is a priority in many jurisdictions. The public entity's sourcing documents should indicate the requirements of the bidder regarding alternative products that are environmentally friendly and the obligations and responsibilities of bidders in the handling of waste shipping and packaging materials. A clause in the sourcing document should address the public entity's requirements in this area. This subject is covered in more detail later in this text under Stewardship and Sustainability.

Safety Stock Levels

Some public entities do not have physical warehouse facilities and rely on their suppliers to provide products, equipment, and furniture on a Just-in-Time (JIT) basis. JIT requires that the supplier maintain safety stock levels that can accommodate a public entity's anticipated short-notice requirements. The Special Conditions section should provide all details relative to the bidder obligations for the maintenance of such inventory and any mechanisms for reporting.

Master Standing Offer (MSO) and Blanket Contract Releases

To take advantage of their efficiencies and economies of volume buying for extended periods of time, a public entity may establish a Master Standing Offer or Blanket Contract. To access these contracts, a designated representative of the public entity issues releases or draw-downs. The Special Conditions section should provide the details of the release, its limitation, eligibility, and any methods of access available. Such access may be permitted by Web-requisition, by purchasing card, in person, by telephone or fax, or by using a supplier or merchant online catalog accessible through their Website.

Packaging

If it is the public entity's intention and a requirement for the bidder to remove all packaging materials promptly after delivery and receipt by the public entity, this should be included in the solicitation document. Some public entities include this clause in all solicitations and purchase orders.

Waste Removal

In addition to a clause regarding packaging and shipping materials, a separate but complementary clause dealing with waste removal should also be included in sourcing documents and agreements. This would cover such items as scrap, building materials, debris for demolition, and any other form of waste product.

Restocking Charges

On occasion, a public entity may inadvertently order more product or equipment than is required, or requirements changed from order date to fulfillment date. It is a good practice to include a restocking charge clause allowing the public entity to return product for a negotiated restocking fee.

Time is of the Essence

This is contractual language that, when inserted in a contract, requires that all references to specific dates and times of day noted in the contract be interpreted exactly. In its absence, extreme delays might be legally acceptable.

This provision means that performance by one party at or within the period specified in the contract is necessary to enable that party to require performance by the other party.

Failure to act within the time required would constitute a breach of the contract. The general rule is that time is not of the essence unless the contract expressly so provides. Time is not of the essence unless the parties have agreed to such intent. This also applies in construction contracts and contracts relating to the manufacture and supply of goods when incorporated into the terms of the agreement between the parties. When time is not of the essence, courts generally permit parties to perform their obligations within a reasonable time.

Performance

Quality Assurance Program

If the public entity has a formal Quality Assurance Program and intends to apply the terms and conditions of this program to the solicitation, details of the program should be incorporated into the document. If a bidder or proponent must pre-qualify prior to submitting a response, this, too, should be indicated.

Safety Procedures Review

If there is a requirement for an industrial health and safety program to be in operation throughout the duration of the contract, specific requirements and provisions for such programs should be included.

Inspection, Testing and Acceptance

If the public entity intends to perform in-progress, post installation inspections, testing, or certifications and acceptance prior to payment, the Special Conditions section should provide details on whom, how, when, and where these shall occur. The obligations of the bidder should be specified if a product or service has been rejected during this inspection period.

Defective Work

The obligations of the bidder for the removal and replacement of defective or unsatisfactory products and/or services should be specified in the document, including any costs which may result in a payment delay.

Claims for Damage, Shortage, or Loss in Transit

The public entity's right to examine products and services for compliance with specifications should be identified in the Special Conditions section. Delivery, in accordance with stated quality and acceptance of products and/or services, should be explained. The Special Conditions section should also indicate that the public entity is not obligated for payment unless and until satisfactory delivery has been confirmed through inspection.

Supplier Obligations for Remedial Action

In the event a supplier delivers unsatisfactory products or provides inadequate services, the solicitation documents should indicate the responsibility and obligation of the bidder in terms of remedial action and costs. It should also indicate at what point the public entity would deem the contract to be in "breach."

Reporting

Regulatory Reporting Requirements

The requirements for reporting incidents and filing reports with regulatory agencies and the public entity should be described in the Special Conditions section.

Reports and Records

If specific requirements exist for the bidder to provide reports, tests, records, financial statements or any other documentation (prior to, during, and post contract fulfillment), these should be identified in the solicitation document. If the requirement is for these reports to be submitted electronically, this process should be explained and clarified.

Records Management

Bidders should be informed of their requirement to maintain all relevant records relating to products and services that will be acquired from the firm. Declaration of the public entity's right to access at any reasonable time with proper or adequate notice should be included. Additionally, the bidder's obligation to retain and maintain in good order all documents relating to the acquisition, including plans, CDs, software, and drawings for a period up to seven years, should be identified. The period may differ depending on jurisdictional requirements after delivery, installation, and acceptance.

Reporting Methods / Frequency

If Corporate Supply Agreements (CSAs), Master Standing Offers (MSOs) or Blanket Contracts (BCs) are to be issued as a result of a solicitation, the bidder should be informed of the method for reporting "releases" or "draw-downs" within the document. For example: Monthly, quarterly, annual, etc.

Audits and Inspections of Financial Reports

Should a public entity wish to view a bidder or proponent's records, logs, financial statements or reports after award, during and/or after the fulfillment of the contract, the public entity's specific terms should be stated. Specific reports or requests for audited financial statements to be submitted with a response must be outlined, detailed, and specified in this section.

Warranty

Warranties and Guarantees

Most new equipment, including supply and install (labor/service) acquisitions, carry a limited warranty for manufacturing defects. Should a public entity require warranties and guarantees that go beyond the limited warranties already provided, these should be identified. In most cases where extended warranties are requested, these may be provided at extra cost to the public entity.

Warranty Briefings

The Special Conditions section should require the supplier or their supplier to provide the public entity with all warranty certificates, registration forms, instruction manuals, and orientation on use, operation, and maintenance. Release of holdback funds should be withheld until the supplier complies with these provisions.

Product-Related Information

Brochures, Catalogs, Operating and Reference Manuals

The requirement for bidders to provide literature with their responses should be identified. Such requests may be for illustrative brochures, operating and reference or training manuals. Details as to content and the number of copies should be included.

New Product Testing and Sampling

Often, during the course of a response, firms will introduce a new or alternate product to that which was specified in the original solicitation. Bidders should be provided with the option or opportunity to propose the new product subject to sampling, testing, and certification. The public entity should include a clause enabling a bidder or proponent to suggest new or alternate products and the mechanisms or criteria for doing so.

Risk of Loss—Demonstration or Trial of Products or Equipment

Bidders are willing to provide products and equipment for demonstration or on a trial basis prior to purchase by a public entity. If this is offered, the public entity would mitigate its risk by including a Risk of Loss clause, which requires the bidder to execute a Risk of Loss Waiver prior to delivery and acceptance. The public entity may choose to include a signed version of this statement as an addendum to be returned with the submission response.

Brand Name or Equal

If a public entity considers alternatives or equals to a specified brand, make or model, the entity should provide the criteria for determination. Any costs incurred to validate "equal" shall be borne by the bidder; and the public entity, in its sole determination, will judge as to equivalency. The Special Conditions section should include any reference to the criteria and a clear statement as to who is responsible for the additional expense.

Royalties and Patents

If royalties and patents are relevant to the solicitation, the Special Conditions section should require the bidder to indemnify the public entity against any claims resulting from the infringement on any patent, copyright, trade secret, trademark, or other intellectual property rights.

Purchase Quantities

The Special Conditions section should state whether the public entity is allowed to increase or decrease the quantities identified within the solicitation document. This section should also indicate whether the bidder could qualify minimum order quantities and units of measures (case lots, broken cases, each, etc.).

System and Equipment Demonstrations

Where specialized equipment or systems are installed, the supplier or equipment supplier should be compelled to provide user training and instruction on maintenance and troubleshooting. The solicitation document should identify the length of time, the frequency of training, stated training times, and indicate what, if any, costs are applied to the public entity.

After Warranty Parts and Repairs

If a supplier is required to supply spare replacement components for equipment during repair and maintenance and after the warranty has expired, this should be specified in the solicitation document.

Inspection and Takeover Procedures

The Special Conditions section should detail the procedures for Inspection and Takeover by the public entity. Prior to application for a Certificate of Substantial Performance, the supplier should be required to carefully inspect all work performed to ensure completeness and compliance and conduct a final inspection with the public entity's designated representative present. A deficiency and defect listing should be prepared and corrected by the supplier. When these have been corrected, the supplier may apply for a Certificate of Substantial Performance.

Manufacturer's Instruction Manual

Public entities should require and specify that the manufacturer's instruction manuals be provided to the public entity with the award of a contract and delivery of products, equipment, and fixtures. The Special Conditions section should require that products and equipment be delivered and installed in accordance with the manufacturer's instructions and guidelines. The conditions should also note that improper installation or erection of products by a supplier will require removal and reinstallation at no cost to the public entity.

Administrative Issues

Agreement Extensions and Renewal Options

The public entity should make provision for its ability to extend, renew or cancel an agreement under specified conditions and terms. The terms of each extension or renewal should be clearly identified. If early termination is permissible the notice period (days) for such termination should be indicated.

Professional Errors and Omissions

This area pertains primarily to consultant and professional services. If a public entity elects to retain a specialist to conduct reviews, design systems, provide professional advice, or develop sourcing documents, the public entity relies on the firm's expertise to provide products and/ or services that are saleable with a high degree of confidence and accuracy. In instances of high risk, technologically sensitive, high value or pioneering (leading edge) acquisitions, the public entity should include a clause to cover errors and omissions. It should also require the bidder to provide adequate insurance coverage for a period following completion and acceptance testing of the work. The duration of the insurance coverage should be determined on the basis of the risk to the public entity for any future or downstream problems.

Alternatives, Equivalents, and Substitutions

In instances of high risk...the public entity should include a clause to cover errors and omissions.

These issues may be subdivided into separate special terms. Essentially, the special terms should offer direction to bidders on how alternatives and equivalents to specifications will be handled. The obligation of the bidder is to establish and certify a product as an equal to any alternative product and/or service. The method of establishing equals, costs, and conditions applicable to bidders should be included. Additionally, if the public entity allows for changes and/or substitutions, this allowance should be specified as well as those conditions when changes and substitutions are acceptable.

Assignments and Conveyance

Should the public entity permit assignments of a contact to another supplier or sub-supplier resulting from a solicitation or portions thereof, language should be included that clarifies administrative provisions and the terms and conditions upon which an assignment can be made. The phrase "with the prior written approval of . . ." should be used. If assignment of a contract or any portion thereof to another supplier is prohibited, this, too, should be stated along with the consequence for violation.

Title—Lien Protection

The Special Conditions section should contain a clause that prohibits a bidder from filing a lien or encumbrance against the items delivered to or against the owned property of the public entity.

Business Registration Required by the Public Entity

Some public entities require Bidders or Proponents to be properly licensed in order to do business in the respective jurisdictions prior to award of the contract. If this is a requirement of the jurisdiction, it should be indicated in the source documents.

Disclosure of Factory Locations

Some public entities require bidders or proponents to disclose the production and/or manufacturing locations for the products that they sell to ensure that the products are not manufactured in plants that engage in child labor or sweat shops.

Debriefing

It is customary to conduct debriefing sessions for bidders under certain types of solicitations. This enables the unsuccessful bidder or proponent to determine their shortfalls and how they can improve and subsequently increase their place in the market. Debriefings are customary in Request for Proposal (RFP) and Request for Qualification (RFQu); therefore, the public entity should provide for the opportunity for debriefings in the sourcing document.

Limitation of Damages

If the public entity elects to use a *Limitation of Damages* clause, the stated damages are normally limited to the lesser of the actual losses, damages or costs, and administration or operational costs to replace the supplier. This information should be included in the solicitation document for bidders to consider, as some may choose to obtain insurance coverage, particularly in high-risk acquisitions.

Sub-suppliers

If sub-suppliers are authorized to perform work on behalf of a bidder, details of the relationship should be stated in the Special Conditions section. The bidder serving as the prime supplier is responsible and accountable for all aspects of the work performed by sub-suppliers.

Travel and Other Related Expenses

Since bidders may be required to travel on behalf of the public entity, the terms and conditions of travel, payment, compliance to policy, and limitations should be specified.

International Labor Organization

The International Labor Organization (ILO) is an organization that is devoted to reducing poverty, achieving fair globalization and advancing opportunities for women and men to obtain decent and productive work in conditions of freedom, equity, security and human dignity. As a tripartite organization the ILO works with governments, employers and workers' organizations to promote the following interlinked aims:

- Social protection
- Social dialogue
- Employment Creation
- Rights at Work

For more information on the ILO, please refer to the following URL: http://www.ilo.org/global/lang--en/index.htm

References

Emanuelli, Paul. (2008) *Government Purchasing*. Ontario: LexisNexis Canada.

National Institute of Governmental Purchasing, Inc. (NIGP) (2007, Rev. 2008). Public procurement *dictionary of terms*. Herndon, VA: NIGP.

National Institute of Governmental Purchasing, Inc. (NIGP) (2007). *Contract Administration (2nd ed.)*. Herndon, VA: NIGP.

Chapter 9

The Sourcing Document:
Technical Specifications or Statement of Work

A critical component of the solicitation document is defining, in technical terms, the desired product or service required by the public entity. There are two general methods for describing these outcomes: a technical specification or a statement of work.

Generally, a technical specification is predominately focused on the provision of goods (products and equipment) but may include an aspect of services required in conjunction with that product. For example, the supplier may be required to furnish shelving for an office based on a technical specification and may also be required to install that shelving as a service. In this case, the technical specification identifies both the qualities of the product and the conditions for completing the services needed in conjunction with the product.

Generally, a Statement of Work (SOW) is primarily focused on the provision of services but may include products or equipment required to perform that service that is supplied and/or installed by the service provider. For example, the service provider may be required to perform detailed landscaping services for a municipal park system but may also be required to provide fertilization or plant and tree replacements. In this case, the statement of work identifies both the requisites for providing the services or work, to include quality and quantity benchmarks as well as performance-based measurements, and the technical characteristics of the associated products.

The purchasing professional must be able to discern whether a technical specification or a statement of work is more appropriate, as this decision will most likely influence the decision on whether to use a bid format or a proposal format. While these formats are interchangeable, typically, a technical specification is more common in Invitation for Bids (IFB) and Invitation to Tender (ITT), as defined earlier in this book. Conversely, the statement of work is more common in a Request for Proposal (RFP) format. Since many solicitations are a hybrid of both goods and services, the purchasing agent must understand the benefits and limits of the IFB and RFP formats and use each method in the most effective manner.

This chapter will address both technical specifications and statements of work, with a major emphasis on the first method. For more detailed information on the statement of work, you may want to reference Developing and Managing Requests for Proposals in the Public Sector, 2nd edition, published by the National Institute of Governmental Purchasing (NIGP, 2007).

Writing Technical Specifications

A detailed analysis on the value and concepts behind a quality specification was provided in Chapter 5. The chapter also identified the three primary types of specifications (design, performance, and combination) as well as variations of specifications that are incorporated into brand names, qualified products, regulatory products, proprietary products, and market grades. The reader should refer to Chapter 5 to understand the differences and applications of these types and variations. With this understanding, the purchasing professional is prepared to write technical specifications into the solicitation document.

Specifications provide a common basis for sourcing, enable a public entity to identify requirements, lead to maximum competition, allow the public entity to measure for compliance in a controlled environment, and result in supply and fulfillment of quality products. Specifications identify to suppliers and manufacturers, in precise terms, the characteristics of what is to be purchased. The development and writing of any specification must be performed in a manner that accurately and concisely represents the requirements or deliverables. Specifications may be developed by:

- a purchaser based on knowledge, experience and expertise of the specific requirement
- a recognized standard public entity, such as the Canadian Standards Association or Underwriters Laboratories
- private firms, including engineers who specialize in specification and drawing development
- quality control and testing agencies
- professional laboratories
- technical and professional associations, such as the Canadian Construction Association or American Water Works Association
- a governmental standards public entity, such as the American National Standards Institute (ANSI) and
- American Society of Testing Materials (ASTM).

Specifications must be developed and written in a manner that accommodates evaluation for compliance during the sourcing process and post-award performance analysis and measurement. Specifications are frequently developed with specific reference to manufacturers' standard products. Every public entity relies on their expertise, knowledge, and skill to develop required specifications as acquisitions are made. These are developed based on standards, changes in the marketplace, and the specific application and use of a product. The requirement to prepare and update specifications is a continuing process. Once valid, specifications may become obsolete based on innovation, product improvement and market changes, making them inappropriate for future use.

Suppliers and manufacturers rely extensively on the specifications provided within the sourcing documents; and, as such, their development and articulation must precisely establish what is being purchased. Specifications must enable the purchaser to evaluate products offered against stated needs. Any omission during the sourcing process may compromise a public entity's ability to successfully acquire the product that best meets the overall requirements. Exclusion of key requirements to be considered during the evaluation stage may compromise the award and result in a formal protest from an unsuccessful supplier. When an error or omission is detected during a sourcing exercise, and prior to the response deadline, an amendment must be issued. If the omission is detected after the response deadline but prior to award, the solicitation must be cancelled and a corrected one issued.

Over specifying a product will result in higher costs and limited competition. Under specifying a product will result in lower quality and possibly long-term higher costs, as the item may need to be replaced earlier; and, subsequently, the operational costs will be higher. Specifications, therefore, should reflect only those requirements that are deemed essential, enable the product to perform as expected, and reflect the quality required.

Specifications must enable the purchaser to evaluate products offered against stated needs.

Specifications should establish maximum and minimum limits that will determine the degree of resulting competition. Restrictive specifications not only limit competition but also decrease the number of items available that could satisfactorily meet the stated requirements. Restrictive specifications may also lead to increased opportunity for supplier collusion. The nature, methodology, and evaluation criteria must be clearly stated in the solicitation document when using subjective evaluation and testing methods. In such circumstances, suppliers are able to more clearly focus their offerings in direct relation to what is written in the specifications.

Well written and developed specifications serve to promote an open, fair, equal, and transparent opportunity to receive a bid, quote, or proposal from the best-suited supplier. Accordingly, specifications should only be developed and written by an individual or firm with specific knowledge, skill, and expertise for the respective products. The services of experts, specialists, or individuals specially trained, such as architects, engineers, testing agencies, standards agencies, or professional associations, can be engaged. Overly complex specifications, contradictory terms within a specification, or excessively restrictive specifications will only add significant risk to a successful acquisition. This will derail a sourcing event and place the public entity into dispute with the supply community.

If a purchaser detects that a specification does not accurately reflect the anticipated require-ments and an award dispute is inevitable, the solicitation should be cancelled and reissued with correct information. For example, consider the situation of a jurisdiction that issued a solicitation document for hearing aids. The end user had developed specifications that were so restrictive that no responses could meet the requirements. The solicitation was cancelled and reissued. This happened a second time for the same product. The end user refused to broaden the specifications, and the purchasing department had to abandon the bid process, resulting in great expense to the public entity and loss of credibility within the industry.

Quality is a measure of compliance with the stated requirements of fulfillment in meeting a specification. Consider paper plates for a picnic and bone china for a fancy dinner party. Both plates perform the same function but meet a different specific need. Specifications that are too rigid or over detailed will inevitably result in less competition and higher costs; and, in some cases, fulfillment may be delayed or difficult to achieve. Equally true, a poorly defined product or service may result in higher costs, increased downtime, and reduced quality or performance. Purchasers and their respective public entities must take care to define their requirements accurately and concisely and take the necessary time to evaluate and analyze products thoroughly in advance of an acquisition solicitation and award.

NIGP has established an extensive library of specifications and sample Tender, Bid, Quotation or Proposal documents that are available to members through its Website at www.nigp.org. In addition, the General Services Administration (GSA) establishes specifications that are used by all federal agencies.

Sources of Specifications

Product specifications continually change and reflect innovative and technological ad-vancements in production, materials, and manufacturing processes. Many larger public entities have the technical expertise and internal resources with the knowledge and skills necessary to develop and prepare comprehensive sourcing documents. Purchasing agents often engage the assistance of their legal services department, financial analysts or auditors, information technology departments, facilities management specialists, researchers, and oth-ers who are available to develop product and/or service requirements as components of sourcing documents.

Nevertheless, it would be impossible for a public entity to stay abreast of every change for every product. For this reason, the public procurement official should rely on the following sources for the development of technical specifications.

Suppliers and Manufacturers

Suppliers are perhaps the single most important source of specifications for the products they manufacture and provide. As products change, the respective specifications are updated with relevant information and brochures.

Specification generation is readily available from manufacturers and suppliers who are eager to sell their products and services to a public entity. Suppliers use a variety of tactics to get their message out regarding their products and services, including:

- marketing mailers
- offers for free trials/demonstrations
- conventional solicitation responses
- radio/television advertising
- direct one-on-one marketing often at the CEO level.
- unsolicited proposals
- conventions and conferences
- eMarketing
- sponsorships

Colleagues and Governmental Sources

Public procurement practitioners at most public agencies are excellent resources to tap for assistance by utilizing the established formal or informal communication networks. Information and history of similar experiences are relatively easy to obtain, as most individuals involved in public procurement and supply management have been faced with similar challenges. This sharing of information with colleagues is instrumental in the effectiveness and efficiencies most public entities demand today.

Federal specifications for the United States Federal Government are administered and issued by the Standardization Division of the General Services Administration's Federal Supply Service for materials, products, and services acquired by agencies. In Canada, the federal, provincial, and local government public entities maintain specifications on a wide variety of products acquired through their respective public entities.

Professional Associations

Professional bodies like the National Institute of Governmental Purchasing (NIGP) and the Institute for Supply Management (ISM) maintain extensive libraries that contain specifications and standards of specifications for sourcing documents and design drawings with links to other public entities. These documents are available to their respective memberships through Internet access. The NIGP also hosts an electronic network that allows members to discuss issues on a wide range of topics, such as bid specification development and sources of supply.

Numerous professional associations exist in virtually every market sector to represent the interest of buyers and sellers within the markets. Several industry-standards public entities also exist to test, certify, and provide advice on products and services. Three of the more prominent public entities are the Underwriters Laboratories (UL), Canadian Standards Association (CSA), and the American Society for Testing and Materials (ASTM).

Online Resources

Public purchasers can search electronic bid boards, scan the bid opportunities, and find public entities involved in acquiring the same or similar products or services through electronic discussion lists. Many public entities are posting their bids, tenders, and quotation or proposal invitations on their own procurement portals or Websites. Access to these opportunities is relatively easy with the Web address. Downloading documents may be a quick source of information if the Website address is known. Typically, this information is available at no cost to agencies and improves the acquisition process.

Other Resources

Specifications are also available from other sources:

- illustrated brochures, catalogs, and literature
- architectural and engineering firms
- trade associations
- Chambers of Commerce
- user agencies
- governmental agencies
- manufacturers
- professional laboratories and testing agencies
- universities, colleges, and technical institutes and
- independent private firms specializing in specification design and development.

Specification Content

Although the content requirements for specifications vary by public entity, some types of specifications are required by all public entities when products and services are purchased. To ensure a complete and comprehensive result, the specification:

- must allow for maximum competition
- must be complete, concise, and free of vague terms

- should reference industry standards, publication, drawings, and reports

- should not duplicate content

- should identify physical, functional, operational, and quality characteristics that can be measured

- should not limit the product to one manufacturer or firm

- should not conflict with referenced material or articles

- should clearly state and identify what should be the exceptions

- should avoid the use of abbreviations, unless clearly illustrated in the text, to mitigate the potential for misunderstanding

- should use "shall," "will," and "must" where the specifications or term is mandatory and is a requirement in the future or is an expression of intent

- include "should" or "may" to indicate non-mandatory provisions

- incorporate the use of "equivalent" only to suggest that name brands meeting the minimum requirements are acceptable

- should avoid the use of "no substitute," as it often limits competition and may be seen as preferential treatment to a specific manufacturer or supplier

- must state all "measurements" —dimension, gauges, capacities, sizes, volumes, temperatures, units of measure, and packaging consistent with industry practice

- should clearly and accurately describe with figures, tables, illustrations, graphics, engineer drawings, plans, etc., the product being purchased

- should use "numerals" in preference to "text" referencing tables

- should use "Arabic numerals" in designations, figures, or illustrations, i.e., Figure 1

- include "Roman numerals" in identifying tables, i.e., Table IV

- incorporate "footnote" references in the text of a specification with consecutive numbering commencing with "1."

- have sections that are "numbered" sequentially and subdivided

- should be written so that responses can be compared against one another and against the specification requirements.

Prior to the release of a specification with any solicitation, the internal end-user must approve the specifications, scope of work, or requirements definition. Technical specifications need to be updated to reflect current product availability. End-user agreement on the specifications is essential to ensure that no misunderstandings will occur during the sourcing, evaluation, and award process. All changes or revisions to specifications should be incorporated into the document, with an indication of who made the updates.

Writing a Scope/Statement of Work (SOW)

The 8th Edition of Purchasing Principles and Applications (1991) asserts that the statement of work is the key to the service contract, as the specification is to the product contract. "A good statement of work will outline the specific services the contractor is expected to perform. It should indicate the type, level, and quality of service."

Preparing the Scope/ Statement of Work (SOW)

The Statement of Work or Scope of Work, predominantly used in RFP's, REI's, RFI's and RFQ's (terms that are used interchangeably) is defined as "a detailed description of the work which a purchasing jurisdiction wants the contractor to perform" (NIGP, 2007). Developing the Statement of Work (SOW) is one of the most difficult challenges in procurement planning. Purchasing must understand the requirements and be able to effectively communicate those requirements to potential offerors. The proposed SOW must accurately reflect the specific work requirement, what needs or is intended to be accomplished, milestones, benchmarks, deliverables, performance measures, etc. It does not specify how the work is to be accomplished, personnel, or what equipment is to be used to perform the work. It provides the purchaser (agency) with expected completion dates.

Agencies should provide as much useful information to offerors as is possible to enable them to attain the best outcomes possible. The subjects that follow are areas many jurisdictions incorporate into their SOW, expectations and deliverables. By providing a historic perspective, environmental scan, and description of physical conditions that may be prevalent and affect the work outcomes, the agency assists considerably in obtaining an accurate proposal response.

A thorough assessment of the needs followed by a refined application of the description and an ability to convey these requirements into a clear and concise document will enable bidders to respond with a precise and reflective submission. The document must be able to clearly communicate the requirements to the supply community.

A purchasing agent normally prepares the sourcing documents with input from end-users and technical specialists. In highly complex, sensitive, or high value acquisitions, the public entity may opt to retain an external expert to develop the SOW. Cross-functional, multi-disciplined teams are often established to formulate SOWs if the nature of the acquisition crosses public organizational boundaries. The public entity's role and responsibility is to advise, guide, and monitor the group's input, while working to ensure that the final document articulates both the scope of work and deliverables.

Within the "Statement" or "Scope of Work," the public entity will normally provide some background information on the public entity using quantitative measures. The inclusion of background information can offer a historical perspective that can reflect the anticipated changes expected from the past environment and the vision, mission, and goals and objectives of the future. Specific outcomes or deliverables are included as well as those aspects that are not to be considered, referred to previously as "out of scope." The more comprehensive the information provided, the more likely the purchasing public entity will experience high-quality and successful competitive outcomes. Care must be taken that the information is not so comprehensive or restrictive that it becomes non-competitive, appearing to be directed to a single supplier.

The question as to whether or not a public entity should include a "budget" value in the background section is a difficult one. It is believed by some that by publishing a budget, a level playing field is created; therefore, enhancing the quality and competitiveness of responses. Others believe that by including a budget figure, the bidders may over or under estimate their effort or quality. Still others believe that if the deliverables are well defined and selection and evaluation criteria are stipulated to include point values, the bidders will know exactly how to compose their bids/proposals. Each procurement public entity must determine on their own the relative merits of including budget figures within the sourcing solicitation.

If a project involves a series of deliverables or the completion of certain work by specific milestones or dates, these, too, must be indicated within the scope of work section. These may be included as a schedule or as an attachment or appendix. The document must include a section on expectations that reflects key contract provisions, performance criteria, changes or unexpected events, and measurements, particularly if progress payments and/or hold-backs will be applied. The following represents specific sections that are typically found in a Statement of Work.

Introduction and Scope of Work/Project

This section provides an overview of the depth and breadth of the project or acquisition requirements. Bidders should be able to review this section and make a determination as to their interest in offering a bid, quote, or proposal. In this section, the public entity should provide some corporate background information on its size, location, existing environment, purpose of the sourcing exercise, objectives, and expectations in broad terms. It may also include key details of the public entity, indicating the business, its goals and objectives, purpose, size, staff, location, etc. Anything relevant to the public entity that would assist the bidder should be included. Specific requirements should be clearly, concisely, and completely stated in the SOW section of the solicitation document.

The document must be able to clearly communicate the requirements to the supply community.

Nature and Description of the Project

The key elements of the project, work, or deliverables should be stated in this section. Issues of duration, complexity, areas that impact the project or work, and any other aspects of the project that would assist the bidder in making a determination of whether or not to respond should be included.

Background

Often, it is useful to provide some details as to how the project or requirements were developed prior to the sourcing stage. An acquisition may be launched due to a natural disaster, a planned project, collaboration among several jurisdictions or public entities, or for any number of other reasons. Public entities should describe the history of the project or acquisition and provide any other relevant information in this section.

Objectives and Purpose of the Solicitation

This section of the Statement of Work clearly and concisely describes the purpose, objectives, and goals of the public entity issuing the solicitation and references the pertinent and subsequent sections of the document that will provide the scope of work, deliverables, expectations, and terms. This section may also provide information about the length of the contract and any potential extensions resulting from the solicitation and award.

Public Entity

Every public entity takes on its own complexity and structure. Bidders and proponents are often guided in their approaches and responses by the nature and hierarchical structure of the public entity. It is helpful to the respondents to know and understand the public organizational climate, reporting requirements, and authorities' matrix of the project/public entity.

Executive Steering Committee

Many highly technical, sensitive or political projects or acquisitions are managed through several committee structures. If the project or acquisition is administered through an Executive Steering Committee, all aspects of the committee, including role responsibility, mandate, etc., should be articulated. Bidders are very interested in the makeup of executive steering committees, and their level and detail of response is often structured in direct relation to the members of the Executive Steering Committee. For example, if an Executive Steering Committee was chaired by an elected official and consisted of predominantly politicians rather then the administrative, technical, or operations officials, a bidder may respond on a more technical note but be very cognizant that the overall decision may be politically swayed. Responses would deliberately be structured to reflect the committee makeup.

Project Advisory Committee

Many projects—technical or specialized acquisitions—often not only have an Executive Steering Committee but also have a technical or advisory committee. This committee is responsible for developing and approving the technical and specialized requirements, identifying the evaluation criteria and ranking factors, and evaluating bid or proposal responses. Normally, it would forward its technical review, evaluation, and recommendation to the Executive Steering Committee for consideration and approval.

Project Coordinator

Every project or major acquisition has one specific individual charged with the responsibilities to coordinate, administer, advise, and collaborate with all participants and stakeholders involved in the solicitation and acquisition. The Statement of Work should indicate the name, title, and public entity of this individual and specifically clarify their role, responsibility, and authority.

Project Team

Project teams are normally associated with acquisitions involving services and construction, or for the supply and installation of technical, specialized, or complex equipment. The project team, headed by a Project Leader, should consist of team members whose skills, knowledge, and experience are needed to achieve the goals and objectives of the acquisition and implementation. Often, teams are established with cross-functional relationships; for example, a financial software or ERP installation may involve team members from finance, audit, information services, procurement, legal and an internal user department representative.

Project Scope of Work and Requirements Definition

The scope of work, requirements definition, and deliverables section of the sourcing document must be written to clearly reflect the deliverables and performance expectations of the public entity. The bidder must be able to establish a clear understanding of the work or product required and be able to define the requirements and respond to these requirements with a best value in such a way that will reflect achievement of the goals and objectives upon work completion. The quality of response will be reflected by the quality of information provided to bidders and proponents for response. As this section represents the end-user requirements, only skilled and knowledgeable individuals should write this section. It should be composed in a manner that will maximize competition as well as afford bidders the ability to propose innovative and creative alternative solutions. The section should be concise and avoid industry expressions and confusing acronyms.

Use of Standard Terms to Define the Scope of Work

As is the case with general and special terms, there may be standard terms developed by the public entity which detail the scope of work and level of responsibility required of the supplier in the performance of the contract. Examples of these standard terms are provided below but are not intended to provide a comprehensive view of the issues to be addressed. As mentioned previously, these standard terms should be reviewed and approved by the entity's legal counsel for compliance with the entity's procurement statutes as well as with laws governing commercial and business practices. Additionally, the public entity may determine to address these issues in the special terms and conditions or a tailored boilerplate of general terms and conditions in its best interest.

Administrative Issues

Commencement of Work. Public entities should specify the earliest date and time when the work is to commence. The public entity should also specify any restrictions prior to issuance of a purchase order or contract and notice of commencement requirements. If penalties will be assessed for work that does not commence as specified, the penalties should be indicated.

[The SOW and Requirements Definition]...should be composed in a manner that will maximize competition as well as afford bidders the ability to propose innovative and creative alternative solutions.

Completion of Work. Bidders should be required to state the earliest completion date of work within their response submissions along with total time required. Any specific delivery or installation requirements or site conditions that may impact the completion of work schedule should be identified.

Delay of Work. Occasionally, work is delayed due to no fault of either the contractor or public entity. In the event a delay of work is to occur (or could be expected), the Special Conditions section should illustrate the notification requirements, reason for delay, impact on the public entity (including costs, commissioning, etc.), and projected completion date. Provision for adjustments, penalties (if applicable), obligations of the contractor, and options available to the public entity for breach of contract should be included.

Hours of Work. If there are restrictions on the hours during which work will be able to be performed, specifics should be included. Because of such limitations, the bidder may have to adjust their pricing or completion date. The Special Conditions section should also mention any weekend and statutory holiday restrictions that may apply. There may also be special considerations if the work site is adjacent to a hospital, nursing home, or school. There may also be some restrictions imposed by municipal or local by-laws that are applicable. Bidders should be made aware of these restrictions in a detailed explanation included in the Special Conditions section.

After-Hours Access. As with security clearance, after-hours access restrictions should be indicated in the sourcing document.

Security Clearance. A public entity's premises may have security restrictions in place. Should this be the case, the public entity should identify these constraints and explain the restrictions that may impact the bidder. The Special Conditions section should enumerate the conditions and any subsequent ramifications for the delivery of the requested work.

Notice of Substantial Completion. The Notice of Substantial Completion is an announcement placed in local newspapers and/or related trade journals that alerts sub-contractors and suppliers of a pending Builders Lien holdback release. This gives the sub-contractors and suppliers an opportunity to notify the public entity of an indebtedness and potential claim by them against the property. If applicable, the Special Conditions section should include a reference that requires contractors and sub-contractors to place the advertisement and cover the costs of such advertisements.

Certificate of Compliance and Completion. The selected contractor may be required to obtain a Certificate of Compliance and Completion prior to any final holdback release from an approving regulatory agency. Should the public entity require this certificate, it should be declared in the solicitation document.

Change Orders. It is not uncommon for a public entity to require and request a change to a Scope of Work during construction or installation. To accommodate these changes, many public entities use the Change Order mechanism. A Change Order is a formal document, signed by the purchasing authority in accordance with the contract, authorizing the contractor to perform additional work not previously anticipated or included in a Scope of Work (NIGP, 2007). Change Orders can substantially increase a project's costs; therefore, all Change Orders should be carefully considered, assessed for cost, and approved prior to commencement of work. The public entity should make provisions within the sourcing document for Change Orders, if they are anticipated. Change Orders are often required when the contractor's experience, hidden or latent defects, or work site conditions are unknown at the time of contract award. A good example is the de-commissioning or demolition of a building.

Structural Integrity—Engineering Certification. Most capital and infrastructure construction projects require architectural and engineering design. During and after various stages of construction, structural and engineering certification by qualified and certified engineers is required. For projects or work requiring this type of certification, all aspects of the requirements by stage and phase should be identified.

Engineering Certification. If required during construction, the contractor should be instructed and required to retain professional registered engineering personnel and secure the required certificates for presentation to the public entity. The Scope of Work should clarify the manner, nature, frequency of inspection (in accordance with building codes), and prompt delivery of the inspection certificates to the public entity.

Project Coordination. The contractor's obligations for coordination of work, progress reports, project management, and update of schedules should be specified. Additionally, the presence of the public entity's representative on site does not imply nor constitute inspection or imply acceptance of work completed to date. The public entity should require that the contractor maintain a copy of all specifications, plans, addenda, drawings, written instructions, and Change Orders on site.

Project Hand-off Upon Completion. Upon notification of substantial completion of a project or work, the public entity and the contractor will visit the site and perform a final inspection to determine compliance with specifications and to document deficiencies requiring remedial repair or replacement. This process and explanation should appear in the solicitation document. At this stage, the representative of the public entity and the contractor will authorize the inspection and deficiency reports. A remedial plan to correct the deficiencies should have been previously agreed upon with alternate time lines established for completion and responsibility for costs established.

Project Coordination Meetings. The requirements and responsibility of the project coordinator should be described in the Scope of Work. This could include coordinating all project meetings, documenting deliberations, authorizing further work, and following up on progress and reporting.

Legal Issues

Permits and License. Certain types of work (primarily construction and renovation) may require building permits, waste removal permits, building development permits, hydro and gas permits, etc. This section of the solicitation document should identify all permits the bidder or proponent is required to obtain prior to, during, and after completion. If a notice of substantial completion is required (as is the case in Canada), these should be inserted in this section.

Temporary Employment Authorization. Should a bidder propose to use out-of-country resources in the form of labor, there may be a requirement to obtain temporary employment authorization from the Federal Government or other governing bodies. Bidders should investigate these requirements, file the appropriate applications, and obtain the required authorization and permits. The public entity should make it clear that the bidder is solely responsible for all applications, documentation, approvals, and costs associated with the bidder's use of workers from outside their respective countries.

Building and Development Permits. Certain types of work may require certain development and building permits to be issued. Often, the public entity obtains these in advance of issuing solicitations for contracts. In some circumstances, it may be more appropriate for the contractor to obtain the permits, such as for a "turnkey" construction project. The contractor is responsible for all aspects of the construction, including permits, inspections and, even, commissioning. The responsibility of both parties should be articulated.

Work and Materials

Material Compliance. The solicitation document should clearly specify deliverables, the work to be performed, performance criteria and measurement and require material compliance. All aspects of the supply, installation, construction, and commissioning is to be fulfilled as specified. The Special Conditions section should also indicate whether no variations or substitutions are allowed.

Workmanship. The Special Conditions section of the solicitation should clearly document the responsibility, obligations, and consequences of incomplete, unsatisfactory, and defective work and/or materials, including the requirement for all workers to have the required skills, qualifications, and expertise associated with the work to be performed. The determination as to quality, appropriateness, and acceptability should rest solely with the public entity.

Repairs to Damages. Contractors performing work on the public entity's property or in their facilities are responsible for repairs to damages caused by their work force. The solicitation document should make provision for the obligations and responsibilities of bidders once a contract for work is issued.

Installation and Removal. In construction, renovation, and maintenance projects, the contractor or supplier shall be required to execute work expeditiously and restore the building and site to its finished-state condition in a prompt manner. The conditions of the movement of materials and works within the work site and the remedial repair to damage caused by the contractor should be stipulated.

Scrap and Salvage. Provisions for the removal of scrap and the contractor's obligations to salvage materials and/or equipment should be detailed. Surplus or excess materials and any item suitable for reuse are to revert to the public entity.

Hoards and Barricades. The Scope of Work should make provisions for erecting hoards or barricades at construction or renovation sites to protect the public, workers, and property from inadvertent damage, noise or worker error until such time as work is complete, inspected, and accepted by the public entity. The contractor, to protect the public from the construction site and any flying debris, erects this perimeter wall.

Dust. During construction, renovation, and restoration, a significant amount of dust and bits and pieces of building material are airborne. Bidders must be made aware of their obligations and requirements to provide and install dust-tight screens or protective partitions to localize dust and particle residue. The Scope of Work should declare that the work site is to be maintained in a dust-free environment for the duration of the project.

Weight Load Requirements. Bidders should be cautioned as to weight load limitations at the public entity's workplace and be aware of their obligation to take protective measures to minimize risk to buildings, property, and the public entity's workers.

Sanitary Facilities. Availability of the public entity's sanitary facilities to the contactor's workers should be included and clarified. If the contractor is to provide its own facilities, the public entity should indicate the location and maintenance of it.

Lighting. If there are any restrictions on the use of the public entity's lighting during specified hours, this should be clarified. If the contractors are required to provide their own portable power supply, this should be indicated in addition to any provision for noise abatement.

Communications—Telephones. The public entity should clarify the availability and use of its telephone infrastructure and that all telecommunication requirements not provided by the public entity, including cellular phones, are the responsibility of the bidder.

Storage. If the public entity provides and allocates storage for building materials, equipment, and construction accessories during construction, the location, access, and use and control of this area should clearly be referenced in the document. The public entity should provide a disclaimer for the responsibility for loss, damage, or theft of any items owned by the contractor.

Fire Protection. If the public entity does not provide fire protection, the contractor should be prepared to do so. The contractor's responsibility and obligation should be clearly defined.

Security—Keys. Where keys are provided to the contractor's workers, the cost of replacement, re-keying of doors due to lost keys shall be borne by the contractor. The contractor should be required to abide by all security provisions of the public entity's security policy.

Building Services. During the period of construction, the contractor should be required to maintain essential building services continuously and keep temporary interruptions to water, power, sewage, and other services to a minimum. Extenuating circumstance and conditions should be included with qualifying criteria for clarity.

Reporting to Maintenance. The Scope of Work should identify provisions for worker access to the site. The contractor's workers should be required to sign-in and maintain login sheets for the duration of the contract or work. The contractor should know at all times which workers are on site and their specific work locations in the event they have to be evacuated from the building site.

Support Structures. During construction, the contractor often is required to use supporting structures, scaffolding, or bracing. The Scope of Work should illustrate the contractor's requirement for the installation, maintenance, and removal of support structures during construction.

References

Heinritz, S. F., Farrell, P.V., Giunpero, & L., Kolchin, M. (1991). *Purchasing principles and applications* (8th ed.). Englewood Cliffs, NJ: Prentice Hall.

National Institute of Governmental Purchasing, Inc. (NIGP) (2007). *Contract administration*, 2nd edition. Herndon, VA: NIGP.

National Institute of Governmental Purchasing, Inc. (NIGP) (2007). *Developing and managing requests for proposals in the public sector* , 2nd edition. Herndon, VA: NIGP.

Chapter 10

The Sourcing Document: The Bid Proposal Form

To assist public entities in their evaluation of the responses, bidders should be required to prepare their response in a consistent and specific format, form and content, commonly referred to as the bid proposal form or solicitation response form. Since these terms are used interchangeably, this chapter will refer to this document as the "bid proposal form."

Public entities should develop and distribute this form to prospective bidders in order to clearly describe the manner in which bidders MUST prepare their responses. Templates and forms may be included to guide the bidder, where they are required to complete each field or section. These entities develop and prepare response documents in format and detail to suit their respective public organizational needs as well to accommodate the specific type of acquisition. Response documents are normally included in a solicitation document in the form of an annex, schedule, attachment, or appendix. Some public agencies require completion of response forms in specific formats as "mandatory." If following a specific format or completion of required forms is deemed "mandatory" by a public entity, the sourcing document should clearly state this requirement and indicate the consequences to the bidder for non-compliance.

Minimum Components of a Bid Proposal Form

The format required by the public entity could be simple or detailed based on the complexity of the solicitation. At a minimum, the format produced by the public entity for use by bidders who submit offers or proposals should include the elements discussed in the following sections.

Proposal Instructions

Public entities should provide guidelines and specific details to bidders submitting responses. Bidders must receive information as to:

- the number of copies required
- acceptable alterations of submitted response documents
- listing of documents that require signatures
- listing of affidavits that require completion and signature
- explanation on how envelopes or packages should be labeled
- any allowances for facsimile or electronic transmissions
- explanation of late submission implications, including the affects of delay in delivery by post office or courier.

Any other details that may be relevant to how a response should be submitted should be included in this section. The public entity should also stipulate in this section the ramifications of incomplete, unsigned, or improper signing by an authority so that there is no doubt as to non-compliance.

Cover Letter

The cover letter in a response provides an overview of the bidder's submission. Public entities should identify what specific items they want a bidder to include in the cover letter; that is, the name of the firm, contact information, and a signature of the senior official authorized to make an offer. This letter officially transacts the tender, proposal, quotation, or bid to the sourcing public entity.

In some cases, this cover letter is replaced by a solicitation response form that is utilized to certify the intent of the bidder to accept the public entity's terms in doing the work for the stated price and under the stated terms and conditions. This is normally where the "offer and acceptance" of the parties is formalized during the solicitation process.

Regardless of which format is utilized, it is essential that the principal and duly authorized officer of the bidding firm provide a signature on one of these documents in order to legally validate the intent of the bidder. As a stated requirement, public entities should declare that a response would be disqualified if it lacks the proper signature.

Technical Proposals

This section of the bid proposal form allows the bidder to explain, in sufficient detail, its business plan to meet the technical requirements of the solicitation.

Proposed Pricing

All pricing associated with delivering the requested goods and services must be detailed on the bid proposal form. This section should also clarify the currency to be used in responses. To remove any potential for bias in the evaluation process, some public entities use the two-envelope process for highly technical or complex solicitations. This approach is commonly referred to as a multi-step bid. In this scenario, bidders are required to submit their pricing or costing responses in a sealed envelope separate from the rest of the submission response. This envelope is opened only after the technical merits of the submission have been evaluated and ranked and the bidders have been determined to be both responsive and responsible.

Exceptions and Variances

The bidder must identify all terms and conditions where its proposal varies from the requirements and/or wishes to take exception. The public entity should exercise care in identifying all requirements that are mandatory as well as the penalty for non-compliance.

Required Attachments

If the public entity requires the inclusion of specified affidavits or documents, such as insurance certificates, bid bonds, etc., these items should be listed on the bid proposal form so that the bidder clearly understands these obligations.

Conflict of Interest Form

"Conflict of Interest," as defined in NIGP's Public Purchasing Dictionary of Terms, is

> A clash between the public interest and the private pecuniary interest of the individual concerned. The term identifies those situations where contractors or public officials may obtain a benefit from a public contract. Conflicts of interest may result in a breach of ethics or an ethical code. (NIGP, 2007)

A conflict of interest statement should be included with the bid proposal form to ensure an impartial and at-arms-length relationship existed between all parties during the solicitation process. Conflict of interest may also be related to a collusive arrangement, and public entities may require that a "Statement of Non-Collusion and Affidavit" be signed.

Optional Components of a Bid Proposal Form

I n addition to the basic requisites, the public entity may also require other submittals or documents based on the specific solicitation. A synopsis of each of these issues follows.

Executive Summary

This section of the bidder's response summarizes (in less than one page) the key features of the response submission.

Bidder's Profile and Information

The public entity should identify the nature and type of information it requires of the bidder, including corporate profile (published), relevant experience on similar projects or work, public organizational structure, confirmation of being a legal entity, years in business, principals and holders of debt/equity, number of employees, size of firm, etc.

Project Approach and Work Plan

All acquisitions are not handled in the same manner and may differ substantially, depending on the nature and type of acquisition; e.g., acquisition of construction will differ from those of services or specific products. Public entities should identify their expectations in terms of the depth and breadth of their bidders' responses; e.g., if a work plan is required for MS Project, then it should be identified as a requirement.

Subcontracting and Alliances

Many projects and solicitations may require the provisions of goods and services, construction, technology, or printing by more than one firm. In these instances, alliances may be formed and subcontractors engaged to assist in fulfillment of the contract. If a public entity permits the use of subcontractors or the formation of alliances, all aspects of the terms, conditions, references, and undertakings must be included in the bid proposal form. Requirements in this section will vary by public entity and will depend on the corporate culture of each public entity, their legal requirements, and the nature, technical merits, and sensitivity of the project or acquisition.

Schedule of Subcontractors

The bidder should be directed to identify all subcontractors that will be engaged in fulfillment of the contract. The solicitation document should explain the type of information to be supplied for each identified subcontractor. This information may be required by some entities to be provided on a standardized form.

References

Bidders may be required to provide references from at least three firms where work of similar scope, complexity, and diversity has been preformed. Reference information should include company names, contacts, phone numbers, etc. Some jurisdictions request that this information be submitted on a standard form.

Financial Guarantees

Depending on the nature and type of work required and the degree of risk to the public entity, different types of guarantees are required by a public entity. Guarantees involving some form of financial value are the most common. The Bid Proposal Form and the Special Conditions section of the solicitation document should identify each of the financial guarantees required, their values, how they will be retained for safekeeping, application of interest, where appropriate, and the return upon fulfillment of the contract. Three major types of financial guarantees frequently requested by a public entity are bid bonds, performance bonds, and material and labor bonds.

- **Bid Bond**. The public entity should identify if and when a bid bond or a security will be required, its value, and how and when it must be filed.

- **Performance Bond**. The public entity should identify if and when a performance bond or security will be required, its value, and how and when it must be filed or delivered.

- **Material and Labor Bond**. The public entity should identify if and when a material and labor bond or security will be required, its value, and how and when it must be filed or delivered.

Ineligibility of Responses

Public entities should identify those criteria that would deem a bidder's response ineligible for consideration. Such decisions may be based on incomplete responses. Improper format, unsigned or illegible documents, responses with arithmetical errors, discrepancies in amounts, or responses that contain irregularities may be deemed ineligible. All potential grounds for elimination should be included in this section.

Agreement Documents

Public entities should provide details of all documents, attachments, or appendices that will form part of the formal agreement to be incorporated into a purchase order or agreement. Clarification should be made here as to which documents will take priority in the event that terms and conditions are in conflict with one another. If a formal agreement is to be executed between the parties, this should be stated in this section with details of the nature, signatures, timing, etc.

Bidder/Proponent Checklist

The organization can provide the bidder with a list that identifies the crucial information and documents that must be submitted with a response. Use of the list by a bidder or proponent is not mandatory and, therefore, does not have to be returned with their response. An example of a "checklist" is illustrated in Figure 11.

1. Everyone involved in putting together the response has read and understands the requirements.	
2. The response meets all the mandatory requirements.	
3. The response addresses everything asked for, particularly those things in the Project Requirements section.	
4. The cover letter has been signed and attached.	
5. The response clearly identifies the bidder or proponent and the project.	
6. The bidder or proponent's name appears on the response envelope.	
7. The appropriate number of copies of the response has been submitted.	
8. The response is submitted at the closing location and before the closing time.	
9. The response is being delivered by hand, courier or mail, but not by fax or email.	
10. All required appendices have been returned, as stipulated in the solicitation document.	

Figure 11. *Bidder checklist for submitting a bid or proposal.*

Stewardship, Social Responsibility and Sustainability

The environment and the impact of manufacturing processes, transportation, product use, recycling disposal has become a highly visible and politicized factor in the supply chain.

Organizations at all levels, and more specifically in the public sector, have become more mindful of their roles and responsibilities in the stewardship of social, environmental and sustainable practices within their respective jurisdictions and communities. Some organizations have committed resources to policies in support of these stewardship considerations. See Appendix E for an example of one organization's Purchasing Services Strategic Objectives and Stewardship Considerations.

The following text outlines various programs and initiatives adopted by the University of Victoria, British Columbia, which highlight the attempts by their organization to address global warming issues and sustainability considerations.

RECYCLING AND REMOVAL OF PACKAGING AND DEBRIS

The supplier is to remove cardboard, packaging materials, pallets, shipping containers, etc. from products at time of installation and is to clear such packaging from each area, as the installation progresses. The supplier is to remove all debris materials from the installation site immediately upon completion of the installation and is to dispose of same within the laws and regulations of the local jurisdiction, using social responsibility principles in its disposal methods.

The bidder or proponent should present a proposal in their response for the recycling of the shipping containers and packaging. Some packaging may be returned to the contractor or supplier for reuse. The contractor or supplier will be responsible for collection and scheduling of packaging returns. This proposal is optional in the response but will be a consideration in the award of the agreement. Bidders or proponents are to indicate in their responses all items eligible for recycling and state credits available towards new item purchase of like kind.

WASTE REMOVAL

The contractor or supplier shall remove all waste products, materials, scrap and debris from the work site regularly and keep the work site clean and safe at all times.

SUSTAINABILITY PROVISIONS AND SOCIAL RESPONSIBILITY

[Organization] strives to conduct business in a sustainable manner. This is an effort to balance economic priorities with environmental and human health. [Organization] may, when economically feasible, do business with companies that can further our sustainable objectives. We are very interested in receiving environmental mission statements, certification details and/or any programs or policies that have to do with sustainable issues.

These programs or policies can be, but are not limited to, reducing, reusing and recycling resources, disposal of organic and other solid waste, conservation efforts in regards to transportation, energy and water, disposal of hazardous waste, and/or giving back to the community. Please include as part of your Proposal Submission any pertinent information in

[Organization] will make its best and reasonable efforts to acquire products and services from local producers, manufacturers, service providers, and contractors... and attain "best-value" on all acquisitions.

reference to any sustainable practices of your firm, if applicable.

Proponents, by making a proposal, certify that no components, parts, and/or accessories used to manufacture or configure any of the products, are manufactured or assembled in sweat shops or below fair trade labor rates.

Proponents are to state their association with ISO and Green Guard Certification, ISO 9000 or ISO 14000 certification, and provide with their proposals, copies of their certifications, environmental mission statement, statement of stewardship principles, policies and stewardship guidelines.

LEADERSHIP IN MAINTAINING SUSTAINABILITY, SOCIAL AND ENVIRONMENTAL RESPONSIBILITY

Purchasing Departments will be called upon with more frequency and under a higher profile to provide leadership in the areas of stewardship pertaining to sustainability, social and environmental responsibility. Internal users and corporate executives will rely upon the purchasing departments of their respective organizations to lead change and work with business and the community to implement these changes. Some responsible supply management considerations may include:

- Non-Sweat Shop/Child Labor
- Moral Issues
- Ethical Issues–Consumption; E-Waste–April 1, 2007 Implementation
- Commercialization - Branding
- Duplex Photocopying
- Fair Trade Coffee Program
- Dischargeable Battery Recycling Program
- Printer Toner/Cartridge Recycling Program
- Technology Recycling Program
- Furniture Recycling and Disposal Program
- Photocopier/Bond Paper - Post-Consumer-Waste Content–30% minimum
- Photocopier/Bond Paper–100% Post Consumer Waste Program
- Virgin Fiber Bond Paper Restrictions
- Chemicals and Hazardous Material Recycling and Disposal Program
- Shipping and Packaging Removal and Recycling Program (plastic, cardboard, metal, wood, Styrofoam, etc.)
- Print shop chemicals–Vegetable Based Product
- Tire Recycling
- Beverage Container Refundable Recycling Program–In Progress

eWaste Program

Proponents are to include within their pricing structure, and show each respective value as a separate line item, environmental or advance disposal surcharges (ADS) or fees for all eligible electronic products. ADS levies/fees are to be collected and remitted on all designated/eligible electronic products to the Provincial Government Agency established by legislation to collect these fees/levies.

Local Preference

[Organization] will make its best and reasonable efforts to acquire products and services from local producers, manufacturers, service providers, and contractors, however, in doing so, [Organization] must comply with various Trade Agreements, competitive sourcing requirements, and attain "best-value" on all acquisitions. [Organization] does not subscribe to any local preference laws or policy due to our requirement to comply with these trade agreements as noted above.

Proponents are required to source and consider supplying products from local producers and manufacturers (Vancouver Island, Lower Mainland, British Columbia) with no price escalation or mark-ups.

Employee, Student and Alumni Discount Programs

Proponents are to indicate within their Proposal Responses if they offer an Employee, Student, and Alumni discount/purchase Program, and if so, to provide details. Proponents are to list any value added services that would be offered as part of this contract.

Disposal Certification

Where specified by [Organization], the supplier may be required to present an executed Affidavit or Certificate of Disposal for all items that have been identified by [Organization] that:

- are traded in
- are hazardous
- are used in the original packaging for shipment purposes
- Other

[Organization] may retain from final payment an amount not to exceed ten (10) percent of the purchase (FOB Delivered) price until such time as the required Affidavit or Certificate of Disposal is presented. This provision shall be included as a Term and Condition in the main Solicitation Document, otherwise, it does not apply.

ENVIRONMENTAL MANAGEMENT ACT - BRITISH COLUMBIA RECYCLING REGULATION

Where levies are applied for recycling of identified product categories under the Act or Regulations, proponents and suppliers are to accept, handle, and dispose of materials in compliance with the Act and Regulations; otherwise, make provisions to enable [Organization] to recycle products and materials in lieu and compensate [Organization] at the tarrifed rates for each category of material or product. Proponents are to specify within their respective proposals on how they intend on carrying out these compliance requirements.

Proponents, suppliers, distributors, or manufacturers by submitting a proposal in response to this RFP, agree to accept for deposit refund all Encorp Canada registered brands (bottles, cans, glass, paper, and other beverage containers).

VEHICLE IDLING

Stationary delivery or service vehicles while on [Organization] property must not remain running in an idling position. Vehicles ignitions are to be turned off when not in use or in motion.

BIO-FUEL DELIVERY VEHICLES

Proponents are encouraged to use bio-fuel type vehicles for delivery of product and performing services at all University of Victoria designated locations.

Reference

National Institute of Governmental Purchasing, Inc. (NIGP) (2007. *Public procurement dictionary of terms.* Herndon, VA: NIGP.

Chapter 11

Receiving, Opening and Evaluating Bid/Proposal Responses

The legal foundation of the solicitation process relies on the integrity of the procurement process. There are some objectives that should be fundamental to any public entity's solicitation process. Fairness, transparency, openness, value for money, and legal effect should be considered during the handling and processing of solicitation response submissions.

There are certain legal and fiduciary core obligations placed on the purchasing official. The public entity is not permitted to accept a bid or proposal response that is not compliant with provisions stipulated in the solicitation document. Additionally, the public entity may be found to be in breach of its contract with a supplier and liable for damages if they deviate from any aspects of the solicitation document. It is, therefore, incumbent upon the procurement official to process all tenders, bids, proposals, and quotations in a manner that complies with all laws applicable to the jurisdiction.

This chapter will discuss appropriate practices for receiving, opening, and evaluating bids and proposals. Since some practices identified in this chapter are too formal for smaller solicitations, such as quotes, the entity needs to determine when to apply these concepts to specific bidding processes. Nevertheless, when the public entity utilizes a formal sealed bid or proposal process to solicit offers from suppliers, the steps listed in this chapter should be followed to the greatest extent possible because the purpose for formal practices is to ensure that public procurement operates in an open environment of integrity and fairness.

Receiving Bids and Proposals

Closing Date and Time

The inclusion of a closing date and time on a solicitation is to ensure that all bidders are treated equally in terms of the time available to them to submit a formal response. Vendors should be given sufficient time to offer a proper and reasonable response. If the time allotted for the solicitation process is inadequate, a bidder may demand an extension, as the solicitation may be deemed to be unfair and unequal. This would be particularly true if the incumbent supplier has an advantage in terms of knowledge and information.

Responsibility for Late or Lost Bids

Clear indications of the "closing date and time" are essential. Bidders have the sole responsibility to deliver and ensure their response submissions are received and time/date stamped prior to the specified date and time, and this should be clearly stated in the solicitation document. Many jurisdictions apply the Greenwich Mean Time clock reference in their solicitation document, e.g., 2:00:00 pm, Pacific Time. A computer or timepiece adjacent to the delivery location for submissions and visible to anyone delivering a response can be used as the formal date and time authentication. Electronic or digital clocks should be calibrated to match this time. Solicitation documents should clearly indicate the clock that will be used for this purpose. The solicitation document should also affirm that the public entity is not responsible or liable for lost or misdirected response submissions and that the responsibility for submission rests with the bidder. Failure to include this clause may lead to a challenge or protest of the award.

Receipt of Bids Prior to Opening

The custodianship of all bid responses is critical to the competitive process to maintain an "equal, open, and transparent" environment. Upon receipt of a bid response, the public entity should ensure the response is:

- promptly received/logged-in
- promptly date and time stamped
- placed in a safe and secure location with limited access and
- handled in a consistent manner.

When accepting solicitation responses from individuals or couriers by hand, the purchasing agent should ensure that the envelope or package is clearly marked with the name from whom the submission was received. Occasionally, a bidder may submit a response in an envelope without identifying it as a response submission to a solicitation invitation. Sent via regular mail or courier, these packages may be inadvertently opened by someone other than the designated purchasing agent. Should this occur, the envelope or package must be re-sealed and marked "opened in error," initialed by the individual who opened the envelope or package and witnessed/initialed by another person. In most cases, the response can be considered to be a valid submission.

Some public entities accept electronic or faxed response submissions. In these cases, the public entity should publicly post a disclaimer as to liability and responsibility for accepting, recording, handling, and storage of responses that are submitted electronically. The terms and conditions within the sourcing document should stipulate which electronic and faxed response submissions will be accepted. With improved Internet security protocols, more and more public entities have begun to accept electronic responses when allowed by law. Public entities employing Internet technologies should designate a specific URL or Internet address for the submission, receipt, and acknowledgement of electronic submissions.

Acknowledgement of Receipt of Response Submittals

Some public entities acknowledge receipt of all bid submissions by issuing a formal acknowledgement document. Technology-supported submissions allow for the bidder to request an online acknowledgement.

Validation of Bid Submittals

If a public entity does not engage a digital, mechanical, or electronic time clock to certify and validate bid submissions, the purchasing official at the designated location should be available at the pre-determined closing date and time to accept and validate receipt of the response. The date, time, and receiver's initials should be indicated on the envelope, package, or document. Occasionally, responses get misdirected to somewhere other than the designated location. Prior to the pending solicitation closing, the purchasing public entity should alert the staff, mailroom, and reception areas of the location and time of the bid opening so that they may facilitate the receipt and validation of on-time delivery and acceptance of all packages. To prevent misdirection, public entities should provide detailed instructions on the delivery location within the solicitation document. Room numbers should be included with street addresses, and post office box numbers should not be utilized.

Security and Safeguards of Bid Submittals

Bidders expect the purchasing public entity to safeguard their submission prior to the designated closing. A public entity is obligated to retain all responses in a safe, secure, and confidential manner. A locked drop-box, a locked filing cabinet, or a locked room with well-marked filing cabinets indicating the solicitation reference number can be used to meet this obligation. When using a "sealed bid or proposal" method of sourcing, there is a legal obligation on the part of the public entity to safeguard response submissions prior to opening.

Modification or Withdrawal of Bid Submittal Prior to Opening

Some public entities permit bidders to modify or withdraw their response submissions prior to the opening date and time. Bidders should be able to correct a detected error or adjust their response prior to the posted closing date and time. Risk to the public entity must be minimized with clear, documented policies and procedures that are to be followed under such circumstances.

If the bidder detects an error prior to the closing date and time, enabling the bidder to issue an alternate, modified, or clarification response, the public entity should accept the revised submission unless specifically indicated otherwise in the terms and conditions. If the public entity allows for modifications and/or withdrawals at any time up to evaluation and award, these conditions must be made clear. A specific clause within the Terms and Conditions section of the solicitation document should identify the conditions under which a response can be withdrawn or changed.

The public entity should carefully consider the denial or non-acceptance of a revised submission due to error prior to the closing date, as the bidder may launch a legal action, which would be difficult to defend.

It is not common practice to permit the withdrawal of the original submission but, rather, to accept an alternate "substitution response" or "supplementary" document. This practice will prevent another bidder or proponent's submission being released inappropriately to a competitor.

Rejection of Late Bid Submittals

The sourcing document must specify the date, time and location for delivery and receipt of response submissions. Late bids (received after the designated time) should be rejected by the public entity and not accepted. Responses that are received after the stated time should be returned unopened to the bidder. Should the public entity be unable to determine the name of the bidder from the marking on the exterior of the fax, envelope or package, the submission should be unopened and filed with the Solicitation file.

Opening Bids and Proposals

Bid Opening and Proceedings

The bid opening and proceedings may be very formal and based on protocol. The official in charge of the proceedings would formally announce the close of the solicitation and announce certain information to the public. The staff assigned to the project may also be introduced. In other public entities, less formal proceedings take place. Irrespective of the manner in which the public entity chooses to handle the opening process details, the process should be clearly described in the solicitation document's terms and conditions.

Two people from the public entity should be present at the opening. As each response is revealed and read aloud by one, the second person should document and record the information on a Bid Tally/Tender Opening Verification and Bid Security Log (Figure 12).

In a formal and public bid opening, the following minimum factors and criteria should be considered based on the entity's purchasing regulations as well as laws (especially those laws governing public records) enacted by the entity or a higher governing authority:

- Announce the solicitation name and reference number.
- If opening a proposal, announce only the name of the proposing firm, unless the entity is legally required to publicly disclose pricing at this time. If this is the case, the attendees should be informed that the total price is not the sole basis for the award and will be reviewed by an evaluation team. The attendees should be informed that the awarded bidders will be announced at a subsequent date.
- If opening bids/tenders, announce individual prices and/or total price.
- Announce any qualifications.
- Announce whether any bidder conditioned or qualified its bid to require the award of all items (commonly known as an "all or none" requirement where the bidder will only accept the award if it receives all of the items on the bid)
- Announce that all prices and responses are subject to evaluation and validation before acceptance by the public entity for award.

Once the bid opening announcements have been completed, it is customary to allow bids to be examined by the public. If allowable, this process should only be conducted under the supervision of an employee of the purchasing department or other official in a similar capacity.

If a public entity does not conduct a formal opening, this should be indicated in the solicitation with details as to how bidders can access the final information. While some agencies may not have a legal requirement to conduct formal bid opening proceedings, it is a recommended practice because it supports the open, fair, and transparent provisions of public sector sourcing. The purchasing agent and public entity has an obligation to provide bidders

Commodity/Service	Bid/Tender Number
Purchasing Officer	Bid/Tender Closing Date

No.	Received Date	Received Time	Company Name	Quoted Price	Delivery	Unique Conditions	Bid Security Type*	Financial Institution	Serial No.	$ Amount

Witnesses

*Bid Security Type
A Security Bond
B Certified Cheque
C Money Order
D Irrevocable Letter of Credit
E Bank Draft

Chairperson/Sponsor	Title	Bid/Tender Opening Date
Purchasing Officer	Title	Time
Audit	Title	Page ___ of ___

Figure 12. *Bid Tally/Tender Opening Verification and Bid Security Log*

with specific information and feedback on the treatment of disqualified or rejected (not accepted) response submissions.

Compliant or Non-Compliant Determination

All sourcing documents, whether an IFB/ITT, RFP/RFI, or and RFQ to some extent have mandatory" bid/proposal/quote requirements. There are those that are absolutely mandatory, and if not met at the time of bid closing/opening the respective submission MUST be set aside from consideration. Appendix D outlines a suggested model that enables public procurement organizations to consider levels of mandatory compliance. This model has been in place for nearly two years at the University of Victoria, and has been acclaimed by internal users, procurement officials, and the supply community as a practical and flexible approach to handling mandatory provisions of public sourcing.

Criteria to determine compliance or non-compliance must be incorporated into the solicitation document. Rules and processes of compliance and implications resulting from non-compliance must be clearly articulated to the bidder. The judicial system looks to the terms and conditions of the solicitation document to determine contested issues of compliance or non-compliance.

If a response is considered to be non-compliant, it is incumbent upon the purchasing agent to provide prompt feedback to the bidder on the bid rejection. The purchasing agent may only consider those responses that have been determined to be compliant for evaluation and award. An established checklist of mandatory requirements to be met by a bidder will result in a compliant response submission. A sample checklist is shown in Figure 13.

Solicitation Item #	Item Description	Solicitation Section Reference #	Compliance Yes	No	Authorized Person's Initials	Comments
4.5.1.1	References					
4.5.1.2	Financial statements for past 3 years					
4.5.1.3	Annual reports for past 3 years					
4.5.1.4	No OHS Infractions for the past one year					
4.5.1.5	Registered and good standing with WCB					
4.5.1.6	Three (3) copies for response					
4.5.1.7	Receipt of response submissions by closing date and time					

4.5.1.8	Licensed/Registered to do business in [Province/State]					
4.5.1.9	Follow and comply with response format explicitly					
4.5.1.10	All sections initials/ signed where required					
4.5.1.11	Agree to comply with Conflict of Interest Clause					
4.5.1.12	Agree to comply with Confidentiality and Protection of Privacy Agreement					
4.5.1.13	Agree to comply with Workplace and Personal Harassment Policy and Guidelines					
4.5.1.14	Agreement to Owner-ship and Intellectual Property Policy					
4.5.1.15	Agreement to Liability and Insurance Require-ments					
4.5.1.16	Agreement to Perfor-mance Security and Bonding					
4.5.1.17	Agreement to Access to Records and Finan-cial Documents for Audit purposes					
4.5.1.18	Agreement to Errors and Omissions Policy					
4.5.1.19	Agreement to Comply with Statement of Non-Collusion Requirements					

Figure 13. *Solicitation document response submission mandatory requirements.*

The purchasing agent is required to examine each response and to determine if all of the stated terms and conditions, including signatures and submission of all supporting documents, have been included. Once determined, only those fully compliant responses should be accepted for subsequent evaluation and award consideration.

Discovery of Bidder Errors or Mistakes after Bid Opening

Mistakes in bids will occur due to human errors, and they may be discovered during or after the bid opening but before contract award. The public entity must have a thorough understanding of the proper procedures required for verifying and correcting mistakes in bids, since this formal process is critically important to the success and integrity of the bidding method of public procurement.

If the bid contains apparent clerical errors, it is appropriate for the public entity to allow the bidder to adjust its bid pricing based on the following conditions and subject to the entity's procurement regulations and governing statutes:

- That there is an obvious clerical mistake (examples: the misplacement of a decimal point, inverted numbers in unit prices, miscalculated extensions, and incorrect units of measure)
- That the public entity, upon discovery of the error, has requested written verification from the bidder regarding the clerical error(s) and
- That the bidder has verified in writing that a clerical mistake was made by providing a copy of the original bid, notating where the error occurred, and re-calculating any and all total amounts.

Assuming that this bid offers the best pricing from responsible, responsive bidders, this re-calculated bid will serve as the basis for contract award.

There are other errors or mistakes in bid documents that are not clerical in nature. These would include errors based on a misunderstanding on the part of the bidder regarding the exact nature of the product or work required as well as errors due to an intentionally low bid. When these errors are discovered by the public entity, the entity has a responsibility to call this to the attention of the bidder in writing. The bidder must be given the opportunity to either withdraw its bid or let it stand, and must convey its desired option in writing.

Bid Surety and Bid Bond Deposits (Bonds, Insurance)

Public entities may require that a Bid Surety or a Bid Bond be posted with the bid submission to ensure that a bidder seriously intends to enter into the contract upon award and does not withdraw their response prior to evaluation and award. It should be a reasonable amount (typically 5% of a total bid) based on the risk and nature of the acquisition in terms of its technical aspects or sensitivity. A bid bond takes the form of a surety bond, irrevocable letter of credit, a bank note or draft, a certified or cashier's check, money order, bearer bond, or an insurance certificate from a registered bonding company.

Under normal practices the bid surety submitted by every bidder is retained by the public entity until the selected bidder executes a contract and insurance certificates have been received.

When a bid bond is identified as mandatory... failure to submit the required surety or bond will deem the bidder non-responsive...

Insurance certificates, if identified as a requirement, are often not required to be filed until a bidder or proponent has been selected for the contract award and prior to commencement of the work. In some cases, however, the public entity has returned the bid surety to all but those who submitted the best two or three bids or proposals. If the entity utilizes this practice, it should be noted in the solicitation document. In some jurisdictions, frequent solicitation responders may file an annual bid surety or bond. When a bid bond is identified as mandatory in the solicitation document, failure to submit the required surety or bond will deem the bidder non-responsive and, therefore, subject to an automatic bid rejection.

If requiring bid surety or bond, the surety or bond can only be encroached upon to off-set damages or additional costs associated with issuing a new solicitation and/or the costs incurred by delay of work due to withdrawal or non-execution of an agreement. The public entity must prove that they incurred additional costs and made reasonable efforts to mitigate costs and/or damages. A bid surety or bond should not be used for leverage against a bidder in agreement execution.

Bid Protests

B id solicitations that result in contract awards are as much about relationships and partnerships as they are about legal attributes. The dynamics of human nature will dictate that any contractual relationship may involve disagreements that can be formal or informal. Formal disagreements will manifest themselves as protests. Informal disagreements may be easily and quickly resolved.

Suppliers that are familiar with public procurement know that some form of protest process is available to them. Most protests are resolved administratively but there is always the possibility that a protest will be advanced through a judicial process. Suppliers may challenge the solicitation at any stage prior to the award of a contract. Since the addressing of protests varies greatly, an agreement on terms and definitions will assist in understanding the general nature of protests. NIGP's *Public Procurement Dictionary of Terms* (NIGP, 2007) offers the following:

- **Protest:** An oral or written objection by a potential interested party to a solicitation or award of a contract, with the intention of receiving a remedial result. May be filed in accordance with agency policy and procedure within predetermined time lines.

- **Dispute:**
    1. A contractual disagreement or misunderstanding between contracting parties specific to contract provisions or language. Resolution is generally through pre-established administrative procedures or agreed upon alternative dispute resolution provisions.
    2. A difference between a contractor/seller and a buyer over a bid, solicitation or contract calling for appropriate administrative action with the intent of achieving a remedial or amicable resolution. When a resolution cannot be achieved the parties may resort to alternative dispute resolution or litigation.

- **Arbitration:**
    1. A process by which a dispute between parties is presented to one or more disinterested parties (arbitrators or neutrals) for a decision whose decision the contending parties agree to accept with no further appeal process also known as binding arbitration.
    2. The resolution of a conflict between parties by a party removed from the dispute.
    3. A form of Alternative Dispute Resolution.

- **Alternate Dispute Resolution (ADR):** A process or procedure used voluntarily between parties to resolve issues in controversy without the need to resort to litigation. ADR may include but are not limited to mediation, fact-finding and arbitration.

- **Claim:** A written assertion or demand, by one of the parties to a contract, which seeks, as a contractual right, payment of money, adjustment of contract terms, or other relief, for injury, loss, or damage arising under or relating to the contract.

- **Change Order:** A written alteration that is issued to modify or amend a contract or purchase order. A bilateral (agreed to by all parties) or unilateral (government orders a contract change without the consent of the contractor) request which directs the contractor to make changes to the contracted scope of work or specifications. In reference to construction contracts, it relates primarily to changes caused by unanticipated conditions encountered during construction not covered by the drawings, plans or specifications of the project.

- **Appeal:** The resubmission of a protest, contract dispute, or claim to a higher authority, with the intent to overturn a decision of a lower authority.

Bidders will normally file protests if they feel that a wrong decision has been made regarding a recommendation to award a contract. Protests are usually filed before the contract is awarded. The public entity's administrative procedures should clearly state the steps an alleged aggrieved supplier must take when filing their protest. Additionally, many public entities will include protest procedures in the solicitation document. At a minimum, protest procedures should include:

- A notification to all bidders of the intent of the jurisdiction to award the contract. This notice should contain the date and time award will be made.
- A timetable indicating the deadline for protest filing. Timeliness is critical in any protest action.
- To whom the aggrieved bidder must submit the protest and in what form.
- A statement regarding the appeal process and how appeals are made.

In many jurisdictions, the legal counsel addresses all protests, claims, and disputes due to the fact that there may be potential litigation. In some jurisdictions, the protest may be as simple as sending a letter to the chief procurement officer. The procurement officer conducts an informal meeting and renders an opinion. If the bidder is not satisfied with the opinion, the only recourse is through the judicial system. In other jurisdictions, an elaborate protest procedure may include a formal hearing by elected officials, an arbitration process, or perhaps an Alternate Dispute Resolution (ADR). Most parties would prefer to avoid litigation and resolve the protest amicably.

A major decision that procurement officials must make, based on legal counsel opinion, is whether the award should be delayed pending the resolution of the protest. When determining whether the protest should impact the award of the contract, administrative procedures usually provide that if the protest is received before contract performance begins and delay would not have an adverse effect on government operations, the award process will be stopped and the start of work delayed until the protest is resolved.

Claims and contract disputes occur after the award of the contract. Frequently, a claim or contract dispute may result in the issuing of a change order to the master contract. Claims and contract disputes, if not quickly resolved to the satisfaction of both parties, may result in payment delays and possibly penalty charges or liquidated damages. Local and state laws frequently stipulate the procedures for resolving contract disputes involving monetary claims against the government and may require a hearing before a governmental body before the contractor can apply to the courts for relief.

Bid Debriefing

Many jurisdictions will debrief unsuccessful bidders before the final award of the contract. When the successful bidder has been selected and a recommendation for award has been made, the unsuccessful offerors are notified and, at their request, may be debriefed as to the basis of the selection process. The debriefing is usually conducted by a procurement official who explains to the unsuccessful bidders the results of the public entity's evaluation of the proposals. This is done without making any point-by-point comparison with other proposals. The debriefing may help avoid or minimize future protest action because it provides the rationale as to why the response was deemed unacceptable for award.

Responding to Protests

Before a public entity can respond to a protest, it is essential that the full nature and extent of the protest be known. An effective protest procedure should state that all protests be in writing and submitted within required time frames. It is essential that the procedures clearly articulate a time line for filing the protest. In addition, the procedures should indicate that the written protest should be sent to the chief procurement official for the jurisdiction. The protest is the first step in the process that could eventually lead to litigation. Frequently, the protest is mailed to the governor, county executive, president of the university, comptroller, etc. When this occurs, it may take weeks before the chief procurement official receives the protest. When the protest is received, it should be reviewed promptly with the jurisdiction's legal counsel.

Many jurisdictions in the solicitation document include a section that details the steps to be taken to file a protest. The following could be used to establish a well-defined procedure:

- Require that all protests be in writing.
- State to whom (name, title, address) the protest should be directed.
- Establish a definition for timely submission of a protest and the specific time after which a protest will not be accepted.
- Review the protest with the appropriate legal counsel.
- Draft a protest response letter and circulate it to the appropriate internal staff (i.e., legal, SOW team, end-user agency) for their approval.
- Mail the protest decision response by registered mail, return receipt requested.

If the protester is not satisfied with the decision, one option is to pursue litigation through the appropriate judicial process. If this occurs and if the courts hear the protester, an injunction may be filed which will stop the contracting process. The public entity might be prohibited from awarding the contract until the process is completed. Many entities have established a hearing process that must be followed prior to appealing to the courts.

Following the written response to the protest, the bidder may be required to have a hearing with the chief procurement official or another public official. This administrative hearing between the entity and the protesting bidder may also be referred to as the ADR. The purpose of the ADR or other forms of administrative hearings is to resolve controversial issues relative to the contracting process so that litigation can be avoided.

Whatever the process, the public entity must be in a position to defend, explain, and justify all of the many decisions manifested in solicitation. As a protest escalates from protest to response to hearing to possible litigation, the burden of proof is on the public entity's procurement and contracting officials. They must demonstrate, without doubt, that the entire process was not arbitrary, capricious, or in bad faith, did not show favoritism, and that it was in the best interests of the jurisdiction.

Evaluating Bids and Proposals

Once the solicitation process is complete, a review and evaluation of the response submissions leading to a recommendation for award must be conducted. The procedures and processes will vary and depend on different factors:

- Was the solicitation a formal Request for Proposal (RFP), Request for Quotation (RFQ), Letters of Interest (LOI), Invitation for Bids/Invitation to Tender, (IFB/ITT) or Request for Qualification (RFQu)?
- Does the public entity have a formal policy or specific protocols for award recommendation?
- Is the response submission for products or goods, services, construction, or technology?
- What is the role of procurement in the review, evaluation, and award?
- Did the solicitation document provide for an Executive Steering Committee, Technical Evaluation Committee, and/or formal presentations of top ranked bidders?

There is no one standard process or procedure that can be used by every jurisdiction; however, all bidders expect that their response submission will be reviewed, evaluated, and considered on an equal, fair, and consistent basis. Accordingly, the public entity must be clear on how the bid offers will be evaluated. Typically, this criterion is outlined in the Special Conditions section; however, its position within the solicitation document is not as critical as the importance of defining the criteria for transparency purposes. As a public institution, the entity must clearly articulate the method of award, as this assures the supplier community that the selection process is fair and impartial.

...the entity must clearly articulate the method of award, as this assures the supplier community that the selection process is fair and impartial.

The NIGP Public Procurement Dictionary of Terms defines a "formal bid" as a "bid, which must be submitted in a sealed envelope and in conformance with a prescribed format to be opened in public at a specified time." An "informal bid" is a competitive bid, price quotation or proposal for supplies or services that is conveyed by a letter, fax, email or other manner that does not require a formal sealed bid or proposal, public opening or other formalities. Generally relegated to requirements that may be considered low value or fall under a stipulated price/cost threshold. Normally, solicitation invitations involving bids and specific types of proposals are handled through a formal process, while routine and non-complex proposals and quotations are handled in an informal manner.

In most cases, award is made to the bidder whose response submission is determined to be the "best-value" based on cost, quality, service, reliability, references, and any other specific factors or criteria itemized in the solicitation document. Successful bidders are determined to have the most responsive and responsible bid—that is to say, the one bid that best meets the specifications and offers the most preferential pricing for the goods and/or services. Formal procurement policy, procedures, and guidelines on the review, evaluation, consideration, and recommendation for award can guide the staff, the internal users, the stakeholders, and the external supply community.

The Evaluation Process

The evaluation process varies with respect to each of the different methods of solicitation. The following is a brief synopsis of the various processes a public entity may deploy when evaluating different solicitation methods.

Small Dollar/Purchasing Card Acquisitions

For small dollar or pCard purchases, typically only one quote is required up to the spending threshold established by the entity. For some agencies, the approved expenditure per transaction is $250; while, for others, it may be between $5,000 and $10,000.

Emergency Purchases

When time is of the essence due to a threat to the public's health or safety, purchasing procedures are suspended with expenditure approvals being obtained after the fact. Typically, the chief executive officer of the agency must give approval for the purchases occurring in excess of the approved threshold amounts.

Sole Source

A sole source (sometimes referred to as directed contract) method of acquisition must clearly document that there is only one capable product or firm that is able to supply the good or service to the agency. In these instances, the process is limited to obtaining an informal quotation from the one supplier and making the award through the established hierarchy of approvals. The public entity must have supporting documentation and evidence confirming that a sole source or directed contract solicitation was essential and appropriate.

Goods, And Goods Related Services

Contract Dollar Level	Commitment Type	Number Of Quotes	Method Of Purchase - Quote Type	Lead Time Guideline (Working Days)	Commitment Issued By (Contract Execution)	Special Conditions
<$2,500 per item or aggregate.Except Restricted Items as per Purchasing Policy 1750	Petty Cash, Purchasing Card, Credit Card, Debit Card, Purchase Order Optional.	One Written Quote, Invoice, or Credit Card or Cash Register Receipt (rotate Suppliers), or two where practical	Telephone, fax, email, written, in person	Delegated to Departments	Delegated	Receipts required with payment claim and monthly reconciliation statement. PO optional.
>$2,500 <$10,000 per item or aggregate	Purchase Order	Minimum of three where practical	Written (fax or email)	3 - 5 days	Purchasing Officer, Assistant Purchasing Officer	Rotate Suppliers invited to quote.
>$10,000 <$30,000 per item or aggregate	Purchase Order	Minimum of three where practical	RFQ/RFP (1 page Spec.)	5 - 10 days	Director, Purchasing Services or Purchasing Officer	Full list of potential Suppliers when less than 8 in marketplace, or BC BID Board.
>$30,000 <$50,000 per item or aggregate	Purchase Order	Minimum 3	ITT/RFQ/RFP (Full Specs.)	5 - 10 days	Director, Purchasing Services, or Purchasing Officer (Initialed by Director)	Full list of potential Suppliers in marketplace, BC Bid Board and/or MERX.
>$50,000 <$200,000 per item or aggregate	Purchase Order or Agreement	Minimum 5	ITT/RFQ/RFP (Full Specs.)	Min. 2 weeks	Director, Purchasing Services, Assistant Manager, and Executive Director, Financial Services	Full list of potential Suppliers in marketplace, BC Bid Board and/or MERX.
Not Specified	Corporate Supply Agreement (CSA), Purchase Order, or Long Form Contract	Open Market - Full List	ITT/RFQ/RFP	4 Weeks	Director, Purchasing Services, or as per Signing Authority Policy 1002	Where required, full list of potential Suppliers in marketplace, BC Bid Board and/or MERX.

Consulting, Training And Professional Services (Non – Academic)						
Contract Dollar Level	**Commitment Type**	**Number Of Quotes**	**Method Of Purchase - Quote Type**	**Lead Time (Working Days)**	**Commitment Issued By**	**Special Conditions**
<$5,000 per item or aggregate	Short Form Contract and Purchase Order	Two (rotate Suppliers where practical)	Written	2 - 5 days	Director, Purchasing Services, Purchasing Officer	Require BFRF. Except where specifically delegated under Purchasing Policy 1750
>$5,000 <$30,000 per item or aggregate	Short Form Contract and Purchase Order	Three where practical (rotate Suppliers where practical)	Written	2 - 5 days	Director, Purchasing Services, Purchasing Officer	Require BFRF. Except where specifically delegated under Purchasing Policy 1750
>$30,000 <$75,000 per item or aggregate	Short Form Contract and Purchase Order	Min. Three (rotate Suppliers where practical)	Written / RFP/RFQ	5 - 10 days	Director, Purchasing Services, Purchasing Officer	Require BFRF. Except where specifically delegated under Purchasing Policy 1750
>$75,000	Long Form Contract or Purchase Order	Full List	ITT/RFP/ RFQ/IPP	MIN. 2 WEEKS	Director, Purchasing Services, Assistant Manager, and Executive Director, Financial Services	Require BFRF. Except where specifically delegated under Purchasing Policy 1750. Full list of potential Service Providers or BC BID Board and MERX where appropriate.
Construction And Facilities Maintenance						
Contract Dollar Level	**Commitment Type**	**Number Of Quotes**	**Method Of Purchase - Quote Type**	**Lead Time (Working Days)**	**Commitment Issued By**	**Special Conditions**
<$2,500 per item or aggregate	Letter of Engagement and/or Purchase Order	One Written, Preferably two where practical	Written Quotations, fax, email, or in person	Delegated	Manager, FMGT	Invoice or Receipts required. Rotate Suppliers invited to quote.

Construction And Facilities Maintenance						
>$2,500 <$10,000 per item or aggregate	Letter of Engagement and/or Purchase Order	Two Written Quotes Where Practical	Written, Fax, email Quotations	Delegated	Manager, FMGT	Rotate Suppliers invited to quote.
>$10,000 <$30,000 per item or aggregate	Letter of Engagement and/or Purchase Order, Contract and CCDC or Consultant Short Form Agreement	Minimum of three written quotations where practical	ITT/RFQ/RFP/RFQu	5 - 10 days	Executive Director, Facilities management or Director, Purchasing Services	Full list of potential Suppliers in marketplace, BC Bid Board
>$30,000 <$100,000	Purchase Order, Long Form Contract, and/or CCDC	Minimum of three written quotations or full list where practical	ITT/RFQ/RFP/RFQu	2 - 4 weeks	Executive Director, Facilities Management or Director, Purchasing Services	Full list of potential Suppliers in marketplace, BC Bid Board and/or MERX.
>$100,000	Purchase Order, Long Form Contract, and/or CCDC	Minimum of three written quotations or full list where practical	ITT/RFQ/RFP/RFQu	2 - 4 weeks	Executive Director, Facilities management or Director, Purchasing Services	Full list of potential Suppliers in marketplace, if <$75,000 must be posted on BC Bid Board and/or MERX. If value >$250,000
>$250,000	Purchase Order, Long Form Contract, and/or CCDC	Posted on BC Bid, and MERX/GETS. Normally posted through the BC Construction Association Bid Depository	ITT/RFP/RFQu	2 plus weeks depending on the nature of the acquisition	President or VPFO; and Executive Director FMGT	University Seal Required
Change Orders from original Contract	Change Order	Single Source, On-Site Contractor	Written	Delegated	Executive Director, Facilities Management or Director, Purchasing Services	First right of refusal from on-site Contractor

Figure 14. *[Agency Name] Purchasing Services Spending and Commitment Authority Levels*

Request for Quotation (RFQ)

Public entities may establish dollar thresholds as guidelines for purchasers to follow for the number of quotations that must be obtained for each acquisition. Often, the dollar amount of the acquisition is directly proportionate to the number of required quotes. After receipt, quotes should be compiled on a spreadsheet and evaluated against the specified requirements. Evaluation and recommendation for award should be based on the quotation that best meets price, quality, delivery, service, past performance, and reliability. A sample of a public entity's Spending Authority Matrix or spending thresholds indicating the number of quotations required under varying dollar thresholds for each respective type of acquisition is included in Figure 14. These typically require executive level approval and sign-off and are often included in formal Procurement Policy.

Invitation for Bids/Invitation to Tender (IFB/ITT)

An Invitation for Bids/Invitation to Tender is used if and when specifications can explicitly describe the product and/or service by product number, make, and model including specific features, design, color, or other identifying features. Within this section, the terms "bid" and "tender" will be used interchangeably. An IFB/ITT document is prepared and issued with a pre-established closing date and time. Upon closing, a public opening of submissions is usually conducted. Particular circumstances usually determine the opening process selected for use. If a public opening is conducted, the bidder's name and line item prices for a total are divulged. The responses are qualified; the award is made by announcement, subject to in-depth review of submissions and validation of prices, terms, and conditions of bid.

A limited bid opening requires that all responses, values, and conditions be recorded and that a communication of the pricing to those firms/bidders submitting a response will be released soon thereafter. In some instances, it is more appropriate to engage a limited opening process, particularly if there are many items, with each individually priced and there is a possibility that many responses will be received. Limited openings are stated as such in the terms and conditions of the solicitation documentation.

The information received is documented, signed, and maintained within the solicitation file. If the low compliant/responsive bid is recommended, the agent will issue a purchase order or contract. If other than the low-compliant bid is recommended, the internal customer will need to support and justify its selection and eventual recommendation for award. Only after the purchasing agent is satisfied with the rationale and that all required approvals have been received should a purchase order or contract be issued.

Request for Proposal (RFP)

Often referred to as the "Competitive Sealed Proposal," the evaluation process for an RFP is more complex and requires additional levels of participation and review. NIGP has produced a separate text dedicated solely to the RFP process; therefore, limited information will be provided here. (NIGP, 2007)

The evaluations of RFP submissions may include a significant element of subjectivity and personal biases and, therefore, have a higher risk of being challenged. Evaluation criteria, methodology, and a framework to eliminate any possibility of subjectivity in the selection and recommendation process must be developed. In addition to all of the steps used in other solicitations, an RFP requires that evaluation relative to mandatory, optional, and desirable criteria is specified within the document. Upon receipt, opening, and recording of responses, an evaluation team whose content is dictated by policy (usually comprised of qualified resources and expertise) begins a detailed review and evaluation process. The committee/team should be under the direction of a senior official of the purchasing department who facilitates the work of the committee and oversees the proceedings to ensure fair and equal treatment of all bidders. The purchasing representative is typically not a voting member of the committee.

Request for Expression of Interest/Request for Information (REI/RFI).

This method of acquisition involves a two-stage process and is more complex than the IFB/ITT and RFP. The preliminary stage is intended to identify only those firms that have an interest in or the capability to supply the required product and/or service. A formal RFP or IFB/ITT is then developed and issued only to those individuals and firms who responded to the REI/RFI. The second stage requires responses to be evaluated using standard evaluation techniques and processes.

Prior to posting of the solicitation:

- Establish mandatory, desirable, or optional criteria.
- Determine evaluation criteria, weights, and values established by category of evaluation factors.
- Establish a technical evaluation team/committee, as appropriate.
- Establish the selection committee, if required.
- Ensure that the evaluation process and methodology are described in the solicitation document.

Following response submission (after closing date and time):

- Responses are opened either in public or limited capacity.
- Responses are documented relative to mandatory terms and conditions.

- Responses are recorded on a summary spreadsheet.
- The Selection Committee is forwarded a copy of the forms and responses for review.
- The Selection Committee meets to review responses and submits short-list recommendations.
- Arrangements are made for presentations, if required or requested.
- Site visits are arranged, if needed.
- Requests are made for additional information, if needed.
- Conduct reference checks.
- Conduct financial or capability reviews, if needed.
- Purchasing Department receives final recommendation to award a contract.

Reverse Auctions

The evaluation process for reverse auctions is quite straightforward and simple. The bidder offering the lowest price at the closing date and time that meets the public entity's specifications is normally awarded the contract. There are no variables to consider or evaluate. Bidders are usually pre-qualified prior to the actual auction to eliminate possible disqualification of bids.

The evaluation process is most successful when a thorough methodology is followed using a pre-established orderly time line. Though available in different formats and with variations, the following is a summary of important points to be considered when developing the process most effective for use by a jurisdiction. Each entity's process will be in line with the public entity's policy and administrative procedures or processes.

The Evaluation Plan

In order to proactively engage all stakeholders, the public entity, with the assistance of the purchasing agent and client representation, should establish a formal evaluation plan. The plan should be included in the solicitation to inform the bidder or respondent as to how their responses will be evaluated and may increase bidder confidence. An identifiable evaluation process will ensure that decisions are based on fair, transparent, and open standards, with special attention being paid to the value for money and legal implications.

The purpose and objective of any evaluation plan is to:

- establish the framework and methodology for evaluation
- establish bidder confidence in the process
- identify evaluation criteria—mandatory, desirable, optional
- identify values and weights by category and/or criteria

- establish evaluation, scoring stages, and methods
- identify the need for formal presentations, site visits, demonstrations, or product testing and
- establish the administrative and approval framework.

Considerable collaboration and input from the user department is required when establishing a plan. Consensus on the evaluation process and methodology prior to the start of the process will improve rather than impede the process.

The Evaluation or Selection Committee/Team

Selection committees or teams are advisory in nature and are often established to advise and assist the public entity in the decision to award. The ultimate recommendation for award rests with the purchasing agent and should be based on best value, life cycle costing, and submission of the most responsible bidder. Teams are typically utilized in conjunction with Request for Proposals, Requests for Expression of Interest, Request for Information, or Request for Qualifications

> *The ultimate recommendation for award...should be based on best value, life cycle costing, and submission of the most responsible bidder.*

The purchasing agent, when determining the appropriate solicitation method, should consider the merits and requirements of a selection committee or team. A skilled purchasing agent can evaluate responses and forward summary documents to the user department for review and recommendation. Detailed and extensive evaluations of the responses may be required of individuals with specific expertise. In these situations, a formal technical evaluation team should be convened. Evaluation teams are often established for information systems, construction, and professional services types of acquisitions.

Should an evaluation committee or team be established to evaluate responses, the team members should consist of qualified and relevant members who can assess, evaluate, rank, select, and recommend the "best-value" submission for award and have a thorough understanding of the solicitation document. The process and procedures of the team should be clearly stipulated prior to starting. Although it is recommended that the purchasing agent chair the team, the user department representative may also serve in this capacity. Individual membership on the committee is based on expertise and one's ability to positively contribute to the evaluation and selection process. Any number of representatives may be asked to serve. The team may consist of any of the following:

- Procurement Services—Chair or Co-Chair
- User Department—Co-Chair or Chair
- Engineer/Architect
- Technical Experts and Industry Specialists
- Systems Developers, Programmers, and Operations Specialists
- Finance Officers or Accountants
- Internal Auditors
- Senior Manager
- Consultants representing public entity
- Others with experience in similar acquisitions

Potential team members should be thoroughly familiar with their roles and responsibilities on the Evaluation or Selection Committee and have the necessary qualifications and background to participate. They should be:

- knowledgeable in the area under consideration
- skilled at technical evaluation
- objective in the evaluation
- free of any conflict of interest and
- of high integrity and able to maintain confidentiality.

As the team is generally comprised of subject matter experts, participation by purchasing services is primarily administrative in nature. They are encouraged to manage the process while not impacting the decision.

Once the team has been formed, the purchasing agent should convene a meeting to identify the process and offer instructions relevant to roles, responsibilities, and requirements. For most entities, the composition of the team and acceptance of its recommendations is considered the responsibility of the purchasing agent. Committee members will need to be familiar with the process of evaluation scoring, response ranking, and how to apply the same objective criteria to each proposal.

It should be understood that discussions among team members during the evaluation process should not occur. In some jurisdictions, evaluation committee members are required to sign confidentiality disclosure statements prior to commencement of the evaluation process. The team will need to retain all evaluation documents, including worksheets, evaluation forms and notes, as the work on the project continues. These will be returned to the purchasing agent for future documentation or reference. This information can provide valuable support material if additional action is required from bidders not selected for final award.

During the evaluation process, should additional information or clarification be required, the purchasing agent will obtain and distribute the requested information to the entire team. Members are not to make contact with any of the bidders but must direct inquiries to the agent for resolution. If a site visit, demonstration, or further presentation is required, such events will need to be coordinated, established, and arranged through the purchasing agent.

In the event that the purchasing agent or chair has reason to believe that any member of the evaluation committee is participating in an inadequate or unacceptable manner, or if there appears to be bias or subjectivity of consideration, the team member can be removed from the evaluation committee.

Safeguarding Original Submittals and Duplication

The solicitation terms and conditions should specify the required number of copies to avoid duplication of documents needed for subsequent team review and evaluation. The request for additional copies ensures that complete information will be distributed to all involved parties and eliminate potential miscommunication on the part of the public entity. The original copy of all response submissions should always be retained in the purchasing department and used as the "master copy" for reference purposes. It is recommended that the solicitation document include a clause providing the public entity with the right to reproduce bids and proposals for internal purposes at the public entity's discretion.

As indicated previously, it is crucial to the integrity of the public procurement solicitation process that all submissions are handled in a consistent manner with due process. Bidders deserve the assurance that their response is submitted to a public entity that will receive, accept, store, and safeguard their submission until the specified date and time of opening. Sealed submissions must be stamped with the date and time immediately upon receipt by the public entity before being placed into safekeeping.

Response Evaluation Process

The evaluation process is designed to identify "best value" to the public entity when all factors and criteria are taken into consideration and to ensure that bidders are treated equitably through an open, fair, and competitive process. The internal client is instrumental in identifying the evaluation factors, criteria, and allocation of weights by category and establishing the points for each factor/criterion. These factors are reviewed prior to release of the solicitation document and ensure that no inadvertent favoritism exists toward a particular bidder. The response evaluation criteria will vary from acquisition to acquisition and by public entity based on the specific and unique considerations of each acquisition as well as the corporate culture of the public entity.

Evaluation Criteria

Solicitation documents should include the basis for evaluation and award of contract, particularly when issuing a Request for Proposal, a Request for Expression of Interest, and a

Request for Qualification. The solicitation document must state the evaluation categories, criteria, factors, weights, and values by category, criteria, or factor, and minimum acceptable score by category, where appropriate.

The evaluation criteria should be listed in order of relative importance. Although there is no mandatory requirement to include specific response values assigned to each identified factor or criteria within a solicitation document, it is of high value to the bidders, as they can respond in direct relationship to the weighting system and assigned points of the criterion. The response criteria should be agreed upon prior to the opening of responses and prior to the release and distribution to team members for review, evaluation, and recommendation.

Mandatory Evaluation Criteria

Certain solicitations may require bidders to meet mandatory response criteria. These mandatory aspects of compliance must be included in the solicitation document. These will vary by type of acquisition and public entity, depending on the specific requirements. Mandatory evaluation criteria reflect the factors and considerations that are essential to the requirement. Bidders must comply with these mandatory criteria. Words such as "must," "will," and "shall" are used to reflect the mandatory nature of each factor. Clauses containing mandatory language criteria must be clear and specific as to expectations of the bidder. It is the responsibility of the purchasing agent to ensure that the bidders can meet the conditions for compliance. Bidders must provide written evidence that they meet or exceed the mandatory evaluation criteria. Responses that do not meet each "mandatory" requirement must be excluded from the evaluation for award consideration.

Examples of criteria that may be deemed mandatory by a public entity include:

- performance considerations in fulfillment of deliverables
- levels of service and delivery reliability
- compliance with regulatory requirements
- compliance with security provisions of the public entities
- meeting minimal or specified knowledge, skills, and expertise of resources allocated to the specific acquisition and
- financial stability and status in the marketplace.

Such criteria will vary by public entity, as does the nature and amount of risk associated with each. For more specific examples of mandatory requirements refer to Appendix D. The public entity's purchasing agent may only change mandatory evaluation criteria prior to the stated closing time and date. Should changes be required to the terms, conditions, specifications, deliverables, scope of work, or evaluation criteria, these should be communicated to the marketplace in the same manner as the original solicitation through "addenda." It is the purchasing agent's responsibility to review all responses for compliance with the mandatory evaluation criteria, and only those responses that meet these provisions can be released to committee/team members for further evaluation for award.

Other Evaluation Criteria

Depending on the nature of the solicitation, one or more of the following criteria will also be mandated by the public entity for a response through the bidder's proposal. The public entity should ensure that this criterion is explained in detail in the bid solicitation document:

- **Price**: All elements of price and life cycle costs that will be taken into account during the evaluation process should be described. Bidders should use this information to develop their responses.

- **Compliance with Specifications**: The solicitation document should clarify how adherence to requirements will be established and how/what criteria will be applied. Since specifications are a fundamental part of an acquisition, bidders should know that compliance to a given specification criteria will impact the value of their response.

- **Value-Added Benefits**. If the public entity decides to recognize and consider factors other than price (quality, responsiveness, service, reliability), such criteria are deemed to be "value-added benefits." These should be clearly identified in the bid solicitation.

- **Quality**. The public entity should provide a definition of its expectations of perceived worth and value. The solicitation document should articulate the desired characteristics associated with the desired levels of an item's quality in regard to specifications, delivery, and installation.

- **Service**. The bid solicitation document should provide benchmarks and measurement parameters used by the public entity in determining service compliance. These should be enumerated to ensure compatibility with stated needs.

- **Reliability**. The public entity should identify the way it measures reliability.

- **Electronic Technology Utilization**. The bid solicitation document should explain the entity's requirements and expectations in the deployment of electronic technology. If demanded by the Scope of Work, this may include utilization of the Internet (www), Electronic Data Interchange (EDI), Electronic Funds Transfer (EFT), or an Enterprise Resources Planning (ERP) system.

- **Past Performance**. The public entity may choose to measure a bidder's previous operational record. Experience, knowledge, specialized skills and expertise, reputation in the industry, market share, and ranking in industry sectors may all be considered as valuable indicators. Such information allows purchasing officials to make better decisions about the future based on a responding firm's history. Electronic databases have been developed that allow suppliers to be evaluated by users, and the collated results are available for reference.

- **Facilities and Distribution**. The public entity may require bidders to have a local presence and/or warehousing or distribution facilities. Such requirements would enable timely request fulfillments. In this case, the bid solicitation document should indicate when and how these factors would be incorporated into the evaluation of responses.

- **Financial Stability**. If fiduciary strength and capacity is of value to the public entity, the bid solicitation document should point out the factors and criteria against which bidders will be measured and evaluated. These may include a firm's financial strength, holdings, and market values.

- **Innovation and Creativity**. If applicable to a solicitation, the document should describe the criteria that will be used to measure and evaluate a bidder's response in terms of their ability to offer pioneering and imaginative solutions to end results. Bidders should be required to demonstrate prior examples of how their innovation and creativity contributed to a superior result that proved to be beyond a normal supply arrangement.

Determining Responsiveness of Proposals to Agency Needs

After the purchasing agent has reviewed responses, all submissions should be evaluated in terms of adequacy and the quality of product or service offered in direct relationship to the scope of work, deliverables, and specifications.

When conducting the evaluations of responses, some guiding principles should be followed:

- Evaluations must be objective, not subjective, and criteria must be applied consistently and carried out in an honest and fair manner.

- The solicitation document's scope of work, deliverables, and supply fulfillment expectations should be evaluated in relation to each response with evaluation criteria, factors, weights, and points administered consistently.

- Team members should fully understand the goals and objectives of the solicitation, the internal client's needs and expectations, and be capable of applying the evaluation factors and criteria.

- The evaluations must be conducted in a manner that serves the best interests of the public entity, including community, resources, socioeconomic, and environmental issues.

- The evaluation process must be carried out on the basis of open and fair competition, without bias or subjectivity.

There are a number of methods which purchasing agents may deploy to determine responsiveness of submissions to a solicitation request and to evaluate these responses for contract award. These will only be identified and briefly described for reference purposes. They are covered in detail in another NIGP text, Developing and Managing RFPs in the Public Sector.

- **Competitive Sealed Bids**. Award is made on the basis of price to the lowest compliant bidder (most responsive and responsible), either in part (by line item) or in whole. No negotiations and no evaluations take place after closing date and time.

- **Competitive Sealed Proposals—(RFP), (REI) (RFI)**. Responses are fully evaluated on the basis of evaluation criteria, and awards are made on a "best-value" or "life-cycle costing" basis.

Variances in Bid Responses

Regardless of the method of solicitation, the evaluation methods are limited to either meeting mandatory requirements, implementing a weight and point rating system, or any combination of the two. While most solicitations receive an adequate number of responses, there are occasions when the public entity is confronted with variation exceptions that should be assessed during the evaluation phase. A few key variances are explained below:

- **One Response**. When only one bid or response is received by the public entity, the purchasing agent will need to consider the costs and time associated with re-sourcing the specific requirement. If it is determined that the award will be made to the sole respondent, the purchasing agent will need to be assured that "best value" is being obtained. If allowable, competitive negotiations should take place with the sole respondent. A limited number of responses may also indicate that the announced specifications were too restrictive, mitigating a competitive solicitation or, possibly, that the item is controlled by the manufacturer or distributor through a geographic or territorial dealer network. It is the responsibility of the purchasing agent to determine the reason for the limited number of responses before acting accordingly.

- **Alternate Item Response**. If a bidder offers an alternate product that exceeds the specifications but is of equal or lower cost, the purchasing agent can make the award on the basis of the increased value-added benefits. It is a good practice to allow for alternates within a solicitation document, as they may enable the public entity to consider another product deemed to be equal or exceed the product specified, often at a lower cost. The bidders may offer alternates that normally would not have been known or considered by the purchasing agent. Regardless of how restrictive the sourcing document is in terms of consideration of alternatives, the purchasing agent should evaluate and consider alternates to ensure that bidders are treated in an equitable manner and with impartiality.

- **Tied or Identical Responses**. Occasionally, a purchasing agent will receive an identical or tie response submission from several bidders or proponents. These may be coincidental or may, in fact, be an attempt at collusion. If the purchasing agent has reason to believe that the bidders are in collusion with one another, all responses may be rejected, and one of several courses of action may be taken.

In most cases, public entities have established regulations on how tie bids should be handled based on workplace certifications, geographic location, past experience, etc. Purchasing professionals should consult with their legal department on the development of a regulation regarding tie bids, if one is not in place.

- **Lump Sum Response**. "Lump sum" or "lot" pricing responses are frequently received for construction solicitations, incorporating all elements of the total cost of the project into one value. Lump sum or lot submissions offer an advantage to the purchasing agent because there is no need to evaluate the various elements of cost. The purchasing agent is at a disadvantage, however, because they are unable to compose the line item costs of each of the responses to determine any areas of lost opportunity. For example, a construction solicitation for a Construction Manager at Risk receives three responses. The electrical component of the lowest response is more than twice the value of the electrical components quoted by the two higher bidders. Without a line item breakdown, the purchasing agent is unable to discern the details and may lose all opportunities to clarify or negotiate on the electrical portion of the contract with the low bidder.

  ...the purchasing agent should evaluate and consider alternates to ensure that bidders are treated in an equitable manner and with impartiality.

- **Low Total Response**. Often, public entities issue solicitations for a group of products that have some commonality, such as stationery and office supplies, janitorial products and supplies, or hardware. Solicitation documents may include terms and conditions that allow the public entity to award in the aggregate (all items), by group, or by line item in its best interest.

This type of award strategy has both advantages and disadvantages. It reduces the administrative costs in analyzing individual line item values and awarding multi contracts. However, by awarding in whole, the public entity may lose the advantage of achieving reduced costs on specific line items. The purchasing agent must weigh the benefits. Some questions to consider when making a "low total" award might be:

Does the bidder supply all items?

With consolidation of all items into one contract, is there opportunity for volume pricing or discounting?

Is there a requirement for compatibility due to the proprietary nature of the item being acquired?

- **"All or None" Responses**. It is not customary for a public entity to issue a solicitation request that includes the phrase "all or none" in its terms or conditions. A bidder responding with a submission that includes an "all or none" offer may fundamentally change the solicitation request and may be deemed a conditional bid and non-responsive based on the jurisdiction's statutes. If it is the intention of the public entity and purchasing agent to award by line item to several bidders or proponents, the terms and conditions by which this will be done should be spelled out in the solicitation document. However, if the solicitation document offers flexibility to the public entity in its method of award, the entity should assess the advantages and disadvantages of awarding the entire contract to a single supplier who requires "all or none," taking into consideration the same analysis suggested for "Low Total Response."

Minor Informalities and Irregularities

In solicitation document preparation, the purchasing agent and user department may not always anticipate every aspect of the requirements definition or content of every response from every bidder. The sourcing document should make provision for the public entity to have adequate discretion in the receipt, evaluation, recommendation, and award decision to account for minor informalities and irregularities. Caution must be used to not inadvertently waive any irregularities that may create an unfair advantage to another bidder. Irregularities may be waived under rare circumstances, for example:

- There is no material variation from the original requirements definition, specifications, scope of work, or deliverable.

- The variation, as noted above, has no impact on quality, delivery, quantity, performance, price, or the bidder's ability to comply with the fulfillment conditions.

- The variation would not restrict or impact the open, fair, and competitive nature of the acquisition.

- The waiver is in the best interest of the agency.

The following are offered as examples of minor irregularities that may be waived by an agency:

- Failure to sign all sections of a response submission, when it is clear from the documentation submitted in the response that the bidder intended to submit the response and that not executing or signing all the stipulated sections of the response was an oversight by the bidder. For example, the bidder's agent may have signed the bid proposal form but failed to sign one of the required affidavits.

- Failure to submit certain required documents or forms regarding the bidder's qualifications or ability to perform. Such documents may be financial statements or execution of non-collusion affidavits that can be submitted prior to award of the contract.

- Failure to submit an executed acknowledgement of receipt of addenda form. As long as the bidder materially complies with all aspects of the scope of work and deliverables, the return of this form is immaterial in the firm's ability to perform.

- Failure to provide an adequate descriptive catalog or brochure for the products being acquired.

- Failure to return the number of executed response submissions.

- Failure to return response submissions to the specified location, but received on time at the official location through secondary delivery (mail room delivery service).

Should the bidder provide sufficient evidence within their response submission that it will comply with all mandatory terms and conditions prior to award of contract, the public entity is able to waive these minor irregularities.

Handling Confidential and Proprietary Information

Each public sector entity has established legislation, regulations, bylaws, ordinances, and policy governing the handling of confidential and proprietary information. Generally, there is consistency in the language, meaning, and intent of this legislation throughout the public sector. Federal, state or provincial legislation and regulations generally cover requirements for handling confidential and proprietary information within their respective jurisdictions. The public purchasing professional must be aware of these regulations and know how to apply them to both the solicitation and evaluation processes.

There is no common statutory or regulatory requirement that a purchasing agent must inform all unsuccessful bidders of the prices and fulfillment conditions. If prices are requested by unsuccessful bidders or proponents, the owner is required to provide same or comply with the respective jurisdictions Freedom of Information (FOI) provisions. However, many public entities post the name of the firm awarded the contract and the contract value on their Websites or telephone message centers. Any information that is deemed confidential by a public entity should be labeled accordingly in the solicitation document. Any information that is received by a purchasing agent that is labeled "proprietary" should not be disclosed to any third party, particularly a competitive bidder. In all cases, prior to the release or disclosure of any information, careful consideration should be given to the effect and impact the disclosure will have on all parties. Again, public statutes determine these parameters, and purchasing officials are strongly encouraged to seek counsel from their legal departments on this issue.

Evaluation of Payment Terms Offered

Payment terms of a public entity are normally established by the Finance Department, and any variation in the payment of invoices should be cleared with the appropriate official prior to exercising or considering the payment discount in the award decision. However, the purchasing agent should be cognizant of the payment terms included in a bidder's response, as they may affect the ranking of a particular response. The public entity usually specifies their payment terms within the solicitation document and, typically, on the actual purchase order or agreement form. Payment terms are negotiable, and there must be agreement as to the specific terms of payment. When clarifying the payment terms, the word "net" without the inclusion of an exact number of days could cause misinterpretation between the purchaser and seller and, therefore, should be avoided.

Documentation and Certification

Bidders are often required to submit specific documents as "mandatory." When reviewing and evaluating response submissions, the purchasing agents should have and maintain a checklist of the required documents and certificates, licenses, letters of compliance, etc. Failure to provide the mandatory documents and certificates listed in the solicitation document would lead to disqualification of the solicitation if the penalty for non-compliance is specified in the solicitation document (i.e., non-responsive and ineligible for award).

Bid proposals that include all specific documents and certificates would be deemed compliant, and the respective submission should be retained in the Master RFP/Bid file. Key documents required to accompany submissions may include:

- Bid Proposal Form or Response Submission Form
- Addenda Acknowledgement
- Executed Confidentiality Agreement
- Executed Statement of Non-Collusion and Affidavit
- Pricing and Costing Form
- Project Implementation Plan
- Financial Capability Certificate, by surety firm
- Equipment Availability Certificate
- Personnel Qualification Certificate
- Corporate Profile
- Subcontractor Schedule and Certificate
- Conflict of Interest Statement
- Drawings or Plans, where applicable
- Bid Bond or Surety
- Material and Labor Board Certificates
- Workers' Compensation Bond Coverage Letter

- Occupational Safety and Health Compliance Certificate
- Insurance Policy and Certificate Forms
- Confidentiality and Protection of Privacy Form
- Brochures, Catalogs, Illustrations, Operating and Reference Manuals
- Permits and Licenses

Site Visits and Demonstrations

During the review and recommendation stages of a response, there may be a need to conduct a site visit, observe demonstrations of equipment, conduct product or equipment trials, observe work-in-progress, or perform laboratory testing. Acquisitions involving infrastructure or capital construction may require bidders to visit the public entity to observe site conditions. Ethically, most public agencies should pay the expenses incurred by their staff to conduct a site evaluation. The air of impartiality and fairness should always be tantamount to unbiased evaluations. Whatever the circumstances, the public entity should clearly detail within the solicitation document the nature and extent of the obligations of the bidder relative to site visits, demonstrations, product or equipment trials, observe work-in-progress, and any other certification or validation protocols.

Samples, Tests and Inspections

The solicitation document may make adequate provisions requiring a bidder to supply samples for testing or on a trial basis at no cost, liability, or obligation to the public entity. It is expected that the bidder cover the cost of samples in order to prove compliance. It should be noted that, in some situations, a public entity might agree to cover the costs of production of the samples or prototypes to ensure that the bidder will produce a better quality example. It is important to document the adequacy and performance of product sample test results at the various stages of testing.

Samples offered by current or potential suppliers for any reason other than testing should be discouraged. The public entity may provide samples or examples of the needed products to ensure that they can replicate or produce a comparable product as in fabric or seating design. In these instances, the bidder may be asked to produce a sample product for testing and evaluation against the sample provided. Testing and inspection may take place prior to commitment and award of a contract, or post award during the work as it progresses.

Determining the Best Value Bid

Critical to the selection of the response offering the "best value" is the necessity for the internal client and purchasing agent to clearly understand the requirements of the solicitation. Best Value is described In the NIGP Public Procurement Dictionary of Terms as

> An assessment of the return which can be achieved based on the total life cycle cost of the item; may include an analysis of the functionality of the item; can use cost/benefit analysis to define the best combinations of quality, services, time, and cost considerations over the useful life of the acquired item. A procurement method that emphasizes value over price. The best value might not be the lowest cost. Generally achieved through the Request for Proposal (RFP) method. (NIGP, 2007).

The fundamental difference in making an award based on "low bid" versus "best value" response lies in the method of solicitation. Awards are made on the basis of "low bid" when using an IFB, ITT, or RFQ. The bidder submits a response based on the specifications, and the award is made to the bidder who complies and has submitted the lowest price. Best value awards are made on the basis of a comprehensive evaluation and analysis of the criteria within the solicitation document and applied independently to each submission. Best value evaluation methodology is deployed for RFPs, REIs, and RFIs. Any of these may achieve the same result; however, the appropriate approach and method of evaluation must be applied based on the type of acquisition.

The selection of which "best value" methodology to apply may differ with each solicitation. Best value selection may be based on:

- highest ranked, based on application of specified criteria
- highest ranked within budget
- lowest cost per point or
- lowest price response.

The bidder receiving the highest point total for technical merit followed by price is typically awarded the contract. Usually, full marks (price category) are awarded to the response with the lowest price with all others proportionally rated. This may mean that a premium price is paid for a marginally better response, thus, increasing the risk associated with the decision. If the submitted technical and price components can be divided into price groups, the lowest cost per point should be the price/point. Award is usually made to the bidder who has submitted the lowest cost per point comparable values.

Negotiations

Depending on the public entity's procurement regulations, negotiations may take place during the review, evaluation, and recommendation stages of the procurement cycle. While negotiations are uncommon in bid solicitations, they are more widely permitted in RFPs. If allowed, the purchasing agent should prepare a checklist of issues and points appropriate for negotiation that can be addressed in a session between the bidder and the public entity. Negotiation sessions require sophisticated skills and strategic thinking to achieve desired results. Extensive preparation prior to the session will increase the public entity's position. Every negotiating team should:

- know and understand the opponent
- be comprised of those who have product-appropriate skill and expertise, i.e., technology, finances and investments, manufacturing, service and maintenance, etc.
- determine in advance their final objective
- know what their opponent considers as a final objective
- determine final acceptable price and
- establish a lead negotiator.

Understanding from the outset that negotiations do not allow for one side to meet every expectation, each side must be willing to compromise. It is important to keep the negotiation session focused and on track. Copious notes should be kept on every issue discussed and its final agreement. Sessions should be summarized and confirmed prior to conclusion. These notes should also be stored in the contracts file for future reference. Individuals involved in extensive negotiations should consider further training to increase their effectiveness.

Best and Final Offer (BAFO)

Prior to award recommendations, the public entity may determine that the "best in market," "best of breed," or "best value" offer has not been achieved. At this stage, the public entity may request the bidder to make a "best and final" offer, if allowable per the entity's statutes and regulations. Typically, best and final offers are not allowed with formal bid solicitations but may be acceptable under the RFP process in those instances where negotiation is allowed. If permitted, a fixed date and time should be established to receive the best and final offer. Should the bidder fail to submit an amended response, the preliminary response is considered its best and final response.

Contract Award

Upon conclusion of the evaluation, the public entity will customarily award a contract and issue an agreement. The nature and type of acquisition and the degree of risk, the value of the contract as well as the term (length of agreement) will determine the type of agreement the public entity will deploy.

The elements of contract execution and administration are fairly rigorous and complex based on the type of purchases. NIGP has produced a separate text, *Contract Administration*, 2nd edition (NIGP, 2007) which can be referenced by the public purchasing official for more specific details of the Contract Administration process. This chapter, therefore, will address a limited number of issues leading to contract award and execution.

A contract is awarded when the purchaser/public entity/agency formally informs or advises the successful bidder or proponent that it has accepted their bid, quotation, proposal, or tender. There is a common belief that once a contract is awarded and a form of agreement issued, the purchasing agents and their respective public entities have completed their work and are no longer involved. In most public entities, this is not the case.

Often, the purchasing agent will be involved with the many aspects of "contract management" involving deliveries, delays, quality assurance, price changes, extension, conflict and dispute resolution, performance, payment, warranty, and removal and disposal. Throughout the fulfillment process, the purchasing agent and support resources will continue to be involved and will be called upon to prepare and maintain documentation on all aspects of the contract fulfillment as well as to provide the required advice and direction relative to past, current, and future acquisition.

Purchasing agents and their respective support public entities are expected to collaborate and consult with internal clients on needs, expectations, and performance in addition to manage relationships with manufacturers, distributors, wholesalers, suppliers, and independent consultants or contractors. They form a link to their counterparts within the various levels of government, professional purchasing associations or cooperative procurement groups, and with industry or regulatory associations.

Award Recommendation and Approval

Specific requirements and expectations are identified in the evaluation and award recommendation stage of the solicitation process. The authority and approval for the award of a contract will depend on the spending limits and signing authority granted through a public entity's policy framework. Regardless of the hierarchy established for award approval and agreement execution, once a "recommendation for award" is issued, accepted, and approved by the appropriate authorities, it may be executed by anyone who has been delegated that authority and responsibility. The specific approvals and authority to sign/execute agreements will vary from one public entity to another and will be dependent on the corporate culture and operating practices of each respective public entity.

When considering an award...the internal client's review acceptance and approval should always be secured prior to award.

User Sign-off

Prior to an award, the internal client (user) should be given the opportunity to acknowledge and accept the recommendation of the team. In situations where the product and/or services are as specified by brand, make or model, user sign-off is not essential because the conditions of "Law of Agency" will have been met. However, any variations from what was specified within the solicitation document require sign-off consensus and initialization. When considering an award as a result of an RFP, REI or RFQ, the internal client's review acceptance and approval should always be secured prior to award.

Finance Office/Funding

During the evaluation process, there may be a need to obtain financial or funding approval. This approval process should be conducted after the technical evaluation but prior to the recommendation for approval. Some public entities require that an acquisition for more than a specified dollar amount be forwarded to and approved by a Finance Committee and/or an allocation of funds. This additional approval is particularly common for infrastructure, capital, or long-term commitment type contracts. Others require rigorous policy, procedures, and processes to be instituted that ensure all involved parties are able to review the decision, examine the funding sources, and assure that the responsible parties have complied with the principles and obligations under consideration.

Executive Level and Governing Body Approval

Large dollar acquisitions, high risk or environmentally, politically, or economically sensitive acquisitions often require executive level approval. The award recommendation is forwarded to the Executive Officer for final decision, who may, in turn, direct the acquisition to higher levels (board, cabinet, council, etc.) for required approval and agreement execution.

The laws, ordinances, and policies of many public entities require that the governing body make the final decision for award. In those cases where research funds are allocated on a cost-sharing basis, approval of the respective funding agencies is required prior to the commitment of funds. Contracts by the public entity cannot be entered into and executed until such time as a formal approval is granted. Often, the financial or funding support of one funding public entity is dependent on another.

Award Notification

Once all required reviews, approvals, internal consultation and collaboration have been completed, a formal award, including notification to the bidder, can be made. A successful bidder should be notified in writing, and the contact should follow with a formal purchase order or agreement. Notifications to unsuccessful bidders may be done through formal written communication, telephone, email or fax, or by posting the winning response submission electronically on a Bid Notification Board or by using a telephone service having a dedicated number for bid notification.

There is no mandatory requirement to notify the unsuccessful bidder, but it is considered to be a common courtesy. Some unsuccessful bidders wish to be informed of a specific solicitation result, status, or evaluation ranking. The public entity should willingly provide this information to ensure that the decision was based on an equitable evaluation. Unsuccessful bidders may be told:

- scores (total)
- winning bidder
- term of contract and
- ranking by category
- winning bidder total score
- value of contract.

A requested or required debriefing session with a bidder supports the public entity's efforts to work in an open and fair environment indicating good faith and enabling the bidder to learn more about the process for subsequent response submissions. The purchasing agent along with the internal client representative can discuss the bidder's strengths, weaknesses, and merits without reference to other offers. The references should be in direct relationship to the terms, conditions, deliverables, specification, and criteria within the sourcing document.

On occasion, an award will not result in a solicitation, or the solicitation may be cancelled because of program changes, changes in organizational priorities, funding withdrawal, or changes in the project requirements. In these instances, all bidders should be informed immediately in writing as to the cancellation or deferral, any reasons for the action, and any expectation to reissue the solicitation. If the date for acceptance and award must be extended beyond the standard acceptance period (typically sixty (60) days), all bidders should be informed in writing. The public entity may be required to issue addenda to validate pricing or delivery.

References

National Institute of Governmental Purchasing, Inc. (NIGP) (2007). *Contract administration* (2nd ed.). Herndon, VA: NIGP.

National Institute of Governmental Purchasing, Inc. (NIGP) (2007). *Developing and managing requests for proposals in the public sector* (2nd ed.). Herndon, VA: NIGP.

National Institute of Governmental Purchasing, Inc. (NIGP) (2007). *Public procurement dictionary of terms.* Herndon, VA: NIGP.

Chapter 12

In Conclusion: Putting it All Together

Sourcing in the public sector takes numerous formats and involves billions of dollars annually. The ability of procurement officials to handle these functions effectively can make a dramatic difference in the public's perception of the professionalism and integrity of governmental processes. Procurements gone awry have become the hallmark stereotype of inefficiency in government. The procurement community must establish sound policies and procedures for determining the best sourcing strategies and techniques by developing guidelines for conduct in each stage of the sourcing process, always keeping in mind the essential goals of the public procurement process.

The Value of Competition

Competition is one of the most important aspects in the public sourcing environment. Fair and open competition is one of the basic tenets for acquiring goods and services in the public sector. Procurement officers should be mindful of the fiduciary responsibility their positions carry, as well as the public scrutiny placed on those that expend tax dollars. More often than not, the sourcing strategy selected can dictate the resulting level of competition. Fostering competition means that procurement public entities need to promote solicitations that encourage competition by using specifications that are not unduly restrictive, open lines of communication between suppliers and public entities, and seek out prospective suppliers to increase source lists. A competitive procurement legally binds the public entity to:

- Fully disclose all known information about public organizational needs which influences the respondents' pricing strategy.
- Award a contract based on information in the sourcing document.
- Treat all respondents equitably through all stages of the sourcing process.

- Avoid bias and conflict of interest between respondents and the evaluation team.
- Employ procurement professionals who act in good faith as representatives of the public entity and represent the interests of the taxpayer.
- Reject proposals that are non-responsive.

With the elimination of the elements and guidelines that structure competitive procurements, none of the legally binding obligations of fair trade would apply, and public officials would be free to make whatever lawful deal they might be able to negotiate. Such actions could encourage decisions that would promote abuse of the system and supplier favoritism. While these actions may be lawful, the perception of favoritism would exist if the same supplier received all of the government's business.

Barriers to Competition

Despite the rules and regulations requiring fair and open competition, there are still several barriers facing public entities that prevent them from fully complying with the mandate to competitively source most acquisitions. Inadequacy in market research, pre-selection of suppliers, lack of planning, and unauthorized commitments are just a few of the hurdles that must be overcome in the public sector. A market survey conducted prior to developing functional or technical requirements is essential. Too often, agency personnel create their requirements from product literature provided by the vendor community. Without adequately conducting some level of independent market analysis, the agency may be unaware of additional sources that could be approached resulting in a better value for their entity. As a result, public entities often solicit a pre-determined solution without fully exploring their options. Increased market research will improve the agency's efforts to increase competition, resulting in more efficient expenditures of tax dollars. NIGP's (2004) book, *Planning, Scheduling, and Requirements Analysis*, provides a detailed assessment of this critical process and its positive impact on stimulating competition.

While communication with suppliers is an important way to gather initial information about product and service availability, outreach to many suppliers will serve to create greater competition, especially among target markets. Resistance to competition stems from the desire to work with a familiar supplier. While certain benefits may result from established relationships, long-term partnerships often become supplier monopolies and, consequently, impact an agency's ability to continue to receive the best and lowest cost for goods and services. A balance must be struck between long-term relationships and new supplier development that continues to foster competition.

Unnecessary "emergency" procurements result in little or no competition and cause the public sector, and ultimately the taxpayer, to pay higher prices for goods and services simply because of inadequate pre-planning. Done with careful attention to planning and forecasting, the procurement process can proceed through its various stages with little or no detraction from critical functions. While some acquisitions are truly an emergency and cannot be planned in advance, many acquisitions that are deemed urgent due to lack of planning could actually have been acquired competitively and, thus, eliminated the potential for poor procurement practices and potential higher costs.

Unauthorized commitments are another barrier to effective competition. While only a duly authorized contracting officer can obligate a public entity, many public officials informally make obligations to suppliers in advance of a solicitation or approved purchase order. These obligations put the public entity at risk for protest should a competitive solicitation be performed or purchase be denied due to funding. If the supplier who had an informal understanding actually was awarded the bid, the public entity is vulnerable to accusations of collusion at worst and favoritism at best. Educating the public entity with respect to appropriate and inappropriate supplier relationships and the importance of ethical behavior at all times may begin to break down this barrier.

The Future of Sourcing in the Public Sector

The field of public procurement is rapidly changing, and the need for public procurement officers to be better prepared to meet the challenges has never been greater. This current environment is a result of:

- a rapidly changing diverse marketplace
- global outreach and expansion
- fewer resources and downsizing in public entities
- more demands and expectations for better service by consumers of public services and
- technological innovation and opportunities.

In order to be able to handle these demands, public procurement officials need to expand their traditional roles and begin to consider themselves as consultants, strategic planners, and technical advisors to programmatic agency organizations that can help in forecasting agency sourcing needs. Procurement officials need to understand the underlying philosophy behind public sector sourcing in order to provide guidance for developing future procurement policies and regulations, and they need to continue to explore ways of meeting the needs of the agency through innovation.

Evaluating the use of new technology to enhance the sourcing process and provide even more efficient and effective strategies is still on the horizon, and will become the answer to stretching the public dollar to its maximum extent. Due to the dynamic nature of technology, it is vital that public procurement officials remain current on the value and limitations of technology in order to make the most prudent decisions on implementation. The following presents an overview of the positive impacts of technology on the profession.

Electronic Sourcing (eSourcing)

Many public entities utilize eSourcing with varying degrees or levels of implementation, including the following:

- A public entity may post solicitations on an electronic bid board or their own Website or portal. All other actions are handled in a conventional manner.
- A public entity may post solicitations electronically but accept faxes and conventional responses.
- An agency may use a third-party company to advertise its sourcing needs. Advantages of this type of service include statistical tracking of information on notifications, bidders, MWBE participation in the solicitation process, as well as the ability to reach a wider audience.

eCommerce and eProcurement technology have made significant improvements in turn-around and fulfillment roles, process and cost reduction, and service improvements. However, security issues continue to exist related to access to bid/proposal information, inclusion of targeted businesses, unsuspecting viruses, potential loss of information, and unauthorized use or sale of a public entity's information and data. There is continual progress in the field of security including improved firewalls and various security installations.

Impact of the Internet on Procurement

Advancements in Internet technology have made a significant impact on a public entity's ability to acquire products and services more effectively and efficiently. Virtually every public sector public entity is engaged in some form of eProcurement. Not only do users obtain products and services in a timely manner, they have the independence of making the acquisition on their own when they want to. This delegation of authority translates into a reduction in administrative costs for hard copy purchase orders, requisitions, checks, envelopes, and postage. Further efficiencies are anticipated in the area of human resources with staff taking on a greater role in front-line procurement activities rather than non-essential process activities and issues.

Electronic Bid Boards and Bid Notification

Using electronic bid boards to post solicitation notices and asset disposals has become easier to access and use over the past decade, and agencies have become more accepting of their use in spite of political ramifications. Government has traditionally played an active role in support of the local economy, and sourcing through the Internet adds a dimension of competition not previously anticipated by elected officials' constituents. While this technology poses fewer security risks and has become more cost-effective, it creates the need for further detail, explanation, and/or justification of purchase awards should a non-local supplier be selected for award. Potential bidders can now access solicitation opportunities from agencies or service providers to participate in a solicitation competition for a nominal fee. In the past, and in some current operations, a master bidder list is still employed as the tool for the distribution of solicitation opportunities. Electronic bid boards are now used to post all types of solicitation and can also be an efficient and effective tool to accommodate reverse auctions as well as facilitate the informal quotation process.

Third-Party Electronic Sourcing

Solicitation and disposal opportunities can be posted on any of number of services. The supplier pays for subscribing to the service, as well as downloading documents. The public entity posting a solicitation is not typically assessed a fee. Suppliers can choose to access the information in the manner most appropriate to their needs.

Final Thoughts

As public agencies engage in the sourcing function in order to save significant public dollars and resources, professionals should remember that a successful procurement is one which:

- supports agency planning
- is driven by results desired
- looks for the best value alternative
- is performed in a timely manner
- minimizes the administrative burden
- expedites routine commodity purchases
- allows flexibility in developing procurement relationships
- encourages competition and
- encourages the participation of quality suppliers.

Resource

National Institute of Governmental Purchasing, Inc. (NIGP) (2004). *Planning, scheduling and requirement analysis.* Herndon, VA: NIGP.

Appendix A

Sample
Sole Source Procurement Request

Submit to: Purchasing Department

Description of Product/Service: _____

RQ Number: _____

Estimated amount of this purchase $ _____

Contract Period: _____

Department: _____ Contact Person: _____ Phone: _____

Due Date: _____ Work must be completed by: _____

Date Material/Equipment/Supplies must be delivered by: _____

Location: _____

Date Service must begin by: _____

Please provide the following information in order to document the sole source request (if $25,000 or more). If the purchase is under $25,000, this information should be placed on the notepad of the RQ.

1. Explain why the product/service requested is the only product/service that can satisfy your requirements, and explain why alternatives are unacceptable. Be specific with regard to specifications, features, characteristics, requirements, capabilities, and compatibility. Describe what steps have been undertaken to make this determination.

2. Explain why this service provider, supplier, or manufacturer is the only practicably available source from which to obtain this product or service, and describe the efforts that were made to verify and confirm whether, or not, this is so. (Obtain and include a letter from the manufacturer confirming claims made by distributors or exclusive distributorships regarding the product or service, if that is cited as a reason for this Sole Source.)

3. Will this purchase obligate us to a particular vendor for future purchases (either in terms of maintenance that only this vendor will be able to perform and/or if we purchase this item, will we need more "like" items in the future to match this one)?

4. Explain why the price for this product or service is considered to be fair and reasonable.

5. Describe the negotiation efforts, if any, that have been made with the supplier to obtain the best possible price.

6. Explain the consequence(s) to the county or public, including a dollar estimate of the financial impact, if this Sole Source is not approved.

I hereby request that a Sole Source be approved for the procurement of the above statement of work, material, equipment, commodity, or service.

_____

Signature   Name   Date

Appendix B

Sample
Directed Contract Procurement Request

Policy

Pursuant to the [Organization name] Purchasing Policy and Operational Procedures Guide:

- Where practical the [Organization name] shall invite quotations from qualified Suppliers for all supplies, equipment and/or services when the estimated cost is in excess of $2,500.00.
- Orders shall normally be awarded to the qualified Supplier offering the most effective life cycle cost (which includes cost, service, warranty, delivery, and support).

Purchasing Services may waive the competitive process and approve a Directed Purchase Award provided the requester can adequately support and document their request.

A Competition may be waived and an award directed to a specific supplier only when an analysis of the specifications and physical requirements determines that the products and/or service is manufactured or available through only one firm and distributed through a single dealer, supplier, or service provider. A Competition may be waived and an award directed to a specific supplier in the following circumstances:

1. **Sole Source** - only one qualified Supplier possesses the unique and singular available capability to meet the requirement of the solicitation, such as technical specifications or ability to deliver at a particular time.

2. **Single Source** - several qualified Suppliers possess the availability and capability to meet the solicitation requirements; however, only a single supplier is selected for an award of an Agreement through negotiation for the reason indicated on page two of this form.

   Note: Certain Procurements are subject to the provisions of NAFTA, AIT (Agreement on Internal Trade), and/or TILMA (Trade, Investment, and Labour Mobility Agreement) and therefore, in specific circumstances a Directed Contract may not be possible.

Process

Purchasing Services will review the reasonability of a sole/single source procurement based on the requester's investigation, evaluation and documentation of alternate sources of supply.

In order to satisfy the requirements of sole/single source award and waiving the requirements for competitive sourcing, the requester must show the inability to locate a similar or compatible product (or the rejection of similar product), is based solely on the product's failure to meet the requester's specific, necessary specifications and operational requirements.

In cases where an alternate Supplier for a similar product cannot be identified, the requester must document that a good faith effort has been made in seeking other sources.

Instructions

Page 2 of this document must accompany a Web Requisition or Purchase Requisition (WR or PR) when a directed contract is requested for products and/or services exceeding $2,500.00. Please include all Supplier quotations and other pertinent information with this form. Please complete the appropriate sections as listed on page 2.

The Directed Contract Request must be signed by the same account holder who signed the accompanying WR or PR. In some cases Purchasing Services may require the requester to obtain additional approval from a Department Head and/or Vice President.

A listing of the unique technical specifications required of the product and/or services and the potential companies that were contacted in the search for alternate sources is necessary. Purchasing may use this information in conducting its own market search.

Please submit with page 2 of this document any documentation, or quotes which support your request for Single/Sole source exemption.

This form must be supported by a Web Requisition or Purchase Requisition (WR or PR) when a Directed Contract review is requested for products and/or services exceeding $2,500.00. Please include all pertinent information to support your request for a review. The completed page 2 may be completed printed and mailed, or completed and e-mailed.

Requestor Information

Department: _____ Phone Number: _____

Requestor Name: _____ E-mail Address _____

Fax Number: _____

Requested Supplier Information

Company: _____ Phone Number: _____

Address: _____ Contact Name: _____

City: _____ E-mail Address: _____

State/Province: _____ Quote Number: _____

Country: _____ Zip/Postal Code: _____

Product or Service Description:

>

Request Justification for Directed Purchase Request:

(Complete A. and B. below)

A. The requested Product or Service is:

☐ An integral repair part or accessory compatible with existing equipment (alternative may void manufacturer's warranty).

☐ A unique design and/or has performance specifications which are essential to my research protocol or other administrative needs and are not available in an alternate and comparable product and/or service provider.

☐ Essential in maintaining experimental or administrative continuity.

☐ One with which I (or my staff) have specialized training and/or extensive experience. Retraining would incur substantial cost and/or time and will not result in the most effective life-cycle net cost.

☐ Urgently required on an emergency basis (e.g. life/death, health, safety, critical equipment or facility break-down)

B. Provide any further information to assist Purchasing Services in assessing your Directed Contract request.

>

Alternative Supplier Information

(quotes may required upon request)

Company 2:	_____	Contact Name:	_____
Phone Number:	_____	E-mail:	_____
Country:	_____	State/province:	_____
Company 2:	_____	Contact Name:	_____
Phone Number:	_____	E-mail:	_____
Country:	_____	State/province:	_____

_____

Authorized Signature: (Must be signed by same person who signed associated WR or PR)

_____

Requestor/Principal Investigator   Date

Appendix C

Sample
Notice Of Intent

REFERENCE NUMBER [_____]
ISSUED: [DATE]
[DESCRIPTION OF PRODUCT AND/OR SERVICE]

Notice is hereby given by the [Organization name] of the intent to renegotiate the [Organization name] [Describe concisely the type of products and services. with [Supplier Name] on an all-inclusive (total portfolio) basis.

The Agreement(s) for various categories of services being provided has a current gross annual value of approximately [$ value]. The new contract is expected to cover a period of [Number] of years to [End Date of Agreement].

The [Organization]'s [Description of Product and/or Service] program contains a multitude of business applications and functions and logistically complex and decentralized. It must be reliable, consistent with and accommodate new technology, and be flexible. [Supplier Name] have demonstrated their commitment to quality, expertise in providing [Description of Product and/or Service] to the University, and are customer service focused. [Supplier Name] provide dedicated on-site service technicians, marketing specialists, and operational, account, and senior management in support of the [Organization's] [Description of Product and/or Service] program.

Firms wishing to submit a written response showing that they are capable of meeting this requirement must do so by FAX to the Manager, Purchasing Services Department at (___) [___-____], no later than 2:00:00 p.m. Pacific Time on [Date]. Your written objections must provide substantive evidence that clearly demonstrates that your products and services are capable of fulfilling the [Organization's] requirements. Responses received after the closing date and time will not be considered. If justified, a Proponent's meeting, with [Organization] representatives present, will be convened to receive Proponent representations regarding this intended Agreement.

The [Organization] will evaluate all submissions based on the following criteria; and, in the event that it receives one or more letters of objection that state compelling reasons for initiating a competitive process, the [Organization] may issue a Request for Proposal.

Criteria that letters of objection will be reviewed against are:

- Fees, costs, and financing structure
- Delivery as per *[Organization]'s* schedule and requirements

- Customer Relationship Management support
- Management Reporting
- Experience in the Marketplace
- Ability to provide complete portfolio of business activities and functions
- Local servicing and corporate offices
- Value-added services and contributions

Appendix D

Levels of Mandatory Requirements
(University of Victoria)

The following criteria and conditions MUST be met in order for a Proponent to become successful in obtaining an award. The mandatory requirements will be considered during evaluation of each proponent's proposal in accordance with the following categories:

LEVEL 1 MANDATORY REQUIREMENTS:

Following are requirements and conditions that **MUST** be met at the time of solicitation closing date and time. Only those proposals which meet **ALL Level 1 Mandatory Requirements** and conditions listed below at the time of closing will be evaluated further. If a proponent fails to meet **ANY of the level 1 Mandatory Requirements** specified in the solicitation, the University will reject that proposal without further evaluation.

Item #	Requirement Description	RFP Section Reference #	Compliance		Authorized Person's Initials	Comments
			Yes	No		
1	Receipt of Proposal by closing date and time					
2	Licensed/Registered to do business in British Columbia (where required)					
3	Signature of Authorized Company Official (Electronic Signatures Accepted)					
4	Enclosure of all specified documents unless specifically "excepted" by other clauses within the Solicitation.					
5	Follow and Comply with Solicitation Format explicitly (Form and Content - where specified)					
6	Submissions and documentation must be in English					
7	Mandatory Technical Specifications have been met.					
8	Sections of Proposals initialed/ signed where required.					
9	Proposal Response MUST not contain Copyrights for any portions of the Proposal Submission					

Level 2 Mandatory Requirements:

Only those Proposals which meet the mandatory requirements and conditions in Section 3.2 will be eligible for consideration of an award (Refer to Section 7.31–Variance to Terms and Conditions Clauses). The following requirements and conditions are to be met during evaluation and prior to the commencement of negotiations, and/or award of contract:

Item #	Requirement Description	RFP Section Reference #	Compliance Yes	No	Authorized Person's Initials	Comments
1	References (at least three, preferable from a Canadian Higher Education Institution)					
2	Proof of no OHS Infractions for the past one year					
3	Registered and in good standing with WCB					
4	Agree to comply with [Organization] Conflict of Interest Clause.					
5	Agreement to [Organization] Errors and Omissions Policy					
6	Agree to comply with [Organization] Confidentiality and Non-Disclosure Agreement (Protection of Privacy)					
7	Agreement to [Organization] Indemnity, Liability, and Insurance Requirements					
8	Agreement to [Organization] Ownership and Intellectual Property Policy					
9	Agreement to [Organization] Access to Records and Financial documents for audit purposes					
10	Agreement to comply with [Organization] Statement of Non-Collusion requirements					
11	Social Responsibility – Agreement to participate in, and comply with [Organization's] Sustainability provisions, including [Organization's] e-Waste Program.					
12	Agree to comply with [Organization's] Workplace and Personal Harassment Policy and Guidelines					
13	Provide Copies of Proposals as Specified within the Solicitation					
14	Enclose current and up-to-date Corporate Profile					

PROPOSAL SIGNING

The Solicitation Submission Form (Appendix -) MUST be completed and executed by a principal duly authorized to bind contracts on behalf of the Proponent.

The Proponent's legal name and the capacity in which the signing officer acts shall be against the signature.

Proposal Submission forms (Appendix -) that do not contain an authorized signature will be deemed "non-compliant and non-responsive" and will not be accepted for evaluation. [*Organization name*] will accept electronic signatures pursuant to Section 11 of the Electronic Transaction Act.

Appendix E

Purchasing Services Strategic Objectives and Stewardship Considerations

Purchasing organizations are usually covered by their Organization's Strategic Plan, Mission Statement and core Goals and Objectives. To be consistent with these principles, a purchasing organization strategic plan also should incorporate values and beliefs that are consistent with the organization's Strategic Plan. Following are several Purchasing Services strategic objectives and stewardship considerations for one public sector organization:

PURCHASING OBJECTIVES:

To develop a framework of measurable practices that balance economic priorities with environmental, ethical and social values and considerations, through campus operations, community, and individuals.

Action: Develop ethical procurement practices for the acquisition of all products, services, technology, and construction required by the [Organization].

Action: Encourage environmentally friendly practices within the campus community with our suppliers, and the community at large.

Action: Encourage our respective organizations, others, and the general supply community to be proactive in examining and implementing environmentally responsible opportunities. For example, Park and Ride; Refundable Beverage Container Return Program; e-Waste.

Action: Respect our customers, employees, and suppliers.

Action: Treat our suppliers, employees, and customers with dignity and fairness.

Action: Avoid complicity in human or employment rights discrimination within the supply community.

Action: Promote a safe environment by continuous deployment of procurement workplace safety practices throughout the organization.

Action: Proactively promote and develop socially diverse suppliers and internal users.

Action: Apply and promote sound financial standards, practices, and behaviors to ensure transparency and fairness.

Action: Conduct audits to determine and improve social responsibility impacts.

Action: Develop a social responsibility and sustainability plan that integrates campus planning, infrastructure development, procurement, and technology deployment in all aspects of operational analysis.

Action: Attain best value over the life cycle of an acquisition that leverages environmental, social and ethical considerations.

Action: Collaborate with other organizations, public sector agencies, suppliers, and the business community to advance sustainable procurement practices.

Appendix F

NIGP Code Of Ethics

The Institute believes, and it is a condition of membership, that the following ethical principles should govern the conduct of every person employed by a public sector procurement or materials management organization.

- Seeks or accepts a position as head or employee only when fully in accord with the professional principles applicable thereto and when confident of possessing the qualifications to serve under those principles to the advantage of the employing organization.

- Believes in the dignity and worth of the service rendered by the organization and the societal responsibilities assumed as a trusted public servant.

- Is governed by the highest ideals of honor and integrity in all public and personal relationships in order to merit the respect and inspire the confidence of the organization and the public being served.

- Believes that personal aggrandizement or personal profit obtained through misuse of public or personal relationships is dishonest and not tolerable.

- Identifies and eliminates participation of any individual in operational situations where a conflict of interest may be involved.

- Believes that members of the Institute and its staff should at no time or under any circumstances accept directly or indirectly, gifts, gratuities, or other things of value from suppliers, which might influence or appear to influence purchasing decisions.

- Keeps the governmental organization informed, through appropriate channels, on problems and progress of applicable operations by emphasizing the importance of the facts.

- Resists encroachment on control of personnel in order to preserve integrity as a professional manager. Handles all personnel matters on a merit basis. Politics, religion, ethnicity, gender and age carry no weight in personnel administration in the agency being directed or served.

- Seeks or dispenses no personal favors. Handles each administrative problem objectively and empathetically without discrimination.

- Subscribes to and supports the professional aims and objectives of the National Institute of Governmental Purchasing, Inc.

Guidelines To The NIGP Code Of Ethics

I. RESPONSIBILITY TO YOUR EMPLOYER

- Follow the lawful instructions or laws of the employer.
- Understand the authority granted by the employer.
- Avoid activities, which would compromise or give the perception of compromising the best interest of the employer.
- Reduce the potential for any charges of preferential treatment by actively promoting the concept of competition.
- Obtain the maximum benefit for funds spent as agents for the employer.

II. CONFLICT OF INTEREST

- Avoid any private or professional activity that would create a conflict between your personal interest and the interests of your employer.
- Avoid engaging in personal business with any company that is a supplier to your employer.
- Avoid lending money to or borrowing money from any supplier.

III. PERCEPTION

- Avoid the appearance of unethical or compromising practices in relationships, actions and communications.
- Avoid business relationships with personal friends. Request a reassignment if the situation arises.
- Avoid noticeable displays of affection, which may give an impression of impropriety.
- Avoid holding business meetings with suppliers outside the office.
- When such meetings do occur, the meeting location should be carefully chosen so as not to be perceived as inappropriate by other persons in the business community or your peers.

IV. GRATUITIES

- Never solicit or accept money, loans, credits or prejudicial discounts, gifts, entertainment, favors or services from your present or potential suppliers which might influence or appear to influence purchasing decisions.
- Never solicit gratuities in any form for yourself or your employer.
- Items of nominal value offered by suppliers for public relations purposes are acceptable when the value of such items has been established by your employer and would not be perceived by the offeror, receiver or others as posing an ethical breach.

- Gifts offered exceeding nominal value should be returned with an explanation or if perishable either returned or donated to a charity in the name of the supplier.
- In the case of any gift, care should be taken to evaluate the intent and perception of acceptance to ensure that it is legal, that it will not influence your buying decisions, and that it will not be perceived by your peers and others as unethical.

V. Business Meals

- There are times when during the course of business it may be appropriate to conduct business during meals. In such instances, the meal should be for a specific business purpose.
- Avoid frequent meals with the same supplier.
- The purchasing professional should be able to pay for meals as frequently as the supplier. Budgeted funds should be available for such purposes.

VI. Confidential Information

- Keep bidders' proprietary information confidential.
- Develop a formal policy on the handling of confidential information.

VII. Relationship With The Supplier

- Maintain and practice, to the highest degree possible, business ethics, professional courtesy, and competence in all transactions.
- Association with suppliers at lunches, dinners or business organization meetings is an acceptable professional practice enabling the buyer to establish better business relations provided that the buyer keeps free of obligation. Accordingly, it is strongly recommended that if a seller pays for an activity that the buyer reciprocate.
- Purchase without prejudice, striving to obtain the maximum value for each dollar of expenditure.
- Preclude from showing favoritism or be influenced by suppliers through the acceptance of gifts, gratuities, loans or favors. Gifts of a nominal value that display the name of a firm which is intended for advertisement may or may not be accepted in accordance with the recipient's own conscience or jurisdictional rules.
- Adhere to and protect the supplier's business and legal rights to confidentiality for trade secrets, and other proprietary information.
- Refrain from publicly endorsing products.

VIII. Relationship With The Employer

- Remain free of any and all interests and activities, which are or could be detrimental or in conflict with the best interests of the employer.

- Refrain from engaging in activities where the buyer has a significant personal or indirect financial interest.
- Exercise discretionary authority on behalf of the employer.
- Avoid acquiring interest or incurring obligations that could conflict with the interests of the employer.

IX. Relationships With Other Agencies And Organizations

- A buyer shall not use his position to exert leverage on individuals or firms for the purpose of creating a benefit for agencies or organizations that he may represent.
- All involvement and transactions shall be handled in a professional manner with the interest of the buyer's employer taking precedent.

X. Relationship With Professional Purchasing Organizations And Associations.

- It is the obligation and the responsibility of the buyer, through affiliation with professional organization, to represent that organization in a professional and ethical manner.
- A buyer shall not use his position to persuade an individual or firm to provide a benefit to an organization.

XI. Policy

- It is the policy of NIGP that any member of the Institute who personally, or on behalf of his local chapter, is involved in the process of acquiring advertisers and/ or exhibitors on behalf of the Institute, shall act only in the capacity of providing referrals of potential or interested parties to the Institute. As a result of such referral, should the Institute form a contractual obligation, appropriate credit shall be given to the individual or chapter.

Index

-A-

Abi-Karam, T., 11
ABL (Approved Brands List), 68-69
Acceptance
    Authority, 84
    test, 69
Accountability, 5-8
Acquisition,
    process, 62, 76, 142
    requirements, 50, 145
    solicitation, 140
    transactions, 86
Adams, M. B., 11
Addenda, 101-102, 189
Administrative Terms, 107
ADR (Alternative Dispute Resolution) , 175
ADS (Advance Disposal Surcharges), 162
Affidavit, 108, 157, 162-163, 196
Affirmative procurement, 35
After-Hours Access, 149
AFV (Alternative Fuel Vehicle), 35
Agent, 82, 84, 192-193
Aggregate pricing, 116
Aggrieved bidder, 176
Agreed-upon notice, 109
Agreement Documents, 160
Agreement
    execution, 174, 200-201
    Extensions, 133
    form, 196
    Number, 110, 122
    on Internal Trade (AIT), 6, 109
    termination, 109
Agreements provisions, 87
AIT (Agreement on Internal Trade), 211
Alliances, 18, 30, 77, 158
Allocation of
    funds, 201
    weights, 188
Allowable costs, 114-115
Alternate Dispute Resolution (ADR), 175-176

Alternate Item Response, 192
Alternative
    Fuel Vehicle (AFV), 35
    goods, 42
    methods, 57
    product and/or service, 134
    sources of revenue, 30
    -powered energy sources, 37
Amended response, 199
Amendments, 22, 102, 108
American
    National Standards Institute (ANSI), 62, 74-75, 138
    Society for Quality Control (ASQC), 75
    Society of Test Materials (ASTM), 74-75, 138, 142
    Water Works Association, 138
ANSI (American National Standards Institute), 62, 74-75, 138
APL (Approved Products List), 68
Appeal process, 175-176
Approval
    Levels, 8, 79, 85-86, 93
    of acquisitions, 92
    of Award, 83
    of products, 87
    of specific requirements, 80
    of specifications, 80
    of tenders, 80
    process, 47, 91, 201
    threshold, 4
Approved
    Brands List (ABL), 68-69
    Equal, 63, 65, 68
    Products List (APL), 68
Arbitration, 175-176
ASQC (American Society for Quality Control), 75
Assignments and Conveyance, 134
ASTM (American Society of Testing Materials), 74-75, 138, 142

At-arms-length
    basis, 84
    relationship, 157
Auger, D. A., 2
Authority levels, 59, 79, 84
Authorization levels, 79
Automated procurement management information systems, 40
Award
    decision, 103, 120-121, 194, 196
    notification, 108, 202
    of a contract, 63, 133, 174, 197, 200
    of the agreement, 161
    process, 70, 108, 143, 176
    recommendation, 83, 178, 200-201

-B-

Background Information, 144-145
BAFO (Best and Final Offer), 28, 30, 199
Barriers to competition, 204
Base specification, 68
BCBid, 53, 60
BCs (Blanket Contracts), 127, 130
Bearer bond, 119, 173
Benchmarks, 71, 137, 144, 190
Best
    and Final Offer (BAFO), 28, 30, 199
    effort estimate, 120
    value evaluation methodology, 198
    -in-market pricing, 31
Bid
    acceptance, 109
    bond, 119, 159, 173-174, 196
    Bond Deposits, 173
    format, 137
    Notification, 28, 53, 202, 206

offers, 173, 178
opening, 21, 167, 169, 173, 183
opportunities, 33, 142
process, 21, 140
Proposal Form, 2, 22, 96, 155-159, 194, 196
/proposal/quote requirements, 171
/Proposal Responses, 165
rejection, 171, 174
Responses, 2, 57, 166, 192
Security Log, 169-170
solicitation document, 2, 190-191
submission, 22, 173
surety, 119, 173-174
Tally/Tender Opening, 169-170
/tender, 62, 170
Bidder
checklist, 160
Conference Calls, 101
/Proponent Checklist, 160
/proponent conference, 101
Bidderís
list, 56
offer, 119
Profile, 158
qualifications, 194
response, 109, 158-159, 191, 196
responsibility, 126
strengths, 202
Bidders conferences, 100
Bidders/proponents, 101
Bids/
Invitation, 117, 178, 183
proposals, 59, 145, 165
tenders, 118, 142, 169
Bill of lading, 88
Binding arbitration, 175
Bio-
based products, 35-36
Fuel Delivery Vehicles Proponents, 163
Blanket Contract (BC), 127, 130
Boilerplate, 2, 58, 104, 148
Bonds, 119, 157, 159, 173
Brand Name, 63-65, 68, 132

Breach of
contract, 149
ethics, 157
Bundling goods, 43
Burden of proof, 177
Business Registration Required, 135
Buyer Supplier Responsibilities, 124
Buyer-supplier relationships, 26

-C-

Calendar of Activities, 97
Canadian
Construction Association, 138
Construction Documents Committee (CCDC), 182
General Standards Board (CGSB), 74-75
International Trade Tribunal (CITT), 63
Standards Association (CSA), 62, 69-70, 74-75, 142
Cancellation
clauses, 46
penalties, 46
Categorization codes, 54
Cavinato J. L., 11
CBD (Commerce Business Daily), 60, 92
CCDC (Canadian Construction Documents Committee), 182
Ceiling cost, 114
Central Purchasing, 18, 82
Centralized procurement, 81, 91
Certificate of
Compliance and Completion, 149
Disposal, 162-16
Substantial Performance, 133
CGSB (Canadian General Standards Board), 74-75
Change Order, 149, 175-176
Chicago
Board of Trade, 71
Buyers Guide, 53
CITT (Canadian International Trade Tribunal), 63
Class-Item-Group-Detail, 55
Closing
dates, 102

location, 160
time, 29, 83, 160, 189
Combination Specifications, 67
Commencement of work, 148-149
Commerce Business Daily (CBD), 60, 92
Commercial standards, 67-68, 72
Commitment Authority, 82, 84
Commodity
codes, 54-55
purchases, 24, 35, 122, 207
request, 24
/service codes, 56
-type products, 71
Common carrier, 124
Communication of Addenda, 60
Communications Guidelines, 101
Comparable product, 69, 197, 213
Competitive
acquisitions, 4, 58
advantage, 30
bidder, 195
negotiations, 28, 192
process, 20, 58, 75, 82, 127, 166, 188, 211, 215
procurement, 22, 53, 59, 203
proposals, 4
Sealed Bids, 21, 192
Sealed Proposal, 184
solicitation, 58, 192, 205
Sourcing, 6, 14, 28, 31, 57, 59, 74, 162, 212
sourcing requirements, 162
strategy, 27, 58
Completion
date, 98, 148-149
form, 115
of Work, 120, 148
Compliance
audits, 45, 86
certification, 88
evaluation, 48-49
requirements, 163
testing, 69
Compliant
bidder/respondent, 90
response submission, 171
responses, 172

/responsive, 183
Components of a Bid Proposal Form, 155, 158
Concealed damages, 124
Confidentiality Agreement, 106, 196
Conflict of Interest, 1, 3, 157, 187, 196, 204, 218, 221-222
Conover-Mast Purchasing Directory, 53
Construction contracts, 85, 120, 128, 175
Consultants, 66, 100, 187, 200, 205
Contract
  Administration, 112-114, 116, 120, 122, 136, 153, 200, 202
  Award, 6, 28, 56, 80, 104, 150, 173-174, 191, 199-200
  Execution, 80, 180, 200
  Formation, 15
  Length, 51
  requirement, 122
Contractorís
  obligations, 150-151
  requirement, 153
  responsibility, 152
Contractual
  disagreement, 174
  language, 128
  relationship, 174
  Risk, 10
COPANT (Pan American Standards Commission), 74
Corporate Supply Agreements (CSAs), 130
Cost
  analysis, 43
  /benefit analysis, 76, 198
  center, 81-82
  comparisons, 44-45
  /complexity, 10-11
  determination, 45
  elements, 42
  factors, 43
  of ownership, 116
  Plus Fixed Fee Contract, 115
  Plus Incentive Fee Contract, 115
  Reimbursement Contracts, 114
  risk, 112, 114

savings, 19, 33, 37, 40, 124
  Sharing Contract, 115
Costley, D. L., 12
Cover Letter, 156, 160
CPPB (Certified Professional Public Buyer)
CPPO (Certified Public Purchasing Officer)
Croner Publications, Inc., 53
CSA (Canadian Standards Association), 62, 69-70, 74-75, 142
Customer service, 7, 32, 76, 92, 215
Customs and Brokerage, 127
Cycle time, 26, 33

-D-

Damages
  clause, 120, 135
  provisions, 120
Dangerous goods, 84
Deadlines, 7, 23, 56
Debriefing session, 202
Debriefings, 135
Decentralization of the procurement process, 18, 58
Decentralized procurement, 8-9, 79, 86
Default, 110, 119
Defect listing, 133
Defective Work, 119, 129, 151
Definite
  Delivery, 122
  quantity, 122
  type, 123
Degree of
  risk, 71, 159, 199
  uncertainty, 11
Delay of Work, 148-149, 174
Delegated authority, 5, 58-59, 84
Delegation of Authority, 4-5, 84, 206
Delivery
  and Receipt Cetification, 80, 88
  approval, 87
  date, 122
  location, 89, 101, 166-167
  requirements, 95

schedule, 122
  terms, 64, 82, 122
  timetable, 22
  vehicle, 81
Derived requirement, 48
Design
  implementation, 50
  Specifications, 66
  -Bid-Build, 32
  -Build, 11, 32
  -Build-Finance, 32
  -Build-Maintain, 32
  -Build-Own-Operate, 32
  -Build-Own-Operate-Transfer, 32
Direct cost, 43
Directed Contract, 10-11, 20, 57, 70, 80, 89-90, 179, 211-213
Disclosure, 106, 135, 187, 195
Disposal
  Certification, 162
  methods, 161
Dispute resolution process, 109
Disqualification, 26, 97, 107, 109-110, 185, 196
Dobler, D. W., 51
Documentation and Certification, 196
Dollar
  threshold, 18, 57-58
  value, 9, 21, 32, 36, 57-58, 82
Domestic preference policies, 6
Draft
  Contract, 27
  Request for Information, 30
Due
  diligence, 57
  process, 56, 188
Dufferin Construction Company, 90

-E-

E-Buy system, 68
Eco-procurement, 35
eCommerce (Electronic Commerce), 60
Economic Price Adjustment, 113
Economies of
  scale, 4, 7-8, 43, 73, 91

volume, 127
EDI (Electronic Data Interchange), 33, 86, 190
Efficiency measures, 4
EFT (Electronic Funds Transfer),
190
Electronic
BID Board, 30, 206
commerce (eCommerce), 60
Data Interchange (EDI), 33,
86, 190
Document Management Tech-
nology Assessment, 48
funds transfer (EFT), 190
Marketing (eMarketing), 141
postings, 57
procurement (eProcurement),
32, 34, 86, 206
Signatures (eSignatures), 86,
217, 219
Solicitations, 86-87
Sourcing (eSourcing), 59-60,
206
submission, 86
Technology Utilization, 190
Waste (eWaste), 162
eMarketing (Electronic Market-
ing), 141
Emergency Purchases, 11,
18-19, 57, 179
End-user agreement, 143
Energy
Policy Act, 35
Star, 37
Engineering Certification, 150
Enterprise Resources Planning
(ERP), 190
Environment Canada, 35
Environmental
Management Act, 163
Stewardship, 51
Environmentally Preferred Pur-
chasing (EPP), 35
EPP (Environmentally Preferred
Purchasing), 35
eProcurement (Electronic Pro-
curement), 32, 86
software, 34
solution, 34
technology, 206
Equipment Availability Certifi-
cate, 196

Equity, 3-4, 7, 30, 55, 62, 136,
158
Equivalents, 134
ERP (Enterprise Resource Planning), 190
Escalation contract, 113
eSign (Electronic Signature), 86
eSourcing (Electronic Sourcing),
59-60, 206
Ethical code, 157
Evaluation
committee, 83, 178, 186-188
Criteria, 22, 90, 96, 139,
145, 147, 184-185, 188-192
factors, 184, 188, 191
methods, 49, 192
of Payment Terms Offered,
196
of products, 75
of responses, 191
of submissions, 56
methodology, 27, 198
phase, 192
Plan, 185
processes, 195
stage, 139
teams, 186
eWaste (Electronic Waste), 162
Exceptions, 97, 104, 111, 143,
157, 192
Exclusivity, 31
Executed Affidavit, 162
Executive
level approval, 183, 201
Steering Committee,
146-147, 178
Summary, 158
Expectations of the bidder, 189
Expenditure authority (Spending
authority), 84
Extensions, 57, 101, 133, 146,
173
External solicitation process, 62

-F-

Facilities Management, 32, 74,
91, 140
Fair competition, 191
FAR (Federal Acquisition Regula-
tions), 24, 68
Farm Bill, 35

Farrell, R. V., 153
FBS (Federal Bureau of Specifi-
cations), 75
Fearon, H. E., 51
Federal
Acquisition Regulation (FAR),
24, 68
Bureau of Specifications
(FBS), 75
Goods and Services Sales Tax
(GST), 121
Fee adjustment formula, 115
Final
inspection, 133, 150
Offer, 28, 199
price, 71, 113
response, 199
solicitation document, 47
Financial
Administration Act, 35
Capability Certificate, 196
Documents, 172, 218
Guarantees, 159
reports, 55, 130
Services, 180
Fixed
closing date, 98
cost, 120
fee, 115
Firm Price Contract, 112
Price Contract, 23, 112
Price with Re-determination
Contract, 114
F.O.B. (Free on Board), 123
–Delivery, 123
Delivered, 63
Destination, 123-124
Origin, 123
Point of Origin, 124
Shipping Point, 125
shipping terms, 124
terms, 123
FOI (Freedom of Information),
17, 106, 195
Force Majeure, 107
Formal
acknowledgement document,
167
agreement, 83, 103, 119,
160
application, 81
approval, 87, 201

contract, 15, 86
response, 166
Frasers Directory, 62
Freedom of Information (FOI),
17, 106, 195
Free on Board (F.O.B.), 123
Freight
Allowed, 123
Collect, 123-124
Collect at Destination, 124
Prepaid, 123-124
Fulfillment process, 200
Funding
allocation, 85
approval, 81, 107, 201
sources, 81, 201
withdrawal, 202

-G-

GAAP (Generally Accepted Ac-
counting Principles), 89
GAO (General Accounting Of-
fice), 69
GATT (General Agreement on
Tariffs and Trades), 6
General Services Administration
(GSA), 140
General Terms/Conditions, 97
Generally Accepted Accounting
Principles (GAAP), 89
George Wimpley Canada Ltd.,
90
Giunpero, L., 153
Global Markets, 51, 73
Good
faith, 118, 202, 204, 212
Standing status, 105
Governing Body Approval, 201
Governmental Sources, 141
Green
Guard Certification, 162
procurement, 6, 34-38
products, 36-37
Grimm, R., 38
GSA (General Services Adminis-
tration), 140
GST (Federal Goods and Ser-
vices Sales Tax), 121

-H-

Hamilton-Wentworth Region, 90
Hand-delivered responses, 98
Harmonized Sales Tax (HST),
121
Harris, S., 38
Historically Under-Utilized Busi-
ness (HUB), 42
Hoards and Barricades, 152
Holdback funds, 131
Holdbacks, 121, 145
HST (Harmonized Sales Tax),
121
HUB (Historically Under-Utilized
Business), 42
Hybrid procurement organiza-
tion, 9
Hybrid structure, 8

-I-

ICB (Informal Competitive Bid-
ding), 20
ICC (International Chamber of
Commerce), 125
Identical Responses, 192
Identifiable evaluation process,
185
Identification of Need, 80
IEC (International Electro-techni-
cal Commission), 74
IFB (Invitation for Bids), 18, 21,
57, 137
IFB/ITT (Invitation for Bid/Invita-
tion to Tender), 83, 171, 178,
183-184
ILO (International Labor Organi-
zation), 136
Immediate need purchases, 19
Implementation Plan, 27, 85,
196
Implied Authority, 85
INCOTERM (International Com-
merce Terms), 125
Indefinite
Delivery, 122
quantity and delivery, 122
Indemnity, 106, 218
Independent
consultants, 200
contractors, 106

Indirect costs, 43
Industry standards, 64-65, 68,
71, 143
Ineligibility of Responses, 159
Informal Competitive Bidding
(ICB), 20
Information Gathering, 2, 11,
14, 20, 23
Informational addendum, 102
Infringement, 106, 132
Inherent Authority, 85
Initial Cost Analyses, 43
Inspection and Takeover Proce-
dures, 133
Inspection, Testing and Accep-
tance, 129
Inspections of Financial Reports,
130
Installation
costs, 117
inspections, 129
Institute for Supply Management
(ISM), 141
Insurance certificate, 119, 173
Intellectual Property, 48,
105-106, 132, 218
Internal
audit, 11
Auditors, 187
International
Chamber of Commerce (ICC),
125
Commercial Terms (INCO-
TERMS), 125
Electro-technical Commission
(IEC), 74
Labor Organization (ILO), 136
Organization for Standardiza-
tion (ISO), 74-75
Invitation
for Bids (IFB), 18, 21, 57,
137
to Negotiate (ITN), 18, 22,
27, 57
Irregularities, 109, 159,
194-195
Irrevocable letter of credit, 119,
170, 173
ISM (Institute for Supply Manage-
ment), 141
ISO (International Organization
for Standardization), 74-75

ITB/ITT (Invitation to Bid/Invitation to Tender), 83, 171, 178, 183-184
ITN (Invitation to Negotiate), 18, 22, 27, 57
ITT (Invitation to Tender), 83, 171, 178, 183-184
ITT/ITB (Invitation to Tender/Invitation to Bid), 83, 171, 178, 183-184

-J & K-

JIT (Just in Time), 127
Joint Solution Procurement (JSP), 29
Journal advertisements, 54
JSP (Joint Solution Procurement), 29
Just-in-Time (JIT), 127
Kansas City Board of Trade, 71
Kelman, S., 12
Kestenbaum, M. I., 12
Killen, K., 51
Kolchin, M., 153
Kwak, M., 38

-L-

Large acquisitions, 75
Late fees, 19
Latent defects, 150
Law of Agency, 5, 82-83, 201
LCC (Life Cycle Costing), 116
LEAP (Learning and Education to Advance Procurement) Program, 22
Lease/rental agreement, 46
Leasing, 45-46
Legal Terms, 104
Leseur, A., 38
Letters of Interest (LOI), 178
Level playing field, 145
Liability, 10, 23, 107, 119, 125, 167, 197, 218
Library of Parliament, 63
Life Cycle Costing (LCC), 116
Limitation of Damages, 135
Limited competition, 58, 139
Liquidated damages clause, 120
LMI (Logistics Management Institute), 7

Local preference, 90-91, 162
Logistics Management Institute (LMI), 7
LOI (Letters of Interest), 178
Long Form Contract, 180
Lost Bids, 166
Low
   Total Response, 193-194
   -Compliant Bid/Quote/Proposal, 90
   -compliant firm, 90
   -compliant quote, 91
   -value acquisitions, 95
Lowest
   bidder, 117
   compliant bidder, 192
   cost, 26, 59, 76, 198, 204
   price, 24, 26, 107, 185, 198
   price response, 198
   response, 193
   responsive bidder, 21
Lump Sum Response, 193

-M-

MacManus, S. A., 12, 38
MacRaeís Blue Book, 53
Maintenance Material, 44
Make or Buy Cost Analysis, 43
Mandatory
   and/or Optional Sourcing Criteria, 76
   Evaluation Criteria, 189
   Requirements, 23, 48, 160, 171-172, 189, 192, 217-218
Mark-ups, 162
Market
   Grades, 65, 71, 138
   research, 16-17, 204
   survey, 42, 204
Master
   bidder list, 207
   RFP/Bid file, 196
   Standing Offer (MSO), 92, 127
Material
   and Labor Bonds, 159
   and Manufacturing Method, 65, 71
   compliance, 151
McCue, C. P., 12
McVay, B. L., 12

Measurable
   performance expectations, 48
   requirements, 48
Measure of compliance, 140
Measurement parameters, 190
MERX (Merix Corp.), 53, 60, 92, 80
Method of Award, 116-117, 178, 194
Methods of Solicitation, 10, 17, 179
Michels, W. L., 38
Minimal element of competition, 21
Minimum
   acceptable levels, 113
   acceptable product, 68
   acceptable score, 189
   requirements, 65, 143
Minneapolis Grain Exchange, 71
Minor
   Informalities, 194
   irregularities, 194-195
Minority
   suppliers, 33, 42
   and women-owned Business Enterprise (MWBE), 42-43, 54, 206
   -owned or Small Businesses, 42-43, 54
Mistakes After Bid Opening, 173
Mitchell, K., 38
Modifications, 70, 101-102, 168
MSO (Master Standing Offer), 92, 127
Multi-step
   Bidding, 116-117
   sourcing process, 29
Multidimensional Model of Public Sourcing, 9
Multiple
   bidders, 116
   suppliers, 58, 116
MWBE (Minority and Women-Owned Business Enterprise), 42-43, 54, 206

-N-

NAFTA (North American Free Trade Agreement), 6

NASPO (National Association of State Procurement Officials), 6
National
Association of State Procurement Officials (NASPO), 6
Bureau of Standards (NBS), 75
Commerce Act, 86
Institute of Governmental Purchasing (NIGP), 1, 7, 39, 54, 61, 110, 138, 141
Institute of Standards and Technology (NIST), 62, 75
Lumber Manufacturers Association (NLMA), 75
Natural
Disasters, 51
Resources Canada, 35
NBS (National Bureau of Standards), 75
New York Mercantile Exchange, 71
NIGP (National Institute of Governmental Purchasing), 38, 77, 94, 136, 153, 202
NIGP Commodity/Service Code, 54-55
NIST (National Institute of Standards and Technology), 62, 75
NLMA (National Lumber Manufacturerís Association), 75
NOI (Notice of Intent), 18, 28
Non-
Collusion, 108, 157, 172, 195-196, 218
competitive negotiations, 28
competitive strategies, 57-58
compliance, 88, 106, 155-157, 171, 196
compliant Determination, 171
Disclosure and Confidentiality Agreement, 106
discrimination, 5, 7
mandatory provisions, 143
negotiable elements of the requirements, 27
performance, 110
proprietary basis, 29-30
responsive, 48, 174, 194, 196, 204, 219

Waiver Clause, 107
North American Free Trade Agreement (NAFTA), 6
Notice
of Intent (NOI), 18, 28
of Letting, 21
of Substantial Completion, 149-150
of termination, 109
period, 57, 133
Notification of Award, 60, 103
Notion of competitive acquisitions, 4

-O-

OASIS (Organization for the Advancement of Structured Information Standards), 74
Obligatory elements of the proposal, 23
Obligatory requirements, 23
Occupational Safety and Health, 70, 74, 105, 197
OEM (Original Equipment Manufacturer), 72
Off-loading facilities, 126
Omissions, 108, 134, 172, 218
Online
Resources, 142
submission of bids, 33
Open competition, 4-6, 42, 57, 203-204
Opening
Bids and Proposals, 169
bids/tenders, 169
date, 168, 170
of responses, 189
process, 169, 183
Optional Components of a Bid Proposal Form, 158
Oral Presentations, 98, 102
Organization for the Advancement of Structured Information Standards (OASIS), 74
Origin of the shipment, 123
Original
Equipment Manufacturer (OEM), 72
solicitation, 28, 101-102, 131, 189
solicitation notice, 28

sourcing document, 102
Out of scope, 95, 145
Output specifications, 44

-P-

P& L Communications v. Library of Parliament, 63
Packaging, 37, 51, 63, 88, 126-128, 143, 161, 163-164
Pan American Standards Commission (COPANT), 74
Part
Drawing, 65, 72
Specification, 65, 72
Partnership, 1-2, 30
Patents, 106, 132
Payment
Authority, 84, 89
Authorization, 89
Bond, 119
delays, 176
Strategy, 27
Terms, 51, 117, 196
pCard (Procurement Card)
acquisitions, 86
procurements, 43
purchases, 179
transactions, 19, 86
PEA (Procurement Executivesí Association), 7
Peat, B., 12
Perception of
favoritism, 204
preferential treatment, 56
Performance
-Based Contract, 113
Bond, 159
criteria, 7, 34, 71, 145, 151
expectations, 47-48, 68, 147
goals, 113
Measurement, 27, 67, 96
measures, 7, 37, 95, 144
outcome measures, 7
parameters, 89
requirements, 36, 67
Risk, 10, 113
schedule, 22
Security, 172
Specifications, 62-63, 67, 213
standards, 7, 37

testing, 65
-based measurements, 137
Personnel Qualification Certificate, 196
Planning Activities, 15, 39
PO (Purchase Order), 110
Point-of-purchase (POP), 31
Policy and Procedure Compliance, 92
Poor performance, 56-57
POP (Point-of-Purchase), 31
Potential
    bidders, 54, 59, 102, 207
    offerors, 30-31, 59-61, 144
PR (Purchase Requisition), 40, 80
Pre-qualification of
    suppliers, 55
    vendors, 56
Pre-qualified suppliers, 16, 28
Pre-response Conference, 100
Pre-selection of suppliers, 204
Preferential treatment, 56, 143, 222
Preferred product, 68
Price
    escalation, 113, 162
    quotation, 178
    reductions, 113
    Risk, 10
Pricing
    and Costing Form, 196
    adjustments, 113
    Errors, 109
    proposals, 117
    responses, 193
    structure, 162
    terms, 112
Prime supplier, 119, 121, 135
Principal-agent relationship, 5
Principle, 5, 85, 91
Privatization, 1-2, 43
Privilege clause, 117-118
Procurement
    Card (pCard), 8, 56
    Executivesí Association (PEA), 7
    Planning, 39, 61, 144
    policies, 6, 8-9, 11, 36-37, 205
    procedures, 4, 7, 13
    processes, 33

Professional Services/Other Services, 32
Program parameters, 48
Project
    Advisory Committee, 147
    Coordinator, 147, 150
    Implementation Plan, 196
    Leader, 147
    Requirements, 96, 160, 202
    Team, 147
Promotion of Domestic Industry, 6
Prompt Payment, 120
Proponent/Bidder Checklist, 160
Proposal
    Invitation, 62, 142
    Risk, 10
    Signing, 219
    Submission forms, 219
Proprietary
    Information, 195, 223
    products, 65
    Specifications, 70
Prospective
    bidders, 102, 155
    suppliers, 7, 44, 203
Protection of Privacy
    Act, 106
    Form, 197
Protest, 28, 139, 166, 174-177, 205
Prototype sample, 64
Provincial Government Agency, 162
Provincial Sales Tax (PST), 121
PST (Provincial Sales Tax), 121
Public
    auction notice, 24
    entityís sourcing documents, 126
    entityís specifications, 185
    notice, 21, 28
    -Private Partnerships (P3s), 18
    Works and Government Services Canada, 35
Purchase
    Order (PO), 110
    Order/Agreement Number, 110
    price, 45-46
    Quantities, 132

Requisition (PR), 40, 80
Purchasing
    authority, 4, 18-19, 58, 149
    card (pCard), 19
    green products, 36
    Handbook, 51
    Organization Authority, 82
    Principles and Applications, 144, 153

-*Q & R*-

Qiao, Y., 23
QPL (Qualified Products List), 65, 67-68
Qualified Products List (QPL), 65, 67-68
Quality
    Assurance Program, 128
    Control (QC), 88, 135
    requirement, 50
Random sample, 88
Range of allowable deviation, 72
Raw materials costs, 113
RCRA (Resource Conservation and Recovery Act), 35
Reasonableness, 120
Receipt and Confirmation Form, 103
Records Management, 130
Recycling, 35-36, 126, 160-161, 163-164
Reference Manuals, 131, 197
Regulatory
    and Testing Agency, 65, 70
    approval and testing, 70
    Reporting Requirements, 130
REI (Request for Expression of Interest), 18, 24, 95
REI/RFI (Request for Expression of Interest/Request for Information), 18, 24, 95
Reimbursement losses, 120
Rejection of Late Bid Submittals, 168
Rejection of Responses, 107
Remedial Action, 129
Renewal Options, 133
Reporting Method, 130
Reputable suppliers, 1, 71

Request for
  Expression of Interest (REI),
    18, 24, 95
  Information/Request for Ex-
    pression of Interest (RFI/REI),
    18, 24, 95
  Qualifications (RFQu), 95
  Quotation, 21, 95, 183
Requirement
  delivery, 123
  Quality, 50
  Relationships, 49
  Specifications, 9, 20, 27, 40,
    59, 64
Requirements
  Analysis, 39, 75-76, 204
  Characteristics, 47
  Definition, 2, 14, 42, 46-47,
    50, 143, 147-148, 194
  Descriptions, 50
  of the bidder, 97, 102, 126
  of the solicitation, 19, 96, 98,
    156, 198
Requisition process, 40
Resource Conservation and
  Recovery Act (RCRA), 35
Response
  criteria, 189
  deadline, 139
  documents, 103, 155-156
  evaluation criteria, 188
  Evaluation Process, 188
  Form, 96, 155-156
  Formats, 97, 172
  submission, 103, 107-108,
    158, 167, 178
  Submission Form, 196
  Submittals, 167
Responsible
  bidder, 21, 111, 116, 118,
    186
  supplier, 20
  bidders, 173
  solicitations, 56
  supplier, 76
Responsiveness,
  of Proposals, 191
  of submissions, 191
Restocking Charges, 128
Restrict competition, 66

Restrictive
  specifications, 70, 139
  tolerances, 72
Return response submissions,
  195
Returns and Refunds, 126
Reusable packaging, 37
Reverse Auction, 11, 18, 24-26,
  57
REI (Request for Expression of
  Interest), 18, 24, 95
RFI (Request for Information),
  18, 24, 95
RFP (Request for Proposal),
  formats, 137
  process, 184, 199
RFQ (Request for Quotation), 21,
  95, 183
RFQu (Request for Qualifications), 135, 186
Risk
  elements, 27
  Management, 119
  of Loss clause, 132
  of Loss Waiver, 132

-*S*-

SAE (Society for Automotive
  Engineers), 75
Safety
  Procedures Review, 129
  Stock Levels, 127
Sale of Goods Act, 126
Sampling, 131
Schedule
  of Events, 98, 100
  of Subcontractors, 159
Schedule Risk, 10
Scope of
  the acquisition, 48
  the proposed procurement,
    24
  the requirement, 50
  Work (SOW), 137, 144
  Work/Project, 145
Scorable Mandatories, 23
Scoring methodology, 23
Scrap and Salvage, 151
Security requirements, 22, 87
Segregation of duties, 89

Selection
  Committee, 184-187
  Committee/Team, 186
  methodology, 96
  of Supplier, 83
  process, 56, 72, 176, 178,
    186
Sensitivity analysis, 45
Service compliance, 190
Set-asides, 6, 42
Shipment installation, 88
Shipping terms, 123-125
Short
  Form Contract, 181
  lead-time, 122
  list of bidders, 117
  -notice requirements, 127
Sign/execute agreements, 200
Sign-off consensus, 201
Signing authority, 16, 94, 180,
  200
Similar products, 20, 66, 142
Single source supplier, 20
Site
  conditions, 102, 148, 150,
    197
  evaluation, 197
  Visits, 30, 57, 102, 185-186,
    197
SKU (Stock Keeping Unit), 41,
  69
Small
  business, 34, 43, 55
  Dollar Purchases, 10, 18-19
  Dollar/Purchasing Card, 18,
    179
SME (Society of Mechanical
  Engineers), 75
Social Responsibility, 160-161,
  218, 220
Society of
  Automotive Engineers (SAE),
    75
  Mechanical Engineers (SME),
    75
Socio-economic Objectives, 6-7
Sole Source, 10-11, 18-20, 57,
  70, 80, 89-90, 179, 209-212
Solicitation
  Categories, 31
  documents, 86-87, 102-104,
    129, 166, 188, 193

file, 168, 183
invitations, 178
method, 29, 186
notice, 28, 60
Process, 14, 63, 79-80, 103, 109, 165-166, 178
reference number, 168
response, 155-156, 165
response form, 155-156
scope of work, 76
Source
 code, 48
 Document, 14
 justification, 89
 list of potential suppliers, 53
 lists, 53-54, 57, 203
Sources of
 Specifications, 140
 Standards, 75
Sourcing,
 activities, 4
 decisions, 7
 document categories, 96
 exercise, 28, 76, 79, 96, 139, 145
 function, 207
 mechanisms, 9, 11, 42
 methods, 13, 17-18
 policies, 7
 Process, 11, 63, 138-139, 203
 requirements, 82, 92, 96, 162
 responsibilities, 9
 solicitation, 145, 207
 stage, 146
 strategies, 9, 13, 32, 57-59, 203
 Suppliers, 53
SOW (Scope/Statement of Work), 137, 144
Special Conditions, 104, 117, 119, 122, 127, 149, 159, 180
Specific Requirements, 47, 69, 80-81, 129-130, 145, 189, 200
Specification Library, 96
Specifications, 14, 20-24, 61-75, 137-143, 190
Spending Authority (Expenditure Authority, 84

Standard
 acceptance period, 202
 Forms, 58, 96
Standardization Program, 73-74, 91
Standards Committee, 74-75
Statement
 of need, 46
 of Non-Collusion and Affidavit, 108, 157, 196
 of Qualification, 11
 /Scope of Work (SOW), 137, 144
Statutory holdbacks, 121
Stewardship
 considerations, 160-161, 220
 guidelines, 162
Stocks, K., 38
Storage, 117, 152, 167
Straight, R. L., 12
Strategic
 Alliance (SA), 30
 plan, 220
 Sourcing, 41
Structural
 Integrity, 150
 Models, 8
Subcontractor Schedule and Certificate, 196
Subcontractors, 158-159
Sub-suppliers, 119, 121, 136
Submission
 deadlines, 23
 response, 97, 132, 157
Submittal Instruction, 23
Submittals, 48, 56, 158, 167-168, 188
Substitutions, 97, 134, 151
Successful bidders, 60, 95, 178
Summary
 documents, 186
 spreadsheet, 185
Supplier
 analysis, 42
 availability, 10
 Bias, 56
 collusion, 139
 evaluation, 72
 favoritism, 204
 lists, 2, 19, 33, 54, 57
 monopolies, 204
 Obligations, 129
 proposals, 27-28, 56-57, 59

Qualification, 18, 28
Responses, 27
selection, 62
source list, 42
Supply
 chain Management, 35
 Management, 15, 91-92, 141, 163
Support Structures, 153
Surety, 10, 119, 173-174, 196
Surety/liability risk, 10
Surplus, 92, 151
Sustainability, 6, 51, 126, 160-161, 163, 218, 220
Sweets Catalog, 53

-T-

Takeover Procedures, 133
Technical
 compliance, 79, 116
 documents, 47
 Evaluation Committee, 83, 178
 Experts, 187
 Proposals, 117, 156
 requirements, 23, 27, 63, 156, 204
 Reviews and Approvals, 91
 Specifications, 23, 40, 42, 57, 96, 137-138, 140, 143
Technology Recycling Program, 164
Tender, 30-31, 82-83, 95, 117-118, 169-170, 183
Tender/Bids, 82
Termination for Convenience, 109
Test performance, 37
Testing methods, 73, 139
Thai, K. V., 38
Third party, 69, 84, 106, 195
TILMA (Trade, Investment, Labour Mobility Agreement), 6
Time
 and Date Imprint, 98
 and Materials Contract, 115
 Is Of The Essence, 128, 179
Title–Lien Protection, 135
Tolerances, 65-67, 71-72

Total
cost, 44, 112, 116, 193
cost of ownership, 116
Trade
agreements, 162
Investment, Labour Mobility
Agreement (TILMA), 6
name, 63
Transparency, 4, 7, 62, 165,
178, 220
Treasury Board Ministers, 35

-U-

UCC (Uniform Commercial Code)
126
UL (Underwriters Laboratories),
69
Uncertainty/risk, 10-11
Underwriters Laboratories (UL),
69
Unfair advantage, 20, 42, 57,
194
Uniform Commercial Code
(UCC), 126
Units of measure, 63, 143, 173
University of Victoria, 29, 76-77,
94, 161, 163, 171, 217
Unofficial response, 100
Unsatisfactory products, 129
Universal Product Code (UPC),
69
Unsuccessful
bidders, 176, 195, 202
offerors, 176
supplier, 139
UPC (Universal Product Code),
69
U.S. Department of Commerce,
60, 92

-V-

Validation of Bid Submittals, 167
Value
analysis, 42, 75
of Competition, 203
-added benefits, 31, 190, 192
-added offering, 31
-added revenue, 31
-added services, 22, 216
Variances, 157, 192

Variations of specifications, 138
VENUS, 29
Volume
Discounts, 121
pricing, 193
purchases, 40, 43, 91

-W-

W. W. Grainger electronic cata-
log, 87
Warranties, 48, 91, 131
Warranty
Briefings, 131
Certificate, 131
Warrillow, C., 2, 12
Waste Removal, 128, 150, 161
Web-requisition, 127
Weighing factor, 23
Weight Load Requirements, 152
WHMIS (Workplace Hazardous
Materials Information System),
105
Winning bidder, 202
Withdrawal
Conditions, 103
of Bid Submittal, 168
of response submissions, 108
Women-owned Business Enter-
prise (WBE), 42-43, 54, 206
Work
Order, 81
site, 149-152, 161
-in-progress inspections, 68,
87
Workplace Hazardous Material
Information System (WHMIS),
105
Writing Technical Specifications,
138
World Trade Organization (WTO),
6
Written
alteration, 175
assertion, 175
protest, 177
WTO (World Trade Organization),
6